'5

The Methuen book of

POEMS *for*
EVERY
DAY

~

The Methuen book of

POEMS *for*
EVERY
DAY

~

Methuen & Co.

10 9 8 7 6 5 4 3 2 1

First published in 2006
by Methuen & Co. Ltd
11–12 Buckingham Gate,
London, SW1E 6LB

Copyright in the selection and editorial material
© Methuen & Co. Ltd 2006

Methuen & Co. Limited Reg. No. 5278590

A CIP catalogue record for this book is
available from the British Library

ISBN 10: 0-413-77456-2

ISBN 13: 978-0-413-77456-9

Designed by Bryony Newhouse

Printed and bound by
The St. Edmundsbury Press, Bury St. Edmunds, Suffolk

CONTENTS

JANUARY

January 1

The Emigrant's Letter

Dear Danny,

I'm takin' the pen in me hand
To tell you we're just out o' sight o' the land;
   In the grand Allan liner we're sailin' in style,
   But we're sailin' away from the Emerald Isle;
And a long sort o' sigh seemed to rise from us all
As the waves hid the last bit of ould Donegal.
   Och! it's well to be you that is takin' yer tay
   Where they're cuttin' the corn in Creeshla the day.

I spoke to the captain – he won't turn her round,
And if I swum back I'd be apt to be drowned,
   So here I must stay – oh! I've no cause to fret,
   For their dinner was what you might call a banquet.
But though it is 'sumpchus,' I'd swop the whole lot,
For the ould wooden spoon and the stirabout pot;
   And sweet Katty Farrell a-wettin' the tay
   Where they're cuttin' the corn in Creeshla the day!

If Katey is courted by Patsey or Mick,
Put a word in for me with a lump of a stick,
   Don't kill Patsey outright, he has no sort of chance,
   But Mickey's a rogue you might murther at wance;
For Katey might think as the longer she waits
A boy in the hand is worth two in the States:
   And she'll promise to honour, to love and obey
   Some robber that's roamin' round Cresshla the day.

Good-bye to you Dan, there's no more to be said,
And I think the salt wather's got into me head,
   For it dreeps from me eyes when I call to me mind,
   The friends and the colleen I'm leavin' behind;

Oh, Danny, she'll wait; whin I bid her good-bye,
There was just the laste taste of a tear in her eye,
    And a break in her voice whin she said "You might stay,
    But plaze God you'll come back to ould Creeshla some day."

Percy French

ON THIS DAY:

In 1892 Ellis Island in upper New York Bay became the main centre for processing immigrants to the USA. Bought by the city of New York in 1807 after the death of its owner Samuel Ellis, it was acquired by the US government in 1808. It has been estimated that almost half of all Americans today can trace in their family history at least one person who entered the country through the port of New York at Ellis Island, the 'Gateway to America'. In 1965 the island was designated as part of the Statue of Liberty National Monument and in 1990 the Ellis Island Immigration Museum was opened.

The Times was first published in 1788.

The BBC was established by Royal Charter in 1927.

The British rail network was nationalised in 1948.

January 2

A Match with the Moon

Weary already, weary miles to-night
    I walked for bed: and so, to get some ease,
    I dogged the flying moon with similes.
And like a wisp she doubled on my sight
In ponds; and caught in tree-tops like a kite;
    And in a globe of film all liquorish
    Swam full-faced like a silly silver fish;–
Last like a bubble shot the welkin's height
Where my road turned, and got behind me, and sent
    My wizened shadow craning round at me,
    And jeered, 'So, step the measure,– one, two, three!'
And if I faced on her, looked innocent.
But just at parting, halfway down a dell,
She kissed me for good-night. So you'll not tell.

Dante Gabriel Rossetti

ON THIS DAY:

In 1893 Louis Daguerre, the pioneering French photographer, took the first photograph of the moon, in Paris.

The Australian scholar Gilbert Murray (1866–1957), Chairman of the League of Nations 1923–1938, was born.

The English composer Sir Michael Tippett (1905–1998) was born in London.

Luna 1 was launched by the USSR in 1959. It was the first man-made object to leave the earth's gravity.

Frank Muir (1920–1998), broadcaster and author, died.

Darren Gough (b.1970), Yorkshire, Essex and England cricketer, became the first English bowler since 1899 to achieve an Ashes 'hat-trick' (Sydney 1999).

January 3

Adlestrop

Yes. I remember Adlestrop—
The name, because one afternoon
Of heat the express-train drew up there
Unwontedly. It was late June.

The steam hissed. Someone cleared his throat.
No one left and no one came
On the bare platform. What I saw
Was Adlestrop—only the name

And willows, willow-herb, and grass,
And meadowsweet, and haycocks dry,
No whit less still and lonely fair
Than the high cloudlets in the sky.

And for that minute a blackbird sang
Close by, and round him, mistier,
Farther and farther, all the birds
Of Oxfordshire and Gloucestershire.

Edward Thomas

ON THIS DAY:

Adlestrop station was closed to passengers on 3rd January 1966, following the 1963 Beeching review of Britain's rail network.

Martin Luther was excommunicated by Pope Leo X in 1521.

Clement Attlee (1883–1967), Prime Minister from 1945 to 1951, was born.

Herbert Morrison, Lord Morrison of Lambeth (1888–1965), was born. Morrison was a cabinet minister in Churchill's wartime coalition government and deputy Prime Minister and leader of the House of Commons in Clement Attlee's government.

The writer J. R. R. Tolkien (1892–1973) was born in South Africa.

William Joyce ('Lord Haw-Haw', 1906–1946) was hanged for treason at Wandsworth Prison, London.

In 1962 Fidel Castro was excommunicated by Pope John XXIII.

January 4

When I Consider how my Light is Spent

When I consider how my light is spent
   Ere half my days, in this dark world and wide,
   And that one talent which is death to hide
   Lodged with me useless, though my soul more bent
To serve therewith my Maker, and present
   My true account, lest he returning chide.
   'Doth God exact day-labour, light denied?'
   I fondly ask; but patience to prevent
That murmur, soon replies, 'God doth not need
   Either man's work or his own gifts; who best
   Bear his mild yoke, they serve him best. His state
Is kingly. Thousands at his bidding speed
   And post o'er land and ocean without rest:
   They also serve who only stand and wait.'

John Milton

ON THIS DAY:

Louis Braille (1809–1852), inventor of the universal system for reading and writing for the blind, was born. Braille was himself blind from the age of three. The poet John Milton (1608–1674) became totally blind in 1652.

Sir Isaac Pitman (1813–1897), inventor of shorthand, was born.

In 1958 Sir Edmund Hillary (b.1919) arrived at the South Pole as a member of the British Commonwealth Trans-Antarctic Expedition.

The poet T. S. Eliot (1888–1965) died.

The novelist Joan Aiken (1924–2004), daughter of writer and poet Conrad Aiken (1889–1973) and author of *The Wolves of Willoughby Chase* and its sequels, died.

January 5

South Pole

There's no reversal now,
Our shadows point the way,
Into the virgin snow,
Into the endless day.

Here at the Southern Pole
We bear the globe, and feel
The burden of the whole,
And know it is not real.

Ocean and continent,
The race of beast and man,
Have shrunk into a point
That turns on a glove-span.

We know that where we stand,
The equatorial wars
Still rage, but in our hand,
Small as the southern stars.

Atlas, who shouldered Earth,
Knew less than we know now;
He sponsored mankind's birth:
We are silent in the snow.

Richard Church

ON THIS DAY:

Sir Ernest Shackleton (1874–1922) died at South Georgia. He had been a member of Captain Scott's Antarctic expedition in 1901–1904. Shackleton subsequently commanded a further expedition in 1907–1909. This expedition reached 88° 23′ S latitude, located the magnetic South Pole and climbed Mount Erebus. Although his colleagues intended to bring his body back to England, Shackleton's wife felt that he should be buried in the place that had meant so much to him. He is buried in the Norwegian Cemetery, South Georgia.

Amy Johnson (1903–1941), aviator and the first woman to fly solo from England to Australia, disappeared, having baled out over the Thames whilst en route to deliver an Airspeed Oxford aeroplane, in her role as a pilot in the Air Transport Auxiliary (ATA). She was the first member of the ATA to die on service.

Requiem for the Plantagenet Kings

For whom the possessed sea littered, on both shores,
Ruinous arms; being fired, and for good,
To sound the constitution of just wars,
Men, in their eloquent fashion, understood.

Relieved of soul, the dropping-back of dust,
Their usage, pride, admitted within doors;
At home, under caved chantries, set in trust,
With well-dressed alabaster and proved spurs
They lie; they lie; secure in the decay
Of blood, blood-marks, crowns hacked and coveted,
Before the scouring fires of trial-day
Alight on men; before sleeked groin, gored head,
Budge through the clay and gravel, and the sea
Across daubed rock evacuates its dead.

Geoffrey Hill

ON THIS DAY:

Richard II (1367–1400, reigned 1377–1399), son of the Black Prince, was born. He was deposed in 1399 by Henry Bolingbroke (1367–1413), who became Henry IV. Richard was imprisoned in Pontefract Castle, where he died in mysterious circumstances.

The last Anglo-Saxon king of England, Harold (c.1020–1066), was crowned in 1066.

Joan of Arc (1412–1431) was born.

Jacques Étienne Montgolfier (1745–1799), inventor, was born. In 1783, together with his brother, Joseph Michel, he built the first successful hot-air balloon.

January 7

Les Ballons

Against these turbid turquoise skies
 The light and luminous balloons
 Dip and drift like satin moons,
Drift like silken butterflies;

Reel with every windy gust,
 Rise and reel like dancing girls,
 Float like strange transparent pearls,
Fall and float like silver dust.

Now to the low leaves they cling,
 Each with coy fantastic pose,
 Each a petal of a rose
Straining at a gossamer string.

Then to the tall trees they climb,
 Like thin globes of amethyst,
 Wandering opals keeping tryst
With the rubies of the lime.

Oscar Wilde

ON THIS DAY:

In 1785 Jean-Pierre Blanchard (1753–1809) and John Jefferies (1744–1819) made the first aerial crossing of the English Channel in a hot-air balloon.

The University of Glasgow was founded in 1451.

Catherine of Aragon (b.1485) died in 1536. She was the first wife of Henry VIII (1491–1547, reigned 1509–1547), and mother of Mary I (1516–1558, reigned 1553–1558).

Nicholas Hilliard (c.1547–1619), court miniaturist, died.

The inaugural transatlantic telephone service, between London and New York, began in 1927. The first call lasted three minutes, and cost £15.00.

John Berryman (1914–1972), poet and novelist, died.

January 8

The Road not Taken

Two roads diverged in a yellow wood,
And sorry I could not travel both
And be one traveller, long I stood
And looked down one as far as I could
To where it bent in the undergrowth;

Then took the other, as just as fair,
And having perhaps the better claim,
Because it was grassy and wanted wear;
Though as for that the passing there
Had worn them really about the same,

And both that morning equally lay
In leaves no step had trodden black.
Oh, I kept the first for another day!
Yet knowing how way leads on to way,
I doubted if I should ever come back.

I shall be telling this with a sigh
Somewhere ages and ages hence:
Two roads diverged in a wood, and I –
I took the one less travelled by,
And that has made all the difference.

Robert Frost

ON THIS DAY:

Marco Polo (1254–1324), merchant and traveller, died. His account of travels in China, *The Description of the World*, was the main source of knowledge of the region for Europeans for centuries.

The novelist Wilkie Collins (1824–1889), author of *The Woman in White* and *The Moonstone*, was born.

The first outside broadcast occurred in 1923 when the BBC transmitted Mozart's *The Magic Flute* from the Royal Opera House in Covent Garden.

Lord Robert Baden-Powell (1857–1941), British General and founder of the Boy Scouts in 1907, died.

In 1959 General Charles de Gaulle (1890–1970) became President of the Fifth French Republic.

François Mitterrand (1916–1996), President of France, died.

January 9

The Miner's Helmet

My father wore it working coal at Shotts
When I was one. My mother stirred his broth
And rocked my cradle with her shivering hands
While this black helmet's long-lost miner's-lamp
Showed him the road home. Through miles of coal
His fragile skull, filled even then with pit-props,
Lay in a shell, the brain's blue-printed future
Warm in its womb. From sheaves of saved brown paper,
Baring an oval into weeks of dust,
I pull it down: its laced straps move to admit
My larger brows; like an abdicated king's
Gold crown of thirty years ago, I touch it
With royal fingers, feel its image firm –
Hands grown to kings' hands calloused on the pick,
Feet slow like kings' feet on the throneward gradient
Up to the coal-face – but the image blurs
Before it settles: there were no crusades.
My father died a draughtsman, drawing plans
In an airy well-lit office above the ground
Beneath which his usurpers, other kings,
Reigned by the fallen helmet he resigned
Which I inherit as a concrete husk.
I hand it back to gather dust on the shelf.

George Macbeth

ON THIS DAY:

In 1816 Sir Humphry Davy's safety lamp was first used in a coalmine.

Thomas Warton (1728–1790), who became Poet Laureate in 1785, was born.

In 1799 William Pitt the Younger (1759–1806), Prime Minister from December 1783 to 1801 and again from 1804 to 1806, introduced income tax ostensibly as a measure designed to finance the Napoleonic Wars.

Admiral Lord Horatio Nelson (1758–1805) was buried at St Paul's Cathedral, London in 1806.

Playwright Karel Čapek (1890–1938) was born.

In 1972 the National Union of Mineworkers called its members out on strike for the first time since 1926, causing widespread disruption.

The Cunard liner *Queen Elizabeth* was destroyed by fire in Hong Kong harbour in 1972.

January 10

Night Mail

I

This is the Night Mail crossing the Border,
Bringing the cheque and the postal order,

Letters for the rich, letters for the poor,
The shop at the corner, the girl next door.

Pulling up Beattock, a steady climb:
The gradient's against her, but she's on time.

Past cotton-grass and moorland boulder,
Shovelling white steam over her shoulder,

Snorting noisily, she passes
Silent miles of wind-bent grasses.

Birds turn their heads as she approaches,
Stare from bushes at her blank-faced coaches.

Sheep-dogs cannot turn her course;
They slumber on with paws across.

In the farm she passes no one wakes,
But a jug in a bedroom gently shakes.

II

Dawn freshens. Her climb is done.
Down towards Glasgow she descends,
Toward the steam tugs yelping down a glade of cranes,
Towards the fields of apparatus, the furnaces
Set on the dark plain like gigantic chessmen.
All Scotland waits for her:
In dark glens, beside pale-green lochs,
Men long for news.

III

Letters of thanks, letters from banks,
Letters of joy from girl and boy,
Receipted bills and invitations
To inspect new stock or to visit relations,
And applications for situations,
And timid lovers' declarations,
And gossip, gossip from all the nations,
News circumstantial, news financial,
Letters with holiday snaps to enlarge in,
Letters with faces scrawled on the margin,
Letters from uncles, cousins and aunts,
Letters to Scotland from the South of France,
Letters of condolence to Highlands and Lowlands,
Written on paper of every hue,
The pink, the violet, the white and the blue,
The chatty, the catty, the boring, the adoring,
The cold and official and the heart's outpouring,
Clever, stupid, short and long,
The typed and the printed and the spelt all wrong.

IV

Thousands are still asleep,
Dreaming of terrifying monsters
Or a friendly tea beside the band in Cranston's or Crawford's:
Asleep in working Glasgow, asleep in well-set Edinburgh,
Asleep in granite Aberdeen,
They continue their dreams,
But shall wake soon and hope for letters,
And none will hear the postman's knock
Without a quickening of the heart.
For who can bear to feel himself forgotten?

W. H. Auden

ON THIS DAY:

The final overnight journey of the Royal Mail's Travelling Sorting Office was made on 9th/10th January 2004. The journey made was between Bristol and Penzance.

January 11

The Heart of Thomas Hardy

The heart of Thomas Hardy flew out of Stinsford churchyard
A little thumping fig, it rocketed over the elm trees.
Lighter than air it flew straight to where its Creator
Waited in golden nimbus, just as in eighteen sixty,
Hardman and son of Brum had depicted Him in the chancel.
Slowly out of the grass, slitting the mounds in the centre
Riving apart the roots, rose the new covered corpses
Tess and Jude and His Worship, various unmarried mothers,
Woodmen, cutters of turf, adulterers, church restorers,
Turning aside the stones thump on the upturned churchyard.
Soaring over the elm trees slower than Thomas Hardy,
Weighted down with a Conscience, now for the first time fleshly
Taking form as a growth hung from the feet like a sponge-bag.
There, in the heart of the nimbus, twittered the heart of Hardy
There, on the edge of the nimbus, slowly revolved the corpses
Radiating around the twittering heart of Hardy,
Slowly started to turn in the light of their own Creator
Died away in the night as frost will blacken a dahlia.

Sir John Betjeman

ON THIS DAY:

The novelist and poet Thomas Hardy (1840–1928) died.

The first national lottery in England was held at St Paul's Cathedral, London in 1569. All the funds raised were donated to support public works.

In 1935 Amelia Earhart (1897–1937) became the first woman to fly solo across the Pacific Ocean when she crossed from Hawaii to California.

When I Heard the Learn'd Astronomer

When I heard the learn'd astronomer,
When the proofs, the figures, were ranged in columns before me,
When I was shown the charts and diagrams, to add, divide, and
    measure them,
When I sitting heard the astronomer where he lectured with much
    applause in the lecture-room,
How soon unaccountable I became tired and sick,
Till rising and gliding out I wander'd off by myself,
In the mystical moist night-air, and from time to time,
Look'd up in perfect silence at the stars.

Walt Whitman

ON THIS DAY:

John Flamsteed (1646–1719), the first Astronomer Royal, died.

The Zulu War, fought between the British forces of the Cape Colony and the people of Zululand, began in 1879.

The National Trust was founded in 1895. The founding members were Miss Octavia Hill (1838–1912), Canon Hardwicke Rawnsley (1851–1920) and Sir Robert Hunter (1844–1913).

The English novelist Nevil Shute (1899–1960), author of *On the Beach* and *The Legacy*, died.

Agatha Christie (1890–1976), creator of the detectives Hercule Poirot and Miss Marple, died.

January 13

The Quiet Snow

The quiet snow
Will splotch
Each in the row of cedars
With a fine
And patient hand;
Numb the harshness,
Tangle of that swamp.
It does not say, The sun
Does these things another way.

Even on hats of walkers,
The air of noise
And street-car ledges
It does not know
There should be hurry.

Raymond Knister

ON THIS DAY:

Edmund Spenser (c.1552–1599), poet and author of *The Faerie Queene*, died.

In 1893 the Independent Labour Party, led by Keir Hardie (1856–1915), was founded in Bradford, Yorkshire.

James Joyce (1882–1941), novelist and poet, died.

January 14

Cinema Paradiso

In the old days at the movies
There were three shows going on at once
As you curled into leather clad seats
Picking the studs down the sides

There was the first show
On the altar screen in front of you
Some exodus for the mind, reeling you in
Only because it was Saturday.

And beyond that, in the screen of your mind
Were the edited bits, the unused footage
Coming together by craft or neglect
A film of parts greater than whole.

And beyond that the greatest show on earth
Light particles dancing with dust
In a shafted energy of their own
Oblivious it seemed, to their starring role

In the longest shot of all
Projecting the art of one mind
To the silver screen and back
Into some other mind's eye

Ann Nadge

ON THIS DAY:

In 1896 the Royal Photographic Society, London presented the first public screening of a motion picture.

A demonstration of the telephone was presented to Queen Victoria (1819–1901, reigned 1837–1901) at Osborne House, Isle of Wight in 1878.

Hal Roach (1892–1992), film producer, was born.

The actor Humphrey Bogart (1899–1957), who appeared in the classic films *Casablanca, The Maltese Falcon, The Treasure of the Sierra Madre* and *The Big Sleep*, died.

In 1943 Franklin D. Roosevelt became the first US President to fly during office – to the Casablanca Conference, where he met Winston Churchill. The conference called for an end to the Second World War and an unconditional surrender by Germany.

January 15

Homage to the British Museum

There is a Supreme God in the ethnological section;
A hollow toad shape, faced with a blank shield.
He needs his belly to include the Pantheon,
Which is inserted through a hole behind.
At the navel, at the points formally stressed, at the organs of sense,
Lice glue themselves, dolls, local deities,
His smooth wood creeps with all the creeds of the world.

Attending there let us absorb the cultures of nations
And dissolve into our judgement all their codes.
Then, being clogged with a natural hesitation
(People are continually asking one the way out),
Let us stand here and admit that we have no road.
Being everything, let us admit that is to be something,
Or give ourselves the benefit of the doubt;
Let us offer our pinch of dust all to this God,
And grant his reign over the entire building.

Sir William Empson

ON THIS DAY:

In 1759 the British Museum opened to the public.

In 1535 Henry VIII became Supreme Head of the Church of England under the Act of Supremacy.

Elizabeth I (1533–1603, reigned 1558–1603), daughter of Henry VIII and Anne Boleyn, was crowned at Westminster Abbey, London in 1559.

The civil rights campaigner Martin Luther King (1929–1968) was born.

January 16

The Fury of Aerial Bombardment

You would think the fury of aerial bombardment
Would rouse God to relent; the infinite spaces
Are still silent. He looks on shock-pried faces.
History, even, does not know what is meant.

You would feel that after so many centuries
God would give man to repent; yet he can kill
As Cain could, but with multitudinous will,
No farther advanced than in his ancient furies.

Was man made stupid to see his own stupidity?
Is God by definition indifferent, beyond us all?
Is the eternal truth man's fighting soul
Wherein the Beast ravens in its own avidity?

Of Van Wettering I speak, and Averill,
Names on a list, whose faces I do not recall
But they are gone to early death, who late in school
Distinguished the belt feed lever from the belt holding pawl.

Richard Eberhart

ON THIS DAY:

In 1943 the RAF carried out the first air raid on the German capital city of Berlin.

Edward Gibbon (1737–1794), author of the *The Decline and Fall of the Roman Empire*, died. His tomb is in St Andrew and St Mary the Virgin Church, Fletching, East Sussex.

January 17

If you would not be forgotten...

If you would not be forgotten
As soon as you are dead and rotten
Either write things worth reading
Or do things worth the writing.

Benjamin Franklin

ON THIS DAY:

Benjamin Franklin (1706–1790), inventor, printer and statesman, was born.

In 1773 Captain James Cook (1728–1779) crossed the Antarctic Circle in his ship, *Resolution.*

The poet and novelist Anne Brontë (1820–1849) was born. She was the youngest of the three literary Brontë sisters.

David Lloyd George (1863–1945), Prime Minister from 1916 to 1922, was born.

January 18

The Way Through the Woods

They shut the road through the woods
Seventy years ago.
Weather and rain have undone it again,
And now you would never know
There was once a road through the woods
Before they planted the trees.
It is underneath the coppice and heath
And the thin anemones.
Only the keeper sees
That, where the ring-dove broods,
And the badgers roll at ease,
There was once a road through the woods.

Yet, if you enter the woods
Of a summer evening late,
When the night-air cools on the trout-ringed pools
Where the otter whistles his mate,
(They fear not men in the woods,
Because they see so few.)
You will hear the beat of a horse's feet,
And the swish of a skirt in the dew,
Steadily cantering through
The misty solitudes,
As though they perfectly knew
The old lost road through the woods...
But there is no road through the woods.

Rudyard Kipling

ON THIS DAY:

Rudyard Kipling (1865–1936), writer and winner of the Nobel Prize for literature, died.

Elizabeth of York, daughter of Edward IV (1442–1483, reigned 1461–1470, 1471–1483), married Henry VII (1457–1509, reigned 1485–1509). After years of bloodshed, the Houses of York and Lancaster were united, symbolised by a rose with white and red petals.

A. A. Milne (1882–1956), creator of Winnie the Pooh, was born.

Arthur Ransome (1884–1967), author of *Swallows and Amazons*, was born.

Captain Robert Falcon Scott (1868–1912) and his party reached the South Pole in 1912. They had failed to beat the Norwegian party, led by Roald Amundsen (1872–1928), by just 35 days.

Sir Cecil Beaton (1904–1980), designer and photographer, died.

January 19

A Last Will and Testament

To my dear wife,
My joy and life,
I freely now do give her
    My whole estate,
    With all my plate,
Being just about to leave her.

A tub of soap,
A long cart-rope,
A frying-pan and kettle;
    An ashes pail,
    A threshing flail,
An iron wedge and beetle.

Two painted chairs,
Nine warden pears,
A large old dripping platter;
    The bed of hay,
    On which I lay,
An old saucepan for butter.

A little mug,
A two-quart jug,
A bottle full of brandy;
    A looking-glass,
    To see your face,
You'll find it very handy.

A musket true
As ever flew,
A pound of shot, and wallet;
    A leather sash,
    My calabash,
My powder-horn, and bullet.

An old sword-blade,
A garden spade,
A hoe, a rake, a ladder;
   A wooden can,
   A close-stool pan,
A clyster-pipe, and bladder.

A greasy hat,
My old ram-cat,
A yard and half of linen;
   A pot of grease,
   A woollen fleece,
In order for your spinning.

A small toothcomb,
An ashen broom,
A candlestick, and hatchet;
   A coverlid,
   Striped down with red,
A bag of rags to patch it.

A ragged mat,
A tub of fat,
A book, put out by Bunyan,
   Another book,
   By Robin Rook,
A skein, or two, of spun yarn.

An old black muff,
Some garden stuff,
A quantity of borage;
   Some Devil's-weed,
   And burdock seed,
To season well your porridge.

A chafing-dish,
With one salt fish,
If I am not mistaken;
    A leg of pork,
    A broken fork,
And half a flitch of bacon.

A spinning-wheel,
One peck of meal;
A knife without a handle;
    A rusty lamp,
    Two quarts of samp,
And half a tallow candle.

My pouch and pipes,
Two oxen tripes,
An oaken dish well carved;
    My little dog,
    And spotted hog,
With two young pigs just starved.

This is my store,
I have no more,
I heartily do give it;
    My days are spun,
    My life is done,
And so I think to leave it.

John Winstanley

ON THIS DAY:
Paul Cézanne (1839–1906), impressionist painter, was born.
John Pudney (1909–1977), poet, was born.

January 20

Death of King George V

"New King arrives in his capital by air…"
Daily Newspaper.

Spirits of well-shot woodcock, partridge, snipe
    Flutter and bear him up the Norfolk sky:
In that red house in a red mahogany book-case
    The stamp collection waits with mounts long dry.

The big blue eyes are shut which saw wrong clothing
    And favourite fields and coverts from a horse;
Old men in country houses hear clocks ticking
    Over thick carpets with a deadened force;

Old men who never cheated, never doubted,
    Communicated monthly, sit and stare
At the new suburb stretched beyond the run-way
    Where a young man lands hatless from the air.

Sir John Betjeman

ON THIS DAY:

George V (1865–1936, reigned 1910–1936) died at Sandringham House, Norfolk. Betjeman's poem commemorates not only the death of the King but the fact that his eldest son Edward VIII arrived in London by aeroplane.

In 1649 Charles I (1600–1649, reigned 1625–1649) was brought before a high court of justice on charges of treason.

The actor David Garrick (1717–1779) died.

The film director Federico Fellini (1920–1993) was born in Rimini, Italy.

President Franklin D. Roosevelt (1882–1945), the 32nd President of the United States of America, began his second term in office in 1937. He held a record four terms in office.

In 1961 John F. Kennedy (1917–1963) was sworn in as the 35th President of the United States of America, the first Roman Catholic elected to the office.

January 21

Relativity

There was a young lady named Bright
Whose speed was far faster than light;
She set out one day,
In a relative way
And returned on the previous night.

A. H. Reginald Buller

ON THIS DAY:

In 1976, British Airways and Air France began supersonic commercial flights with Concorde. The inaugural routes were from London to Bahrain and Paris to Rio de Janeiro. Concorde was taken out of service in 2003.

In 1793 Louis XVI of France (1754–1793) was guillotined, and over a thousand years of the French monarchy came to an end.

Lenin (1870–1924), whose real name was Vladimir Ilyich Ulyanov, died and Petrograd was renamed Leningrad in his honour (the city reverted to its original name of St Petersburg in 1991).

George Orwell (1903–1950), whose real name was Eric Blair, author of *Animal Farm* and *1984*, died.

On This Day I Complete My Thirty-Sixth Year

'Tis time this heart should be unmoved,
　　Since others it hath ceased to move:
Yet, though I cannot be beloved,
　　Still let me love!

My days are in the yellow leaf;
　　The flowers and fruits of love are gone;
The worm, the canker, and the grief
　　Are mine alone!

The fire that on my bosom preys
　　Is lone as some volcanic isle;
No torch is kindled at its blaze –
　　A funeral pile.

The hope, the fear, the jealous care,
　　The exalted portion of the pain
And power of love, I cannot share,
　　But wear the chain.

But 'tis not *thus* – and 'tis not *here* –
　　Such thoughts should shake my soul, nor *now*,
Where glory decks the hero's bier,
　　Or binds his brow.

The sword, the banner, and the field,
　　Glory and Greece, around me see!
The Spartan, borne upon his shield,
　　Was not more free.

Awake! (not Greece – she *is* awake!)
　　Awake, my spirit! Think through *whom*
Thy life-blood tracks its parent lake,
　　And then strike home!

Tread those reviving passions down,
    Unworthy manhood! – unto thee
Indifferent should the smile or frown
    Of beauty be.

If thou regrett'st thy youth, *why live?*
    The land of honourable death
Is here: – up to the field, and give
    Away thy breath!

Seek out – less often sought than found –
    A soldier's grave, for thee the best;
Then look around, and choose thy ground,
    And take thy rest.

George Gordon, Lord Byron

ON THIS DAY:

George Gordon, Lord Byron (1788–1824) was born. He died in Greece a few months after writing this poem.

August Strindberg (1849–1912), playwright, poet and painter, was born.

Queen Victoria died in 1901.

In 1924 Ramsay MacDonald (1866–1937) became Prime Minister in Britain's first Labour government.

An Irish Airman Foresees His Death

I know that I shall meet my fate
Somewhere among the clouds above;
Those that I fight I do not hate,
Those that I guard I do not love;
My country is Kiltartan Cross,
My countrymen Kiltartan's poor,
No likely end could bring them loss
Or leave them happier than before.
Nor law, nor duty bade me fight,
Nor public men, nor cheering crowds,
A lonely impulse of delight
Drove to this tumult in the clouds;
I balanced all, brought all to mind,
The years to come seemed waste of breath,
A waste of breath the years behind
In balance with this life, this death.

W. B. Yeats

ON THIS DAY:

Major Robert Gregory, Royal Flying Corps, was killed in action by friendly fire over northern Italy in January 1918. He was the son of Yeats' friend, and patron, Lady Augusta Gregory. Yeats wrote several other poems to commemorate Major Gregory.

The French impressionist painter Édouard Manet (1832–1883) was born.

In 1849 Elizabeth Blackwell (1821–1910) became the first woman doctor in the USA.

January 24

The Rolling English Road

Before the Roman came to Rye or out to Severn strode,
The rolling English drunkard made the rolling English road.
A reeling road, a rolling road, that rambles round the shire,
And after him the parson ran, the sexton and the squire;
A merry road, a mazy road, and such as we did tread
The night we went to Birmingham by way of Beachy Head.

I knew no harm of Bonaparte and plenty of the Squire,
And for to fight the Frenchman I did not much desire;
But I did bash their baggonets because they came arrayed
To straighten out the crooked road an English drunkard made,
Where you and I went down the lane with ale-mugs in our hands,
The night we went to Glastonbury by way of Goodwin Sands.

His sins they were forgiven him; or why do flowers run
Behind him; and the hedges all strengthening in the sun?
The wild thing went from left to right and knew not which was which,
But the wild rose was above him when they found him in the ditch.
God pardon us, nor harden us; we did not see so clear
The night we went to Bannockburn by way of Brighton Pier.

My friends, we will not go again or ape an ancient rage,
Or stretch the folly of our youth to be the shame of age,
But walk with clearer eyes and ears this path that wandereth,
And see undrugged in evening light the decent inn of death;
For there is good news yet to hear and fine things to be seen
Before we go to Paradise by way of Kensal Green.

G. K. Chesterton

ON THIS DAY:

All Souls' Cemetery, Kensal Green, was consecrated in 1833, having been established by an Act of Parliament in July 1832.

William Congreve (1670–1729), English playwright and poet, was born. His first play was entitled *The Old Bachelor*. Later works included *The Mourning Bride* and *The Way of the World*.

Sir Winston Churchill (1874–1965), politician and statesman, died. His State Funeral was held on 30th January.

January 25

Sir Winston Churchill

The Divine Fortune, watching Life's affairs,
Justly endowed him with what Fortune may,
With sense of Storm and where the Centre lay,
With tact of deed, in some wise witty way,

Fortune of parents came in equal shares,
With England's wisest mingling with the West,
A startling newness, making better best,
A newness putting old things to a test...

So, when convulsion came, and direst need,
When, in a mess of Nations overthrown,
This England stood at bay, and stood alone,
His figure, then commanding, stood as stone,

Or, speaking, uttered like the very breed
Of Francis Drake, disaster being near,
One solemn watchword, to have done with fear.
Thence, without other drum-beat, all took cheer,
Content with such a Captain, such a Creed.

John Masefield

ON THIS DAY:

In 1965, *The Times* published this poem by Poet Laureate, John Masefield (1878–1969), as a tribute to Churchill, who had died the previous day.

Edward III (1312–1377, reigned 1327–1377) acceded to the throne. He laid claim to the French throne (through his mother, Isabella (1292–1358), daughter of Philip IV of France), which resulted in the Hundred Years War. The English were initially very successful with notable victories at Crécy (1346) and Poitiers (1356).

In 1533 Henry VIII secretly married Anne Boleyn (1501–1536).

The poet Robert Burns (1759–1796) was born. His birthday is celebrated annually as Burns Night.

The novelist Virginia Woolf (1882–1941) was born.

January 26

Advance Australia Fair

Australians all let us rejoice,
For we are young and free;
We've golden soil and wealth for toil;
Our home is girt by sea;
Our land abounds in nature's gifts
Of beauty rich and rare;
In history's page, let every stage
Advance Australia Fair.
In joyful strains then let us sing,
Advance Australia Fair.
Beneath our radiant Southern Cross
We'll toil with hearts and hands;
To make this Commonwealth of ours
Renowned of all the lands;
For those who've come across the seas
We've boundless plains to share;
With courage let us all combine
To Advance Australia Fair.
In joyful strains then let us sing,
Advance Australia Fair.

Peter Dodds McCormick

ON THIS DAY:

In 1788 Captain Arthur Phillip landed at Port Jackson, Sydney Cove, Australia (now Sydney, the capital of New South Wales). This day, Australia Day, is now a public holiday. Captain Phillip, who commanded a fleet of eleven ships carrying immigrants (mostly convicts), eventually became the first governor of New South Wales.

In 1836 the first Australia Day Regatta was held in Sydney Harbour.

January 27

Buna

Torn feet and cursed earth,
The long line in the grey morning.
The Buna smokes from a thousand chimneys,
A day like every other day awaits us.
The whistles terrible at dawn:
'You multitudes with dead faces,
On the monotonous horror of the mud
Another day of suffering is born.'
Tired companion, I see you in my heart.
I read your eyes, sad friend.
In your breast you carry cold, hunger, nothing.
You have broken what's left of the courage within you.
Colourless one, you were a strong man,
A woman walked at your side.
Empty companion who no longer has a name,
Forsaken man who can no longer weep,
So poor you no longer grieve,
So tired you no longer fear.
Spent once-strong man.
If we were to meet again
Up there in the world, sweet beneath the sun,
With what kind of face would we confront each other?

28th December 1945

Primo Levi

ON THIS DAY:

In 1945 the Allies liberated Nazi concentration camps at Auschwitz and Birkenau in Poland. The date is now observed as Holocaust Memorial Day. Primo Levi (1919–1987) had been held at Auschwitz.

The Reverend Charles Lutwidge Dodgson (1832–1898), writer (as Lewis Carroll), was born.

Thomas Sopwith (1888–1989), aircraft designer, died.

Christopher Lloyd (1921–2006), renowned horticulturalist and writer, died.

In Flanders Fields

In Flanders fields the poppies blow
Between the crosses, row on row,
    That mark our place; and in the sky
    The larks, still bravely singing, fly
Scarce heard amid the guns below.

We are the Dead. Short days ago
We lived, felt dawn, saw sunset glow,
    Loved and were loved, and now we lie
        In Flanders fields.

Take up our quarrel with the foe:
To you from failing hands we throw
    The torch; be yours to hold it high.
    If ye break faith with us who die
We shall not sleep, though poppies grow
        In Flanders fields.

John McCrae

ON THIS DAY:

John McCrae (1872–1918), poet and Canadian Army Surgeon, killed in action during the last year of the First World War.

Henry VIII died. His son, Edward VI (1537–1553, reigned 1547–1553), the only child from his third marriage, to Jane Seymour, succeeded him.

The poet W. B. Yeats (1865–1939) died.

January 29

On the Sea

It keeps eternal whisperings around
    Desolate shores, and with its mighty swell
    Gluts twice ten thousand Caverns, till the spell
Of Hecate leaves them their old shadowy sound.
Often 'tis in such gentle temper found,
    That scarcely will the very smallest shell
    Be moved for days from where it sometime fell,
When last the winds of Heaven were unbound.
Oh ye! who have your eyeballs vexed and tired,
    Feast them upon the wideness of the Sea;
        Oh ye! whose ears are dinned with uproar rude,
    Or fed too much with cloying melody –
        Sit ye near some old Cavern's Mouth, and brood,
Until ye start, as if the sea nymphs choired!

John Keats

ON THIS DAY:

In 1616 William Schouten (c.1580–1625) became the first man to sail around Cape Horn (in the *Unitie*). He was seeking a swifter route to the Far East. He sailed through the treacherous waters of Cape Horn on an unusually calm day.

Thomas Paine (1737–1809), political writer, was born.

In 1856 the Victoria Cross was instituted by Royal Warrant and awarded retrospectively to 1854. The first 62 crosses, awarded mostly for service in the Crimea (1854–1856), were presented by Queen Victoria at an investiture in Hyde Park on 26th June 1857.

Alfred Sisley (1839–1899), impressionist painter, died.

H. E. Bates (1905–1974), creator of Pop Larkin, died.

Robert Frost (1874–1963), poet, died.

On the Funeral of Charles the First
at Night, in St George's Chapel, Windsor

The castle clock had tolled midnight:
   With mattock and with spade,
And silent, by the torches' light,
   His corse in earth we laid.

The coffin bore his name, that those
   Of other years might know,
When earth its secrets should disclose,
   Whose bones were laid below.

'Peace to the dead' no children sung,
   Slow pacing up the nave, –
No prayers were read, no knell was rung,
   As deep we dug his grave.

We only heard the winter's wind,
   In many a sullen gust,
As, o'er the open grave inclined,
   We murmured, 'Dust to dust!'

A moonbeam from the arch's height
   Streamed, as we placed the stone;
The long aisles started into light,
   And all the windows shone.

We thought we saw the banners then,
   That shook along the walls,
Whilst the sad shades of mailèd men
   Were gazing on the stalls.

'Tis gone! again on tombs defaced
   Sits darkness more profound;
And only by the torch we traced
   The shadows on the ground.

And now the chilling, freezing air
    Without blew long and loud;
Upon our knees we breathed one prayer,
    Where he slept in his shroud.

We laid the broken marble floor, –
    No name, no trace appears, –
And when we closed the sounding door,
    We thought of him with tears.

William Lisle Bowles

ON THIS DAY:

Charles I was beheaded outside the Banqueting Hall at Whitehall, London.

Adolf Hitler (1889–1945) was named Chancellor of Germany by President Hindenburg in 1933.

The State Funeral of Sir Winston Churchill (1874–1965) was held.

January 31

1901

When Queen Victoria died
The whole of England mourned
Not for a so recently breathing old woman
A wife and a mother and a widow,
Not for a staunch upholder of Christendom,
A stickler for etiquette
A vigilant of moral values
But for a symbol.
A symbol of security and prosperity
Of 'My Country Right or Wrong'
Of 'God is good and Bad is bad'
And 'What was good enough for your father
Ought to be good enough for you'
And 'If you don't eat your tapioca pudding
You will be locked in your bedroom
And given nothing but bread and water
Over and over again until you come to your senses
And are weak and pale and famished and say
Breathlessly, hopelessly and with hate in your heart
"Please Papa I would now like some tapioca pudding very much indeed"'
A symbol too of proper elegance
Not the flaunting, bejewelled kind
That became so popular
But a truly proper elegance,
An elegance of the spirit,
Of withdrawal from unpleasant subjects
Such as Sex and Poverty and Pit Ponies
And Little Children working in the Mines
And Rude Words and Divorce and Socialism
And numberless other inadmissible horrors.
When Queen Victoria died
They brought her little body from the Isle of Wight
Closed up in a black coffin, finished and done for,
With no longer any feelings and regrets and Memories of Albert
And no more blood pumping through the feeble veins

And no more heart beating away
As it had beaten for so many tiring years.
The coffin was placed upon a gun-carriage
And drawn along sadly and slowly by English sailors.

But long before this the people had mourned
And walked about the streets and the Parks and Kensington Gardens
Silently, solemnly and dressed in black.
Now, with the news already a few days old
The immediate shock had faded.
The business of the funeral was less poignant than the first realization
    of death,
This was a pageant, right and fitting, but adjustments were already
beginning to be made.
This was something we were all used to,
This slow solemnity
This measured progress to the grave.
If it hadn't been for the gun-carriage
And the crowds and all the flags at half mast
And all the shops being closed
It might just as well have been Aunt Cordelia
Who died a few months earlier in Torquay
And had to be brought up to London by the Great Western
In a rather large coffin
And driven slowly, oh so slowly
To the family burial ground at Esher
With all the relatives driving behind
Wearing black black black and peering furtively out of the carriage windows
To note for a moment that life was going on as usual.
For Aunt Cordelia was no symbol really
And her small death was of little account.
She was, after all, very old indeed
Although not quite so old as Queen Victoria
But on the other hand she didn't have so much prestige
Except of course in her own personal mind
And that was snuffed out at the same moment as everything else
Also, unlike Queen Victoria, she had few mourners

Just the family and Mrs Stokes who had been fond of her
And Miss Esme Banks who had looked after her in Torquay
And two remote cousins
Who couldn't rightly be classed as family
Because they were so very far removed
And only came to the cemetery because it was a sign of respect,
Respect, what is more, without hope
For there was little or no likelihood of their being mentioned in the will
But there they were all the same
Both tall and bent, in black toques with veils,
And both crying.

When Queen Victoria died
And was buried and the gun-carriage was dragged empty away again
The shops reopened and so did the theatres
Although business was none too good.
But still it improved after a while
And everyone began to make plans for the Coronation
And it looked as if nothing much had happened
And perhaps nothing much had really
Except that an era, an epoch, an attitude of mind, was ended.

There would be other eras and epochs and attitudes of mind.
But never quite the same.

Sir Noël Coward

ON THIS DAY:

Queen Victoria's body rested at Osborne House for the last time prior to travelling to London on 1st February for her funeral.

Guy Fawkes (1570–1606) was executed in London for his part in the Gunpowder Plot of November 1605.

In 1858 the SS *Great Eastern*, designed by Isambard Kingdom Brunel (1806–1859), was launched.

A. A. Milne (1882–1956), author, died.

FEBRUARY

February 1

Ceremonies for Candlemasse Eve

Down with the Rosemary and Bayes,
  Down with the Mistleto;
In stead of Holly, now up-raise
  The greener Box (for show.)

The Holly hitherto did sway;
  Let Box now domineere;
Until the dancing Easter-day,
  Or Easters Eve appeare.

Then youthfull Box which now hath grace,
  Your houses to renew;
Grown old, surrender must his place,
  Unto the crispedYew.

When Yew is out, then Birch comes in,
  And many Flowers beside;
Both of a fresh, and fragrant kinne
  To honour Whitsontide.

Green Rushes then, and sweetest Bents,
  With cooler Oken boughs;
Come in for comely ornaments,
  To re-adorn the house.
Thus times do shift; each thing his turne do's hold;
New things succeed, as former things grow old.

Robert Herrick

ON THIS DAY:

In 1587 Elizabeth I signed the death warrant of Mary, Queen of Scots (1542–1587). Mary was executed on 8th February 1587.

Mary Wollstonecraft Shelley (1797–1851), writer, creator of *Frankenstein*, and second wife of Percy Bysshe Shelley (1792–1822), died.

Sir Stanley Matthews (1915–2000), footballer, was born.

A Song for Candlemas

There's never a rose upon the bush,
And never a bud on any tree;
In wood and field nor hint nor sign
Of one green thing for you or me.
Come in, come in, sweet love of mine,
And let the bitter weather be!

Coated with ice the garden wall;
The river reeds are stark and still;
The wind goes plunging to the sea,
And last week's flakes the hollows fill.
Come in, come in, sweet love, to me,
And let the year blow as it will!

Lizette Woodworth Reese

ON THIS DAY:

The festival of Candlemas is celebrated on 2nd February (forty days after Christmas Day).

In 1709 Alexander Selkirk, a Scottish sailor, was rescued from an island near Chile, after being marooned for over four years. His story provided inspiration for Daniel Defoe's *Robinson Crusoe*.

James Joyce (1882–1941), was born. His work *Ulysses* was published on this day in 1922 in Paris.

The funeral of Queen Victoria took place at St George's Chapel, Windsor in 1901. The Queen was interred in Frogmore Mausoleum, next to her husband, Prince Albert (1819–1861).

Bertrand Russell, the third Earl Russell (1872–1970), mathematician, philosopher and campaigner for nuclear disarmament, died.

February 3

To the Lady May

Your smiles are not, as other womens bee,
Only the drawing of the mouth awrye;
For breasts and cheekes and forehead wee may see,
    Parts wanting motion, all stand smiling by.
Heaven hath noe mouth, and yet is sayd to smile
      After your stile;
Noe more hath Earth, yet that smyles too,
      Just as you doe.

Noe sympering lipps nor lookes can breed
Such smyles as from your face proceed.
The sunn must lend his goulden beames,
    Soft windes their breath, green trees their shade,
Sweet fields their flowers, cleare springs their streams,
    Ere such another smyle bee made.
But these concurring, wee may say,
So smiles the spring, and soe smyles lovely May.

Aurelian Townshend

ON THIS DAY:

In 1616 Sir Humphrey May, Lord Chamberlain of the Household (from 1629), married his second wife Judith and this poem is believed to have been written in her honour.

Felix Mendelssohn (1809–1847), composer, was born.

Sidney Lanier (1842–1881), poet, was born.

Hugh Montague Trenchard, first Viscount Trenchard (1873–1956), founder of the police college at Hendon and principal architect of the establishment of the RAF in 1918, was born.

Woodrow Wilson (1856–1924), President of the United States of America (1913–1921) and Nobel Peace laureate (1919), died.

February 4

The Snow Storm

Announced by all the trumpets of the sky,
Arrives the snow, and, driving o'er the fields,
Seems nowhere to alight: the whited air
Hides hills and woods, the river, and the heaven,
And veils the farmhouse at the garden's end.
The sled and traveller stopped, the courier's feet
Delayed, all friends shut out, the housemates sit
Around the radiant fireplace, enclosed
In a tumultuous privacy of storm.

Come see the north wind's masonry.
Out of an unseen quarry evermore
Furnished with tile, the fierce artificer
Curves his white bastions with projected roof
Round every windward stake, or tree, or door.
Speeding, the myriad-handed, his wild work
So fanciful, so savage, nought cares he
For number or proportion. Mockingly,
On coop or kennel he hangs Parian wreaths;
A swan-like form invests the hidden thorn;
Fills up the farmer's lane from wall to wall,
Maugre the farmer's sighs; and, at the gate,
A tapering turret overtops the work.
And when his hours are numbered, and the world
Is all his own, retiring, as he were not,
Leaves, when the sun appears, astonished Art
To mimic in slow structures, stone by stone,
Built in an age, the mad wind's night-work,
The frolic architecture of the snow.

Ralph Waldo Emerson

ON THIS DAY:

Charles Lindbergh (1902–1974), aviator who in 1927 completed the first non-stop solo transatlantic flight, between New York and Paris, was born.

Gavin Ewart (1916–1995), poet, was born.

Louise Bogan (1897–1970), poet, died.

Patricia Highsmith (1921–1995), author, and creator of the character Tom Ripley, died.

Poetry

I, too, dislike it: there are things that are important beyond all this fiddle.
  Reading it, however, with a perfect contempt for it, one discovers in
  it after all, a place for the genuine.
      Hands that can grasp, eyes
      that can dilate, hair that can rise
          if it must, these things are important not because a

high-sounding interpretation can be put upon them but because they are
  useful. When they become so derivative as to become unintelligible,
  the same thing may be said for all of us, that we
      do not admire what
      we cannot understand: the bat
          holding on upside down or in quest of something to

eat, elephants pushing, a wild horse taking a roll, a tireless wolf under
  a tree, the immovable critic twitching his skin like a horse that feels
  a flea, the base-
      ball fan, the statistician –
      nor is it valid
          to discriminate against 'business documents and

school-books'; all these phenomena are important. One must make a
          distinction
  however: when dragged into prominence by half poets, the result is not
          poetry,
      nor till the poets among us can be
      'literalists of
      the imagination' – above
          insolence and triviality and can present

for inspection, 'imaginary gardens with real toads in them', shall we have
  it. In the meantime, if you demand on the one hand,
      the raw materials of poetry in
      all its rawness and
      that which is on the other hand
          genuine, you are interested in poetry.

Marianne Moore

ON THIS DAY:

Marianne Moore (1887–1972), poet, died.

February 6

Stanley Matthews

Not often *con brio*, but *andante, andante,*
   horseless, though jockey-like and jaunty,
Straddling the touchline, live margin
   not out of the game, nor quite in,
Made by him green and magnetic, stroller
Indifferent as a cat dissembling, rolling
A little as on deck, till the mouse, the ball,
   slides palely to him,
And shyly, almost with deprecatory cough, he is off.

Head of a Perugino, with faint flare
Of the nostrils, as though Lipizzaner-like,
   he sniffed at the air,
Finding it good beneath him, he draws
Defenders towards him, the ball a bait
They refuse like a poisoned chocolate,
   retreating, till he slows his gait
To a walk, inviting the tackle, inciting it.

At last, unrefusable, dangling the ball at the instep
He is charged — and stiffening so slowly
It is rarely perceptible, he executes with a squirm
Of the hips, a twist more suggestive than apparent,
   that lazily disdainful move *toreros* term
     a Veronica — it's enough.
Only emptiness following him, pursuing some scent
Of his own, he weaves in towards,
   not away from, fresh tacklers,
Who, turning about to gain time, are by him
   harried, pursued not pursuers.

Now gathers speed, nursing the ball as he cruises,
Eyes judging distance, noting the gaps, the spaces
Vital for colleagues to move to, slowing a trace,
As from Vivaldi to Dibdin, pausing,
    and leisurely, leisurely, swings
To the left upright his centre, on hips
His hands, observing the goalkeeper spring,
    heads rising vainly to the ball's curve
Just as it's plucked from them; and dispassionately
Back to his mark he trots, whistling through closed lips.

Trim as a yacht, with similar lightness
    — of keel, of reaction to surface—with salt air
Tanned, this incomparable player, in decline fair
    to look at, nor in decline either,
Improving like wine with age, has come far—
    born to one, a barber, who boxed
Not with such filial magnificence, but well.
'The greatest of all time,' *meraviglioso*, Matthews—
    Stoke City, Blackpool and England.
Expressionless enchanter, weaving as on strings
Conceptual patterns to a private music, heard
Only by him, to whose slowly emerging theme
He rehearses steps, soloist in compulsions of a dream.

Alan Ross

ON THIS DAY:

George VI (1895–1952, reigned 1936–1952) died and his eldest daughter acceded to the throne, as Elizabeth II, (b.1926).

Women received the right to vote in 1918.

In 1965 the *London Gazette* published the notification that Stanley Matthews (1915–2000) had received a knighthood.

February 7

Winter: My Secret

I tell my secret? No indeed, not I:
Perhaps some day, who knows?
But not today; it froze, and blows, and snows,
And you're too curious: fie!
You want to hear it? well:
Only, my secret's mine, and I won't tell.

Or, after all, perhaps there's none:
Suppose there is no secret after all,
But only just my fun.
Today's a nipping day, a biting day;
In which one wants a shawl,
A veil, a cloak, and other wraps:
I cannot ope to every one who taps,
And let the draughts come whistling thro' my hall;
Come bounding and surrounding me,
Come buffeting, astounding me,
Nipping and clipping thro' my wraps and all.
I wear my mask for warmth: who ever shows
His nose to Russian snows
To be pecked at by every wind that blows?
You would not peck? I thank you for good will,
Believe, but leave that truth untested still.

Spring's an expansive time: yet I don't trust
March with its peck of dust,
Nor April with its rainbow-crowned brief showers,
Nor even May, whose flowers
One frost may wither thro' the sunless hours.

Perhaps some languid summer day,
When drowsy birds sing less and less,
And golden fruit is ripening to excess,
If there's not too much sun nor too much cloud,
And the warm wind is neither still nor loud,
Perhaps my secret I may say,
Or you may guess.

Christina Rossetti

ON THIS DAY:

Sir Thomas More (1478–1535), scholar and politician, was born.

Charles Dickens (1812–1870), author, was born.

Lament of Mary, Queen of Scots
On the Approach of Spring

Now Nature hangs her mantle green
    On every blooming tree
And spreads her sheets o' daisies white
    Out o'er the grassy lea;
Now Phoebus cheers the crystal streams
    And glads the azure skies;
But nought can glad the weary wight
    That fast in durance lies.

Now laverocks wake the merry morn,
    Aloft on dewy wing;
The merle, in his noontide bower,
    Makes woodland echoes ring;
The mavis wild wi' monie a note,
    Sings drowsy day to rest:
In love and freedom they rejoice,
    Wi' care nor thrall opprest.

Now blooms the lily by the bank,
    The primrose down the brae;
The hawthorn's budding in the glen,
    And milk-white is the slae:
The meanest hind in fair Scotland
    May rove their sweets amang;
But I, the Queen of a' Scotland,
    Maun lie in prison strang.

I was the Queen o' bonnie France,
    Where happy I hae been;
Fu' lightly raise I in the morn,
    As blythe lay down at e'en:
And I'm the sov'reign of Scotland,
    And monie a traitor there;
Yet here I lie in foreign bands,
    And never-ending care.

But as for thee, thou false woman,
   My sister and my fae,
Grim Vengeance yet shall whet a sword
   That thro' thy soul shall gae!
The weeping blood in woman's breast
   Was never known to thee;
Nor th' balm that draps on wounds of woe
   Frae woman's pitying e'e.

My son! my son! may kinder stars
   Upon thy fortune shine;
And may those pleasures gild thy reign
   That ne'er wad blink on mine!
God keep thee frae thy mother's faes,
   Or turn their hearts to thee:
And where thou meet'st thy mother's friend,
   Remember him for me!

O! soon, to me, may Summer suns
   Nae mair light up the morn!
Nae mair to me the Autumn winds
   Wave o'er the yellow corn!
And in the narrow house o' death
   Let winter round me rave;
And the next flowers that deck the spring,
   Bloom on my peaceful grave.

Robert Burns

ON THIS DAY:

Mary, Queen of Scots was executed at Fotheringhay Castle by order of Elizabeth I for her alleged participation in a plot to overthrow Elizabeth. Her son, James VI of Scotland, succeeded Elizabeth in 1603 and became James I of England.

Sir Giles Gilbert Scott (1880–1960), son of George Gilbert Scott Jr (1839–1897), architect of the Anglican cathedral in Liverpool and designer of the red telephone boxes, died.

Halley's Comet

My father saw it back in 1910,
The year King Edward died.
Above dark telegraph poles, above the high
Spiked steeple of the Liberal Club, the white
Gas-lit dials of the Market Clock,
Beyond the wide
Sunset-glow cirrus of blast-furnace smoke,
My father saw it fly
Its thirty-seven-million-mile-long kite
Across Black Combe's black sky.

And what of me,
Born four years too late?
Will I have breath to wait
Till the long-circuiting commercial traveller
Turns up at his due?
In 1986, aged seventy-two,
Watery in the eyes and phlegmy in the flue
And a bit bad tempered at so delayed a date,
Will I look out above whatever is left of the town –
The Liberal Club long closed and the clock stopped,
And the chimneys smokeless above damped-down
Furnace fires? And then will I
At last have chance to see it
With my own as well as my father's eyes,
And share his long-ago Edwardian surprise
At that high, silent jet, laying its bright trail
Across Black Combe's black sky?

Norman Nicholson

ON THIS DAY:

In 1986 Halley's Comet was visible from earth as it made its passage on its 76-year orbit. Named after Edmund Halley (1656–1742) it passed closer to the sun on this occasion than on previous recorded orbits.

The body of Charles I was buried at Windsor. Kings and Queens were traditionally buried at Westminster Abbey but the measure was taken in order to avoid any disturbances caused by supporters of the monarchy. The King had been beheaded on 30th January.

Brendan Behan (1923–1964), writer, was born.

Of Poor B.B.

I

I, Bertolt Brecht, came out of the black forests.
My mother moved me into the cities as I lay
Inside her body. And the coldness of the forests
Will be inside me till my dying day.

II

In the asphalt city I'm at home. From the very start
Provided with every last sacrament:
With newspapers. And tobacco. And brandy
To the end mistrustful, lazy and content.

III

I'm polite and friendly to people. I put on
A hard hat because that's what they do.
I say: they are animals with a quite peculiar smell
And I say: does it matter? I am too.

IV

Before noon on my empty rocking chairs
I'll sit a woman or two, and with an untroubled eye
Look at them steadily and say to them:
Here you have someone on whom you can't rely.

V

Towards evening it's men that I gather round me
And then we address one another as 'gentlemen'.
They're resting their feet on my table tops
And say: things will get better for us. And I don't ask when.

VI

In the grey light before morning the pine trees piss
And their vermin, the birds, raise their twitter and cheep.
At that hour in the city I drain my glass, then throw
The cigar butt away and worriedly go to sleep.

VII

We have sat, an easy generation
In houses held to be indestructible
(Thus we built those tall boxes on the island of Manhattan
And those thin aerials that amuse the Atlantic swell).

VIII

Of those cities will remain what passed through them, the wind!
The house makes glad the eater: he clears it out.
We know that we're only tenants, provisional ones
And after us there will come: nothing worth talking about.

IX

In the earthquakes to come, I very much hope
I shall keep my cigar alight, embittered or no
I, Bertolt Brecht, carried off to the asphalt cities
From the black forests inside my mother long ago.

Bertolt Brecht

ON THIS DAY:

Bertolt Brecht (1898–1956), playwright and poet, was born.

Charles Lamb (1775–1834), poet, was born.

Samuel Plimsoll (1824–1898), reformer whose name was given to the load-line on ships, was born.

Harold Macmillan (1894–1986), Prime Minister from 1957 to 1963, was born.

Photograph of Haymaker, 1890

It is not so much the image of the man
that's moving – he pausing from his work
to whet his scythe, trousers tied
below the knee, white shirt lit by
another summer's sun, another century's –
as the sight of the grasses beyond
his last laid swathe, so living yet
upon the moment previous to death;
for as the man stooping straightened up
and bent again they died before his blade.

Sweet hay and gone some seventy years ago
and yet they stand before me in the sun,
stems damp still where their neighbours' fall
uncovered them, succulent and straight,
immediate with moon-daisies.

Molly Holden

ON THIS DAY:

William Fox Talbot (1800–1877), photography pioneer who, in 1835, took the earliest surviving photograph, was born.

In 1531 Henry VIII's position as Supreme Head of the Church of England was recognised by the clergy.

Thomas Edison (1847–1931), inventor, and the first man to record sound (in 1877), was born.

John Buchan (1875–1940), first Baron Tweedsmuir and writer, died.

In 1929 the Vatican became an independent papal state within the city of Rome.

In 1990 Nelson Mandela (b.1918) was released from jail.

The Solitude of Alexander Selkirk

I am monarch of all I survey;
My right there is none to dispute;
From the centre all round to the sea
I am lord of the fowl and the brute.
O Solitude! where are the charms
That sages have seen in thy face?
Better dwell in the midst of alarms
Than reign in this horrible place.

I am out of humanity's reach,
I must finish my journey alone,
Never hear the sweet music of speech;
I start at the sound of my own.
The beasts that roam over the plain
My form with indifference see;
They are so unacquainted with man,
Their tameness is shocking to me.

Society, Friendship, and Love
Divinely bestow'd upon man,
O had I the wings of a dove
How soon would I taste you again!
My sorrows I then might assuage
In the ways of religion and truth,
Might learn from the wisdom of age,
And be cheer'd by the sallies of youth.

Religion! what treasure untold
Resides in that heavenly word!
More precious than silver or gold,
Or all that this earth can afford.
But the sound of the church-going bell
These vallies and rocks never heard,
Ne'er sigh'd at the sound of a knell,
Or smil'd when a sabbath appear'd.

Ye winds that have made me your sport,
Convey to this desolate shore
Some cordial endearing report
Of a land I shall visit no more:
My friends, do they now and then send
A wish or a thought after me?
O tell me I yet have a friend,
Though a friend I am never to see.

How fleet is a glance of the mind!
Compared with the speed of its flight,
The tempest itself lags behind,
And the swift-wingéd arrows of light.
When I think of my own native land
In a moment I seem to be there;
But alas! recollection at hand
Soon hurries me back to despair.

But the seafowl is gone to her nest,
The beast is laid down in his lair;
Even here is a season of rest,
And I to my cabin repair.
There's mercy in every place,
And mercy, encouraging thought!
Gives even affliction a grace
And reconciles man to his lot.

William Cowper

ON THIS DAY:

Alexander Selkirk (1676–1721), the inspiration for the character of Robinson Crusoe, was born.

Abraham Lincoln (1809–1865), the 16th President of the United States (1861–1865), was born. He was assassinated by John Wilkes Booth.

Charles Darwin (1809–1882), explorer, scientist and writer, was born. His ground-breaking work *On the Origin of Species by Natural Selection* was published in 1859.

February 13

February 13, 1975

Tomorrow is St Valentine's:
tomorrow I'll think about
that. Always nervous, even
after a good sleep I'd like
to climb back into. The sun
shines on yesterday's new-
fallen snow and yestereven
it turned the world to pink
and rose and steel-blue
buildings. Helene is restless:
leaving soon. And what then
will I do with myself? Some-
one is watching morning
TV. I'm not reduced to that
yet. I wish one could press
snowflakes in a book like flowers.

James Schuyler

ON THIS DAY:

The first trading mission of the East India Company departed from London in 1601.

Richard Wagner (1813–1883), composer, died.

Georges Simenon (1903–1989), writer and creator of the French detective Maigret, was born.

In 1924 Howard Carter supervised the opening of Tutankhamun's sarcophagus during an archaeo-logical expedition funded by the Earl of Carnarvon.

The German town of Dresden was bombed by the RAF in 1945.

H. M. Bateman (1887–1970), cartoonist, died.

February 14

Air and Angels

Twice or thrice had I lov'd thee,
Before I knew thy face or name;
So in a voice, so in a shapeless flame,
Angels affect us oft, and worshipped be;
    Still when, to where thou wert, I came,
Some lovely glorious nothing I did see,
    But since my soul, whose child love is,
Takes limbs of flesh, and else could nothing do,
    More subtle than the parent is
Love must not be, but take a body too,
    And therefore what thou wert, and who
      I bid love ask, and now
That it assume thy body, I allow,
And fix itself in thy lip, eye, and brow.

Whilst thus to ballast love, I thought,
And so more steadily to have gone,
With wares which would sink admiration,
I saw, I had love's pinnace overfraught,
    Every thy hair for love to work upon
Is much too much, some fitter must be sought;
    For, nor in nothing, nor in things
Extreme, and scatt'ring bright, can love inhere;
    Then as an angel, face and wings
Of air, not pure as it, yet pure doth wear,
    So thy love may be my love's sphere;
      Just such disparity
As is 'twixt air and angels' purity,
'Twixt women's love, and men's will ever be.

John Donne

ON THIS DAY:

14th February is the feast day of St Valentine.

In 1895 *The Importance of Being Earnest*, the last play written by Oscar Wilde (1854–1900), opened at St James's Theatre in London.

Richard II (1367–1400, reigned 1377–1399), died at Pontefract Castle, Yorkshire in 1400.

Sir Pelham G. Wodehouse (1881–1975), writer and creator of characters such as Bertie Wooster and his manservant Jeeves, died at his home in America.

Maple and Sumach

Maple and sumach down this autumn ride—
Look, in what scarlet character they speak!
For this their russet and rejoicing week
Trees spend a year of sunsets on their pride.
You leaves drenched with the lifeblood of the year—
What flamingo dawns have wavered from the east,
What eves have crimsoned to their toppling crest
To give the fame and transience that you wear!
Leaf-low he shall lie soon: but no such blaze
Briefly can cheer man's ashen, harsh decline;
His fall is short of pride, he bleeds within
And paler creeps to the dead end of his days.
O light's abandon and the fire-crest sky
Speak in me now for all who are to die!

C. Day Lewis

ON THIS DAY:

Canada flew its new flag, depicting the maple leaf, for the first time in 1965.

Jeremy Bentham (1748–1832), philosopher, was born.

Sir Ernest Shackleton (1874–1922), explorer, was born.

H. M. Bateman (1887–1970), cartoonist, was born.

Herbert Asquith (1853–1928), Prime Minister 1908–1916, died.

In 1971 decimal currency was introduced in Britain.

February Evening in New York

As the stores close, a winter light
   opens air to iris blue,
   glint of frost through the smoke
   grains of mica, salt of the sidewalk.
As the buildings close, released autonomous
   feet pattern the streets
   in hurry and stroll; balloon heads
   drift and dive above them; the bodies
   aren't really there.
As the lights brighten, as the sky darkens,
   a woman with crooked heels says to another woman
   while they step along at a fair pace,
   'You know, I'm telling you, what I love best
   is life. I love life! Even if I ever get
   to be old and wheezy – or limp! You know?
   Limping along? – I'd still... 'Out of hearing.
To the multiple disordered tones
   of gears changing, a dance
   to the compass points, out, four-way river.
   Prospect of sky
   wedged into avenues, left at the ends of streets,
   west sky, east sky: more life tonight! A range
   of open time at winter's outskirts.

Denise Levertov

ON THIS DAY:

In 1659 Nicholas Vanacker wrote the first cheque, for the sum of £10.

The Battle Creek Toasted Cornflake Company was founded in 1906 by J. H. Kellogg and W. K. Kellogg.

Leslie Hore-Belisha (1893–1957), Minister of Transport who was responsible for the introduction of beacons at zebra crossings, died.

Celandine

Thinking of her had saddened me at first,
Until I saw the sun on the celandines lie
Redoubled, and she stood up like a flame,
A living thing, not what before I nursed,
The shadow I was growing to love almost,
The phantom, not the creature with bright eye
That I had thought never to see, once lost.

She found the celandines of February
Always before us all. Her nature and name
Were like those flowers, and now immediately
For a short swift eternity back she came,
Beautiful, happy, simply as when she wore
Her brightest bloom among the winter hues
Of all the world; and I was happy too,
Seeing the blossoms and the maiden who
Had seen them with me Februarys before,
Bending to them as in and out she trod
And laughed, with locks sweeping the mossy sod.

But this was a dream: the flowers were not true,
Until I stooped to pluck from the grass there
One of five petals and I smelt the juice
Which made me sigh, remembering she was no more,
Gone like a never perfectly recalled air.

Edward Thomas

ON THIS DAY:

In 1938 the first public transmission of colour television occurred with a broadcast from Crystal Palace to the Dominion Theatre in central London.

André Maginot (1877–1932), French politician and Minister of Defence, was born. His name was given to a line of concrete fortifications, tank obstacles, machine gun posts and other defences which the French constructed along their border with Germany after the First World War.

In 1972 President Richard Nixon (1913–1994) departed for China, the first such visit by a US president.

February 18

To the Moon

The glittering colours of the day are fled–
    Come, melancholy orb! that dwell'st with night,
Come, and o'er earth thy wandering lustre shed,
    Thy deepest shadow, and thy softest light.
To me congenial is the gloomy grove,
    When with faint rays the sloping uplands shine;
That gloom, those pensive rays, alike I love,
    Whose sadness seems in sympathy with mine.
But most for this, pale orb! thy light is dear,
    For this, benignant orb! I hail thee most,
That while I pour the unavailing tear,
    And mourn that hope to me in youth is lost–
Thy light can visionary thoughts impart,
And lead the Muse to soothe a suffering heart.

Helen Maria Williams

ON THIS DAY:

The Pilgrim's Progress by John Bunyan (1628–1688), written mostly whilst he was imprisoned for illegal preaching, was published in 1678.

In 1504 Prince Henry (the future king Henry VIII) was invested as Prince of Wales.

Mary I, only daughter of King Henry VIII and his first wife, Catherine of Aragon, was born.

Martin Luther (1483–1546), Protestant reformer, died.

J. Robert Oppenheimer (1904–1967), theoretical physicist, died.

In 1979 snow fell in the Sahara.

The Sun Rising

Busy old fool, unruly Sun,
　　Why dost thou thus,
Through windows, and through curtains call on us?
Must to thy motions lovers' seasons run?
　　Saucy pedantic wretch, go chide
　　Late school-boys and sour 'prentices,
　Go tell court-huntsmen that the King will ride,
　Call country ants to harvest offices;
Love, all alike, no season knows, nor clime,
Nor hours, days, months, which are the rags of time.

　　Thy beams, so reverend and strong
　　Why shouldst thou think?
I could eclipse and cloud them with a wink,
But that I would not lose her sight so long:
　　If her eyes have not blinded thine,
　　Look, and tomorrow late tell me,
　Whether both the Indias of spice and mine
　Be where thou left'st them, or lie here with me.
Ask for those kings whom thou saw'st yesterday,
And thou shalt hear, 'All here in one bed lay.'

　　She's all States, and all Princes I;
　　Nothing else is.
Princes do but play us; compared to this,
All honour's mimic; all wealth alchemy.
　　Thou, Sun, art half as happy as we,
　　In that the world's contracted thus;
　Thine age asks ease, and since thy duties be
　To warm the world, that's done in warming us.
Shine here to us, and thou art everywhere;
This bed thy centre is, these walls thy sphere.

John Donne

ON THIS DAY:

David Garrick (1717–1779), actor and student of Samuel Johnson, was born.

Georg Büchner (1813–1837), poet and dramatist, died from typhus.

Thomas Edison (1847–1931) patented the phonograph, the first piece of equipment which could record sound, in 1878.

February 20

Blow, Blow, Thou Winter Wind

Blow, blow, thou winter wind,
Thou art not so unkind
As man's ingratitude;
Thy tooth is not so keen
Because thou art not seen
Although thy breath be rude.
Heigh ho! sing heigh ho! unto the green holly:
Most friendship is feigning, most loving mere folly:
Then, heigh ho, the holly!
This life is most jolly.

Freeze, freeze, thou bitter sky,
Thou dost not bite so nigh
As benefits forgot:
Though thou the waters warp,
Thy sting is not so sharp
As friend remember'd not.
Heigh ho! sing heigh ho! unto the green holly:
Most friendship is feigning, most loving mere folly:
Then, heigh ho! the holly!
This life is most jolly.

William Shakespeare

ON THIS DAY:

The steamer *John Rutledge* was abandoned after it hit an iceberg on the journey from Liverpool to New York in 1856. Only one passenger survived out of a total of 136.

Adam Black (1784–1874), founder of A. & C. Black Publishers (in 1807), was born.

Dame Marie Rambert (1888–1982), ballerina and founder of a dance company, was born.

Earl Mountbatten of Burma (1900–1979) was appointed Viceroy of India in 1947, the last person to hold the office. India became an independent Dominion within the Commonwealth later that year.

A Winter Night

It was a chilly winter's night;
   And frost was glittering on the ground,
And evening stars were twinkling bright;
   And from the gloomy plain around
      Came no sound,
But where, within the wood-girt tower,
The churchbell slowly struck the hour;
As if that all of human birth
   Had risen to the final day,
And soaring from the worn-out earth
   Were called in hurry and dismay,
      Far away;
And I alone of all mankind
Were left in loneliness behind.

William Barnes

ON THIS DAY:

W. H. Auden (1907–1973), poet, was born.

The siege of Verdun began on this day in 1916. It lasted ten months, during which time both sides suffered heavy losses. The German troops were eventually defeated by the French.

The magazine the *New Yorker* was first published in 1925.

Dame Margot Fonteyn (1919–1991), prima ballerina, died.

The Mangel-Bury

It was after war; Edward Thomas had fallen at Arras –
I was walking by Gloucester musing on such things
As fill his verse with goodness; it was February; the long house
Straw-thatched of the mangels stretched two wide wings;
And looked as part of the earth heaped up by dead soldiers
In the most fitting place – along the hedge's yet-bare lines.
West spring breathed there early, that none foreign divines.
Across the flat country the rattling of the cart sounded;
Heavy of wood, jingling of iron; as he neared me I waited
For the chance perhaps of heaving at those great rounded
Ruddy or orange things – and right to be rolled and hefted
By a body like mine, soldier still, and clean from water.
Silent he assented; till the cart was drifted
High with those creatures, so right in size and matter.
We threw with our bodies swinging, blood in my ears singing;
His was the thick-set sort of farmer, but well-built –
Perhaps, long before, his blood's name ruled all,
Watched all things for his own. If my luck had so willed
Many questions of lordship I had heard him tell – old
Names, rumours. But my pain to more moving called
And him to some barn business far in the fifteen acre field.

Ivor Gurney

ON THIS DAY:

George Washington (1732–1799), who in 1789 became the first President of the United States, was born.

In 1879 Frank Winfield Woolworth (1852–1919) opened his first store in Utica, New York. All goods were sold at a price of just five cents.

Sir John Mills (1908–2005), actor who appeared in films such as *Ice Cold in Alex* and *Ryan's Daughter*, was born.

February 23

When I have Fears

When I have fears that I may cease to be
  Before my pen has gleaned my teeming brain,
Before high piled books, in charactry,
  Hold like rich garners the full ripened grain;
When I behold, upon the night's starred face,
  Huge cloudy symbols of a high romance,
And think that I may never live to trace
  Their shadows, with the magic hand of chance;
And when I feel, fair creature of an hour,
  That I shall never look upon thee more,
Never have relish in the fairy power
  Of unreflecting love; – then on the shore
Of the wide world I stand alone, and think
Till love and fame to nothingness do sink.

John Keats

ON THIS DAY:

John Keats (1795–1821), poet, died in Rome.

Samuel Pepys (1633–1703), diarist, was born.

Sir Joshua Reynolds (1723–1792), painter and first President of the Royal Academy of Arts, died.

The Cato Street conspiracy of 1820 was uncovered on this day. The conspirators planned to assassinate all members of the British Cabinet. Five of the conspirators were tried for treason and subsequently executed.

L. S. Lowry (1887–1976), painter, died.

Sir Stanley Matthews (1915–2000), footballer, died.

Frost at Midnight

The Frost performs its secret ministry,
Unhelped by any wind. The owlet's cry
Came loud – and hark, again! loud as before.
The inmates of my cottage, all at rest,
Have left me to that solitude, which suits
Abstruser musings: save that at my side
My cradled infant slumbers peacefully.
'Tis calm indeed! so calm, that it disturbs
And vexes meditation with its strange
And extreme silentness. Sea, hill, and wood,
This populous village! Sea, and hill, and wood,
With all the numberless goings-on of life,
Inaudible as dreams! the thin blue flame
Lies on my low-burnt fire, and quivers not;
Only that film, which fluttered on the grate,
Still flutters there, the sole unquiet thing.
Methinks its motion in this hush of nature
Gives it dim sympathies with me who live,
Making it a companionable form,
Whose puny flaps and freaks the idling Spirit
By its own moods interprets, everywhere
Echo or mirror seeking of itself,
And makes a toy of Thought.

But O! how oft,
How oft, at school, with most believing mind,
Presageful, have I gazed upon the bars,
To watch that fluttering *stranger*! and as oft
With unclosed lids, already had I dreamt
Of my sweet birthplace, and the old church tower,
Whose bells, the poor man's only music, rang
From morn to evening, all the hot Fair-day,
So sweetly, that they stirred and haunted me
With a wild pleasure, falling on mine ear
Most like articulate sounds of things to come!

So gazed I, till the soothing things, I dreamt,
Lulled me to sleep, and sleep prolonged my dreams!
And so I brooded all the following morn,
Awed by the stern preceptor's face, mine eye
Fixed with mock study on my swimming book:
Save if the door half opened, and I snatched
A hasty glance, and still my heart leaped up,
For still I hoped to see the *stranger's* face,
Townsman, or aunt, or sister more beloved,
My playmate when we both were clothed alike!

Dear Babe, that sleepest cradled by my side,
Whose gentle breathings, heard in this deep calm,
Fill up the interspersèd vacancies
And momentary pauses of the thought!
My babe so beautiful! it thrills my heart
With tender gladness, thus to look at thee,
And think that thou shalt learn far other lore,
And in far other scenes! For I was reared
In the great city, pent 'mid cloisters dim,
And saw nought lovely but the sky and stars.
But *thou*, my babe! shalt wander like a breeze
By lakes and sandy shores, beneath the crags
Of ancient mountain, and beneath the clouds,
Which image in their bulk both lakes and shores
And mountain crags: so shalt thou see and hear
The lovely shapes and sounds intelligible
Of that eternal language, which thy God
Utters, who from eternity doth teach
Himself in all, and all things in himself.
Great universal Teacher! he shall mould
Thy spirit, and by giving make it ask.

Therefore all seasons shall be sweet to thee,
Whether the summer clothe the general earth
With greenness, or the redbreast sit and sing
Betwixt the tufts of snow on the bare branch

Of mossy apple tree, while the nigh thatch
Smokes in the sun-thaw; whether the eave-drops fall
Heard only in the trances of the blast,
Or if the secret ministry of frost
Shall hang them up in silent icicles,
Quietly shining to the quiet Moon.

Samuel Taylor Coleridge

ON THIS DAY:

Originally one of the feast days of St Matthias, it was said that if a frost fell on St Matthias's day it would last from a week to two months before thawing. In 1969 St Matthias's day was moved to 14th May.

In 1582 Gregory XIII (Pope 1572–1585) issued a papal bull introducing the Gregorian calendar, which replaced the Julian calendar. It was adopted first by Italy, France, Spain and Portugal.

In 1923 the *Flying Scotsman*, number 4472, first entered service with the London and North Eastern Railway. After steam locomotives were withdrawn from service, the *Flying Scotsman* had a number of owners but it is now in the National Railway Museum in York.

D.G.B.: In Memoriam

Written in February 2001, on the death of Sir Donald Bradman

The spell alas is over now:
A sea of silence lies.
Great things were conqueringly done
That illumined the skies.

Minds cannot justly comprehend
The prizes that were gained –
Mind and muscle finely tuned:
But not to be explained.

The memory of a soaring hour,
Of wrists and eye so vivid yet,
Which could remove men from their squalor
And in its place a fortune set.

A fortune not of wealth or riches
But of sky-blue faultlessness,
Through skill and power – and centuries –
Put forth with ripened peerlessness.

The volcano, awesome in its might, is stilled,
The present from the past unties.
The spell alas is over now:
A sea of silence lies.

Irving Rosenwater

ON THIS DAY:

Sir Donald Bradman (1908–2001), record-breaking Australian cricketer, died.

Edward II (1284–1327, reigned 1307–1327) was crowned King of England in succession to his father, Edward I (1239–1307, reigned 1272–1307).

Sir Christopher Wren (1632–1723), architect of St Paul's Cathedral, died. His tomb is in the cathedral.

Tennessee Williams (1911–1983), playwright, died.

Keats

The young Endymion sleeps Endymion's sleep;
   The shepherd-boy whose tale was left half told!
   The solemn grove uplifts its shield of gold
   To the red rising moon, and loud and deep
The nightingale is singing from the steep;
   It is midsummer, but the air is cold;
   Can it be death? Alas, beside the fold
   A shepherd's pipe lies shattered near his sheep.
Lo! in the moonlight gleams a marble white,
   On which I read: 'Here lieth one whose name
   Was writ in water.' And was this the meed
Of his sweet singing? Rather let me write:
   'The smoking flax before it burst to flame
   Was quenched by death, and broken the bruised reed.'

Henry Wadsworth Longfellow

ON THIS DAY:

The poet John Keats (1795–1821) was buried in the Protestant Cemetery in Rome, three days after his death.

In 1797 the Bank of England issued £1 notes for the first time.

The Grand National (originally known as the Grand Liverpool Steeplechase) was held for the first time at Aintree Racecourse in 1839. The winning horse was called Lottery.

In 1848 *The Communist Manifesto* was published for the first time.

The inventor Sir Robert Watson-Watt (1892–1973) demonstrated radar (radio detection and ranging) for the first time in 1935. The invention would prove invaluable during the Second World War.

Snow-Flakes

Out of the bosom of the Air,
  Out of the cloud-folds of her garments shaken,
Over the woodlands brown and bare,
  Over the harvest-fields forsaken,
    Silent, and soft, and slow
    Descends the snow.

Even as our cloudy fancies take
  Suddenly shape in some divine expression,
Even as the troubled heart doth make
  In the white countenance confession,
    The troubled sky reveals
    The grief it feels.

This is the poem of the air,
  Slowly in silent syllables recorded;
This is the secret of despair,
  Long in its cloudy bosom hoarded,
    Now whispered and revealed
    To wood and field.

Henry Wadsworth Longfellow

ON THIS DAY:

The poet Henry Wadsworth Longfellow (1807–1882) was born. Very popular during his lifetime, he was also Professor of Modern Languages and Literature at Harvard University.

The writer John Steinbeck (1902–1968) was born.

Benjamin Disraeli (1804–1881) became Prime Minister for the first time in 1868. He was Prime Minister again from 1874 to 1880.

In 1900 the Labour Representation Committee (LRC) was set up in order to establish a distinct Labour Group in Parliament. Labour candidates had first stood in 1892. In 1906 the LRC became known as the Labour Party.

The Year's Awakening

How do you know that the pilgrim track
Along the belting zodiac
Swept by the sun in his seeming rounds
Is traced by now to the Fishes' bounds
And into the Ram, when weeks of cloud
Have wrapt the sky in a clammy shroud,
And never as yet a tinct of spring
Has shown in the Earth's apparelling;
   O vespering bird, how do you know,
     How do you know?

How do you know, deep underground,
Hid in your bed from sight and sound,
Without a turn in temperature,
With weather life can scarce endure,
That light has won a fraction's strength,
And day put on some moments' length,
Whereof in merest rote will come,
Weeks hence, mild airs that do not numb;
   O crocus root, how do you know,
     How do you know?

Thomas Hardy

ON THIS DAY:

Michel de Montaigne (1533–1592), writer and courtier, was born.

In 1900, in the first few months of the Second Anglo-Boer War, the British garrison at Ladysmith was relieved after a siege lasting four months.

Henry James (1843–1916), writer, died in London.

February

The robin on my lawn,
He was the first to tell
How, in the frozen dawn,
This miracle befell,
Waking the meadows white
With hoar, the iron road
Agleam with splintered light,
And ice where water flowed:
Till, when the low sun drank
Those milky mists that cloak
Hanger and hollied bank,
The winter world awoke
To hear the feeble bleat
Of lambs on the downland farms:
A blackbird whistled sweet;
Old beeches moved their arms
Into a mellow haze
Aerial, newly-born:
And I, alone, agaze,
Stood waiting for the thorn
To break in blossoms white,
Or burst in a green flame…
So, in a single night,
Fair February came,
Bidding my lips to sing
Or whisper their surprise,
With all the joy of spring
And morning in her eyes.

Francis Brett Young

ON THIS DAY:

St Hilarius, the forty-sixth pope (?–468, Pope 461–468), died. His feast day is celebrated on 28th February.

St Oswald (?–992), Archbishop of York, died. His feast day is celebrated on 28th February.

There is an old custom that during a leap year ladies may propose marriage, and if refused, claim a silk gown.

MARCH

March 1

First Snow in Alsace

The snow came down last night like moths
Burned on the moon; it fell till dawn,
Covered the town with simple cloths.

Absolute snow lies rumpled on
What shellbursts scattered and deranged,
Entangled railings, crevassed lawn.

As if it did not know they'd changed,
Snow smoothly clasps the roofs of homes
Fear-gutted, trustless and estranged.

The ration stacks are milky domes;
Across the ammunition pile
The snow has climbed in sparkling combs.

You think: beyond the town a mile
Or two, this snowfall fills the eyes
Of soldiers dead a little while.

Persons and persons in disguise,
Walking the new air white and fine,
Trade glances quick with shared surprise.

At children's windows, heaped, benign,
As always, winter shines the most,
And frost makes marvellous designs.

The night guard coming from his post,
Ten first-snows back in thought, walks slow
And warms him with a boyish boast:

He was the first to see the snow.

Richard Wilbur

ON THIS DAY:

Richard Wilbur, poet and translator, was born in 1921.

Today is the feast day of St David, the patron saint of Wales.

The first issue of the *Spectator* was published in 1711.

Robert Lowell (1917–1977), poet, was born.

March

Slayer of the winter, art thou here again?
O welcome, thou that bring'st the summer nigh!
The bitter wind makes not thy victory vain,
Nor will we mock thee for thy faint blue sky.
Welcome, O March! whose kindly days and dry
Make April ready for the throstle's song,
Thou first redresser of the winter's wrong!

Yea, welcome March! and though I die ere June,
Yet for the hope of life I give thee praise,
Striving to swell the burden of the tune
That even now I hear thy brown birds raise,
Unmindful of the past or coming days;
Who sing: 'O joy! a new year is begun:
What happiness to look upon the sun!'

Ah, what begetteth all this storm of bliss
But Death himself, who crying solemnly,
E'en from the heart of sweet Forgetfulness,
Bids us 'Rejoice, lest pleasureless ye die.
Within a little time must ye go by.
Stretch forth your open hands, and while ye live
Take all the gifts that Death and Life may give.'

William Morris

ON THIS DAY:

This is the feast day of St Chad (?–672), patron saint of mineral springs.

Kurt Weill (1900–1950), composer and collaborator with Bertolt Brecht (1898–1956) on *The Threepenny Opera*, was born.

D. H. Lawrence (1885–1930), writer and poet, died.

Howard Carter (1874–1939), Egyptologist, died.

March the Third

Here again (she said) is March the third
And twelve hours' singing for the bird
'Twixt dawn and dusk, from half-past six
To half-past six, never unheard.

'Tis Sunday, and the church-bells end
When the birds do. I think they blend
Now better than they will when passed
Is this unnamed, unmarked godsend.

Or do all mark, and none dares say,
How it may shift and long delay,
Somewhere before the first of Spring,
But never fails, this singing day?

And when it falls on Sunday, bells
Are a wild natural voice that dwells
On hillsides; but the birds' songs have
The holiness gone from the bells.

This day unpromised is more dear
Than all the named days of the year
When seasonable sweets come in,
Because we know how lucky we are.

Edward Thomas

ON THIS DAY:

Edward Thomas (1878–1917), poet, was born. He fought in France during the First World War and
died at the battle of Arras.

The poet and politician Edmund Waller (1606–1687) was born.

Alexander Graham Bell (1847–1922), the inventor of the telephone, was born.

Edward Herbert (1582–1648), poet and statesman, was born.

March 4

After the Shipwreck

Lost, drifting on the current, as the sun pours down
Like syrup, drifting into afternoon,

The raft endlessly rocks, tips, and we say to each other:
Here is where we will store the rope, the dried meat, the knife,

The medical kit, the biscuits, and the cup.
We will divide the water fairly and honestly.

Black flecks in the air produce dizziness.
Somebody raises a voice and says: Listen, we know there is land

Somewhere, in some direction. We must know it.
And there is the landfall, cerulean mountain-range

On the horizon: there in our minds. Then nothing
But the beauty of ocean,

Numberless waves like living, hysterical heads,
The sun increasingly magnificent,

A sunset wind hitting us. As the spray begins
To coat us with salt, we stop talking. We try to remember.

Alicia Ostriker

ON THIS DAY:

The Royal National Lifeboat Institution (RNLI) was founded in 1824 by Sir William Hillary (1771–1847).

In 1675 John Flamsteed (1646–1719) was appointed the first Astronomer Royal.

The Forth Rail Bridge was opened in 1890 by Edward, Prince of Wales.

William Carlos Williams (1883–1963), poet, died.

In 1975 Charles Chaplin (1889–1977) was knighted.

March 5

Letty's Globe

When Letty had scarce pass'd her third glad year,
   And her young, artless words began to flow,
One day we gave the child a colour'd sphere
   Of the wide earth, that she might mark and know,
By tint and outline, all its sea and land.
   She patted all the world; old empires peep'd
Between her baby fingers; her soft hand
   Was welcome at all frontiers. How she leap'd,
And laugh'd, and prattled in her world-wide bliss;
   But when we turned her sweet unlearned eye
On our own isle, she raised a joyous cry,
   'Oh! yes, I see it, Letty's home is there!'
And, while she hid all England with a kiss,
   Bright over Europe fell her golden hair.

Charles Turner

ON THIS DAY:

Gerardus Mercator (1512–1594), cartographer, was born. He devised the method of map drawing using longitude and latitude lines. Originally used for nautical maps, the method was adapted and is now used on land maps.

Henry II (1133–1189, reigned 1154–1189), was born.

The Spitfire fighter aeroplane took off on its maiden flight from Eastleigh airport in Hampshire on this day in 1936. The plane was designed by R. J. Mitchell (1895–1937).

Joseph Stalin (1879–1953), died.

March 6

If it's ever Spring again

If it's ever spring again,
  Spring again,
I shall go where went I when
Down the moor-cock splashed, and hen,
Seeing me not, amid their flounder,
Standing with my arm around her;
If it's ever spring again,
  Spring again,
I shall go where went I then.

It it's ever summer-time,
  Summer-time,
With the hay crop at the prime,
And the cuckoos – two – in rhyme,
As they used to be, or seemed to,
We shall do as long we've dreamed to,
If it's ever summer-time,
  Summer-time,
With the hay, and bees achime.

Thomas Hardy

ON THIS DAY:

Francis Beaumont (1584–1616), playwright, died. His earliest known play was *The Woman Hater* (first performed in c.1605).

The poet Elizabeth Barrett Browning (1806–1861) was born in Durham.

Ivor Novello (1893–1951), actor and composer of musicals, died.

Georgia O'Keeffe (1887–1986), painter, died.

Note on Local Flora

There is a tree native in Turkestan,
Or further east towards the Tree of Heaven,
Whose hard cold cones, not being wards to time,
Will leave their mother only for good cause;
Will ripen only in a forest fire;
Wait, to be fathered as was Bacchus once,
Through men's long lives, that image of time's end.
I knew the Phoenix was a vegetable.
So Semele desired her deity
As this in Kew thirsts for the Red Dawn.

Sir William Empson

ON THIS DAY:

In 1804 The Royal Horticultural Society (RHS), originally known as The Royal Horticultural Society of London, was founded at Hatchard's in Piccadilly, London by Sir Joseph Banks (1744–1820) and John Wedgewood (1766–1844).

Thomas Aquinas (1225–1274), theologian, philosopher and author of *Summa Theologica*, died.

The HMS *Beagle*, captained by Robert FitzRoy, and with Charles Darwin as one of her passengers, set sail from Chile in 1835.

In 1876 Alexander Graham Bell (1847–1922) patented the invention of the telephone.

March 8

from Summer's Last Will and Testament

Spring, the sweete spring, is the yeres pleasant King,
Then bloomes eche thinge, then maydes daunce in a ring,
Cold doeth not sting, the pretty birds doe sing,
Cuckow, jugge, jugge, pu we, to witta woo.

The Palme and May make countrey houses gay,
Lambs friske and play, the Shepherds pype all day,
And we heare aye birds tune this merry lay,
Cuckow, jugge, jugge, pu we, to witta woo.

The fields breathe sweete, the dayzies kisse our feete,
Young lovers meete, old wives a sunning sit;
In every streete, these tunes our eares doe greete,
Cuckow, jugge, jugge, pu we, to witta woo.
Spring, the sweete spring.

Thomas Nashe

ON THIS DAY:

In 1702, Anne (1665–1714) acceded to the throne when William III (1650–1702) was killed in a riding accident. In 1711 the Queen introduced horse racing on Ascot Heath.

Kenneth Grahame (1859–1932), author of *The Wind in the Willows*, was born.

Life

Animula, vagula, blandula.

> Life! I know not what thou art,
> But know that thou and I must part;
> And when, or how, or where we met,
> I own to me's a secret yet.
> But this I know, when thou art fled,
> Where'er they lay these limbs, this head,
> No clod so valueless shall be,
> As all that then remains of me.
> O whither, whither dost thou fly,
> Where bend unseen thy trackless course,
>   And in this strange divorce,
> Ah tell where I must seek this compound I?
>
> To the vast ocean of empyreal flame,
>   From whence thy essence came,
>   Dost thou thy flight pursue, when freed
>   From matter's base encumbering weed?
>   Or dost thou, hid from sight,
>   Wait, like some spell-bound knight,
> Through blank oblivious years th'appointed hour,
> To break thy trance and reassume thy power?
> Yet canst thou without thought or feeling be?
> O say what art thou, when no more thou 'rt thee?
>
>   Life! we've been long together,
>   Through pleasant and through cloudy weather;
>   'Tis hard to part when friends are dear;
>   Perhaps 't will cost a sigh, a tear;
>   Then steal away, give little warning,
>   Choose thine own time;
>   Say not Good night, but in some brighter clime
>   Bid me Good morning.

Anna Laetitia Barbauld

ON THIS DAY:

Anna Laetitia Barbauld (1743–1824), poet and editor, died.

March 10

Am I to Lose You?

'Am I to lose you now?' The words were light;
　　You spoke them, hardly seeking a reply,
　　That day I bid you quietly 'Good-bye,'
And sought to hide my soul away from sight.
The question echoed, dear, through many a night, –
　　My question, not your own – most wistfully;
　　'Am I to lose him?' – asked my heart of me;
'Am I to lose him now, and lose him quite?'

And only you can tell me. Do you care
　　That sometimes we in quietness should stand
　　As fellow-solitudes, hand firm in hand,
And thought with thought and hope with hope compare?
What is your answer? Mine must ever be,
　　'I greatly need your friendship: leave it me.'

Louisa S. Guggenberger

I So Liked Spring

I so liked Spring last year
Because you were here; –
    The thrushes too –
Because it was these you so liked to hear –
    I so liked you.

This year's a different thing, –
    I'll not think of you.
But I'll like Spring because it is simply Spring
    As the thrushes do.

Charlotte Mew

ON THIS DAY:

The Luddite Riots began on the night of 11th March 1811. The group known as the Luddites, led by the mythical 'Ned Ludd', were hand-loom weavers who feared the changes that the introduction of machinery into their workplaces would bring. The riots began in Nottingham when looms were destroyed. The disturbances continued over the next year and spread to Lancashire and Yorkshire before dying out in 1816. The Luddites were later severely punished. Some were transported to Australia and others were executed.

Sir Henry Tate (1819–1899), sugar merchant who endowed the Tate Gallery on Millbank, was born.

Three years into the First World War, Baghdad was captured by the British in 1917.

Sir Harold Wilson (1916–1995), politician and Prime Minister 1964–1970 and 1974–1976, later Baron Wilson of Rievaulx, was born.

The bacteriologist Sir Alexander Fleming (1881–1955) died. His experiments led to the discovery of penicillin, a widely used antibiotic.

Upon Arch-bishop Laud, Prisoner in the Tower. 1641

Our Canterburye's great Cathedrall Bell
Seldome rings out, but makes a fatall knell.
Her loud unpleasing warring-jarring sound
The noyse of all our well-tun'd Bells hath drown'd.
Shee lately rang so loud, I am in doubt
Shee had almost struck Lincolne's clapper out.

It is reported by the men of Kent,
Shee sound's such discord, shee gives no content;
But that shee's ponderous, and so great, the People
Would very gladly pull her out o'th'steeple.

Shee makes an hideous noyse with her Bum-Bom,
As did the roaring Bull that came from Rome.
Shee'le serve for nothing, shee's so full of brasse,
But for to ring the Catholicks to Masse.

Except the Parliament will take this Bell,
And cast her new agayne, or hang her well;
And make both her, and all the rest, that are
So bigge, more tuneable, though lesse by farre.

Then they, that wont to ring so seldome well,
May prove each one a constant Sermon-Bell.
So shall wee have good Musick, and lesse noyse;
And have our Church purg'd from new-fangled toyes.

Anonymous

ON THIS DAY:

The trial of Archbishop William Laud (1573–1645) began in 1644. Favoured by Charles I, Laud attempted to impose the King's authority and liturgical uniformity throughout the kingdom but faced opposition from the Scots and fellow clergymen. The trial proved inconclusive and Laud was condemned by special decree of the House of Commons and the House of Lords and was beheaded in 1645.

The University of Cambridge challenged the University of Oxford to a boat race in 1829. The first race was held in June of the same year. Oxford won.

Edward Albee, playwright and author of *Who's Afraid of Virginia Woolf?*, was born in 1928.

The BBC began to broadcast its programmes from Broadcasting House in 1932.

March 13

The Coronet

When for the Thorns with which I long, too long,
    With many a piercing wound,
    My Saviours head have crown'd,
I seek with Garlands to redress that Wrong:
    Through every Garden, every Mead,
I gather flow'rs (my fruits are only flow'rs)
    Dismantling all the fragrant Towers
That once adorn'd my Shepherdesses head.
And now when I have summ'd up all my store,
    Thinking (so I my self deceive)
    So rich a Chaplet thence to weave
As never yet the king of Glory wore:
    Alas I find the Serpent old
    That, twining in his speckled breast,
    About the flow'rs disguis'd does fold,
    With wreaths of Fame and Interest.
Ah, foolish Man, that would'st debase with them,
And mortal Glory, Heavens Diadem!
But thou who only could'st the Serpent tame,
Either his slipp'ry knots at once untie,
And disentangle all his winding Snare:
Or shatter too with him my curious frame:
And let these wither, so that he may die,
Though set with Skill and chosen out with Care.
That they, while Thou on both their Spoils dost tread,
May crown thy Feet, that could not crown thy Head.

Andrew Marvell

ON THIS DAY:

Halley's Comet passed through its perihelion in 1759. Edmond Halley (1656–1742) had predicted that the comet would return around 1757 and in December 1758 it did. His accurate prediction meant that earlier references to the comet's appearances, in historical records, could be authenticated.

In 1781 the planet Uranus was discovered by William Herschel (1738–1822). It was then the seventh known planet of the Solar System and the most distant from the sun. Herschel first named the planet Georgium Sidus in honour of George III.

Isabelle Beeton (1836–1865), author of *The Book of Household Management*, was born.

Sir Hugh Walpole (1884–1941), novelist, was born.

Titwillow (*from* The Mikado)

On a tree by a river a little tom-tit
  Sang 'Willow, titwillow, titwillow!'
And I said to him, 'Dicky-bird, why do you sit
  Singing "Willow, titwillow, titwillow"?'
'Is it weakness of intellect, birdie?' I cried,
'Or a rather tough worm in your little inside?'
With a shake of his poor little head, he replied,
  'Oh, willow, titwillow, titwillow!'

He slapped at his chest, as he sat on that bough,
  Singing 'Willow, titwillow, titwillow!'
And a cold perspiration bespangled his brow,
  Oh, willow, titwillow, titwillow!
He sobbed and he sighed, and a gurgle he gave,
Then he plunged himself into the billowy wave,
And an echo arose from the suicide's grave –
  'Oh, willow, titwillow, titwillow!'

Now I feel just as sure as I'm sure that my name
  Isn't Willow, titwillow, titwillow,
That 'twas blighted affection that made him exclaim
  'Oh, willow, titwillow, titwillow!'
And if you remain callous and obdurate, I
Shall perish as he did, and you will know why,
Though I probably shall not exclaim as I die,
  'Oh, willow, titwillow, titwillow!'

W. S. Gilbert

ON THIS DAY:
The Mikado by Gilbert and Sullivan opened at the Savoy Theatre, London in 1885.
Albert Einstein (1879–1955) was born.
Karl Marx (1818–1883) died.
John Wain (1925–1994), poet, novelist and critic, was born.

The Donkey

When fishes flew and forests walked
    And figs grew upon thorn,
Some moment when the moon was blood,
    Then surely I was born;

With monstrous head and sickening cry
    And ears like errant wings,
The devil's walking parody
    On all four-footed things.

The tattered outlaw of the earth,
    Of ancient crooked will;
Starve, scourge, deride me: I am dumb,
    I keep my secret still.

Fools! For I also had my hour;
    One far fierce hour and sweet:
There was a shout about my ears,
    And palms before my feet!

G. K. Chesterton

ON THIS DAY:

This is the earliest date on which Palm Sunday, the next before Easter Day, can occur.

The Ides of March is notorious for the assassination of Julius Caesar by a group of Senators including Marcus Junius Brutus in 44BC. Ostensibly staged to restore Rome's freedoms and wrest control from Caesar's hands, little of benefit was achieved by the act, and further civil war followed.

In 1493 Christopher Columbus (1451–1506) returned to Spain.

In 1649 the poet John Milton was appointed Cromwell's Latin (foreign language) secretary.

The first cricket Test match was held in Melbourne between Australia and England in 1877. Australia won by 45 runs.

London Bridge is falling down

London Bridge is falling down,
Falling down, falling down,
London Bridge is falling down,
My fair Lady.

Build it up with wood and clay,
Wood and clay, wood and clay,
Build it up with wood and clay
My fair Lady.

Wood and clay will wash away,
Wash away, wash away,
Wood and clay will wash away,
My fair Lady.

Build it up with bricks and mortar,
Bricks and mortar, bricks and mortar,
Build it up with bricks and mortar,
My fair Lady.

Bricks and mortar will not stay,
Will not stay, will not stay,
Bricks and mortar will not stay,
My fair Lady.

Build it up with iron and steel,
Iron and steel, iron and steel,
Build it up with iron and steel,
My fair Lady.

Iron and steel will bend and bow,
Bend and bow, bend and bow,
Iron and steel will bend and bow,
My fair Lady.

Build it up with silver and gold,
Silver and gold, silver and gold,
Build it up with silver and gold,
My fair Lady.

Silver and gold will be stolen away,
Stolen away, stolen away,
Silver and gold will be stolen away,
My fair Lady.

Set a man to watch all night,
Watch all night, watch all night,
Set a man to watch all night,
My fair Lady.

Suppose the man should fall asleep?
Fall asleep, fall asleep,
Suppose the man should fall asleep?
My fair Lady.

Give him a pipe to smoke all night,
Smoke all night, smoke all night,
Give him a pipe to smoke all night,
My fair Lady.

Anonymous

ON THIS DAY:

In 1973 HM Queen Elizabeth II opened the new London Bridge. The previous bridge had been sold and was later rebuilt in Arizona, USA.

Aubrey Beardsley (1872–1898), illustrator, died.

The Lamb

Little Lamb, who made thee?
Dost thou know who made thee?
Gave thee life, and bid thee feed
By the stream and o'er the mead;
Gave thee clothing of delight,
Softest clothing, wooly, bright;
Gave thee such a tender voice,
Making all the vales rejoice?
Little Lamb, who made thee?
Dost thou know who made thee?

Little Lamb, I'll tell thee,
Little Lamb, I'll tell thee:
He is called by thy name,
For he calls himself a Lamb.
He is meek, and he is mild;
He became a little child.
I a child, and thou a lamb,
We are called by his name.
Little Lamb, God bless thee!
Little Lamb, God bless thee!

William Blake

ON THIS DAY:

In 1337 Edward III created the Duchy of Cornwall for his son Edward (1330–1376), known as the Black Prince.

The feast day of St Patrick, the patron saint of Ireland, is celebrated.

Seed

The first warm day of spring
and I step out into the garden from the gloom
of a house where hope had died
to tally the storm damage, to seek what may
have survived. And finding some forgotten
lupins I'd sown from seed last autumn
holding in their fingers a raindrop each
like a peace offering, or a promise,
I am suddenly grateful and would
offer a prayer if I believed in God.
But not believing, I bless the power of seed,
its casual, useful persistence,
and bless the power of sun,
its conspiracy with the underground,
and thank my stars the winter's ended.

Paula Meehan

ON THIS DAY:

In 1834 six farm labourers from Tolpuddle in Dorset were found guilty of taking a seditious oath in the course of forming a trade union. They were sentenced to be transported to Australia. In 1836, after a public outcry, the Tolpuddle Martyrs, as they became known, were pardoned.

Wilfred Owen (1893–1918), poet and soldier, was born.

Neville Chamberlain (1869–1940), Prime Minister 1937–1940, was born.

Robert Donat (1905–1958), film actor who appeared in the first film version of John Buchan's *The Thirty-Nine Steps*, was born.

Maundy Thursday

Between the brown hands of a server-lad
The silver cross was offered to be kissed.
The men came up, lugubrious, but not sad,
And knelt reluctantly, half-prejudiced.
(And kissing, kissed the emblem of a creed.)
Then mourning women knelt; meek mouths they had,
(And kissed the Body of the Christ indeed.)
Young children came, with eager lips and glad.
(These kissed a silver doll, immensely bright.)
Then I, too, knelt before that acolyte.
Above the crucifix I bent my head:
The Christ was thin, and cold, and very dead:
And yet I bowed, yea, kissed—my lips did cling
(I kissed the warm live hand that held the thing.)

Wilfred Owen

ON THIS DAY:

Maundy Thursday, the day before Good Friday, commemorates the institution of the Eucharist and the washing of the disciples' feet by Jesus. Traditionally in the UK on Maundy Thursday, the reigning monarch distributes specially minted silver coins to selected pensioners, representing 'the poor'.

In 1932 the Sydney Harbour Bridge was opened (construction work on the bridge had started in December 1926).

The Great St Bernard Tunnel between Switzerland and Italy was opened in 1964.

March 20

Endpiece

The bells of hell,
Go ting-a-ling-a-ling,
For you but not for me,
Oh death, where is thy sting-a-ling-a-ling?
Or grave thy victory?
If you meet the undertaker,
Or the young man from the Pru,
Get a pint with what's left over,
Now I'll say good-bye to you.

Brendan Behan

ON THIS DAY:

Brendan Behan (1923–1964), writer and playwright, died in Dublin. His plays include *The Quare Fellow* and *The Hostage*.

Henry V (1387–1422, reigned 1413–1422) died. Although shortlived his reign had been notable for the defeat of the French at the battle of Agincourt in October 1415. He was succeeded by his one-year-old son, Henry VI (1421–1471, reigned 1422–1461, 1470–1471).

In 1602 the Dutch East India Company was founded.

Sir Isaac Newton (1642–1727), who established the principles of the law of gravity, died.

Henrik Ibsen (1828–1906), playwright, was born.

Jacques Chirac (b.1932) was elected Prime Minister of France for the second time in 1986.

The Spring

Now that the winter's gone, the earth hath lost
Her snow-white robes, and now no more the frost
Candies the grass, or casts an icy cream
Upon the silver lake or crystal stream;
But the warm sun thaws the benumbèd earth
And makes it tender; gives a sacred birth
To the dead swallow; wakes in hollow tree
The drowsy cuckoo, and the humble-bee.
Now do a choir of chirping minstrels bring
In triumph to the world the youthful Spring.
The valleys, hills, and woods in rich array
Welcome the coming of the long'd-for May.
Now all things smile, only my love doth lour;
Nor hath the scalding noonday sun the power
To melt that marble ice, which still doth hold
Her heart congeal'd, and makes her pity cold.
The ox, which lately did for shelter fly
Into the stall, doth now securely lie
In open fields; and love no more is made
By the fireside, but in the cooler shade:
Amyntas now doth with his Chloris sleep
Under a sycamore, and all things keep
Time with the season; Only she doth carry
June in her eyes, in her heart January.

Thomas Carew

ON THIS DAY:

Spring begins on 21st March, coinciding with the vernal equinox.

Archbishop Thomas Cranmer (1489–1556) was burnt at the stake after being found guilty of treason and heresy by the Catholic regime of Mary I.

Robert Southey (1774–1843), writer and poet, died.

Easter

Most glorious Lord of Lyfe! that on this day,
  Didst make Thy triumph over death and sin;
And, having harrowd hell, didst bring away
  Captivity thence captive, us to win:
  This joyous day, deare Lord, with joy begin;
And grant that we, for whom thou diddest dye,
  Being with Thy deare blood clene washt from sin,
May live for ever in felicity!
And that Thy love we weighing worthily,
  May likewise love Thee for the same againe:
And for Thy sake that all lyke deare didst buy,
  With love may one another entertayne!
    So let us love, deare Love, lyke as we ought,
    Love is the lesson which the Lord us taught.

Edmund Spenser

ON THIS DAY:

The earliest date on which Easter Day can fall is 22nd March. Easter last fell on this day in 1818.

Thomas Carew (c.1594/5–1640), poet, died.

In 1903 Niagara Falls ran dry because of a sustained period of drought.

Lines Written in Early Spring

I heard a thousand blended notes,
While in a grove I sate reclined,
In that sweet mood when pleasant thoughts
Bring sad thoughts to the mind.

To her fair works did Nature link
The human soul that through me ran;
And much it grieved my heart to think
What man has made of man.

Through primrose tufts, in that green bower,
The periwinkle trailed its wreaths;
And 'tis my faith that every flower
Enjoys the air it breathes.

The birds around me hopped and played,
Their thoughts I cannot measure: –
But the least motion which they made,
It seemed a thrill of pleasure.

The budding twigs spread out their fan,
To catch the breezy air;
And I must think, do all I can,
That there was pleasure there.

If this belief from heaven be sent,
If such be Nature's holy plan,
Have I not reason to lament
What man has made of man!

William Wordsworth

ON THIS DAY:

In 1956 HM Queen Elizabeth II laid the foundation stone for the new Coventry Cathedral. The previous building had been destroyed by German bombs in the Second World War.

Michael Ramsay (1904–1988), Archbishop of Canterbury, met Pope Paul VI in Rome in 1966. This was the first official meeting between the leaders of the Roman Catholic and Anglican churches for 400 years.

On the Tombs in Westminster Abbey

Mortality, behold, and fear,
What a change of flesh is here!
Think how many royal bones
Sleep within this heap of stones,
Hence removed from beds of ease,
Dainty fare, and what might please,
Fretted roofs, and costly shows,
To a roof that flats the nose:
Which proclaims all flesh is grass;
How the world's fair glories pass;
That there is no trust in health,
In youth, in age, in greatness, wealth;
For if such could have reprieved
Those had been immortal lived.
Know from this the world's a snare,
How that greatness is but care,
How all pleasures are but pain,
And how short they do remain:
For here they lie had realms and lands,
That now want strength to stir their hands;
Where from their pulpits sealed with dust
They preach: 'In greatness is no trust'.
Here's an acre sown indeed
With the richest royalest seed,
That the earth did e'er suck in
Since the first man died for sin.
Here the bones of birth have cried,
'Though Gods they were, as men they died'.
Here are sands (ignoble things)
Dropped from the ruined sides of kings;
With whom the poor man's earth being shown
The difference is not easily known.
Here's a world of pomp and state,
Forgotten, dead, disconsolate;
Think, then, this scythe that mows down kings

Exempts no meaner mortal things.
Then bid the wanton lady tread
Amid these mazes of the dead;
And these truly understood
More shall cool and quench the blood
Than her many sports aday,
And her nightly wanton play.
Bid her paint till day of doom,
To this favour she must come.
Bid the merchant gather wealth,
The usurer exact by stealth,
The proud man beat it from his thought,
Yet to this shape all must be brought.

Francis Beaumont

ON THIS DAY:

In 1560 Elizabeth I founded the Collegiate Church of St Peter at Westminster Abbey.

James VI of Scotland (1566–1625, reigned 1567–1625), son of Mary, Queen of Scots, great-grandson of Margaret Tudor and great-great grandson of Henry VII, became James I of England in 1603 on the death of Elizabeth I.

William Morris (1834–1896), poet and founder of the Society for the Protection of Ancient Buildings (SPAB), was born.

J. M. Synge (1871–1909), playwright and author of *The Playboy of the Western World*, died.

Queen Mary (1867–1953), widow of George V, died.

March 25

I Sing of a Maiden

I sing of a maiden
That is makeless:
King of alle kinges
To her son she ches.

He came also stille
Where his mother was
As dew in Aprille
That falleth on the grass.

He came also stille
To his mother's bower
As dew in Aprille
That falleth on the flower.

He came also stille
Where his mother lay
As dew in Aprille
That falleth on the spray.

Mother and maiden
Was never none but she –
Well may such a lady
Godes mother be.

Anonymous

ON THIS DAY:

Today is Lady Day which commemorates the Annunciation of the Virgin Mary. Until 1752 Lady Day also marked the beginning of the legal year. If Good Friday fell on this day it was considered to be bad luck.

Sir A. J. P. Taylor (1906–1990), historian, was born.

Sir David Lean (1908–1991), film director, was born.

When I have Fears

When I have fears, as Keats had fears,
Of the moment I'll cease to be
I console myself with vanished years
Remember laughter, remembered tears,
And the peace of the changing sea.

When I feel sad, as Keats felt sad,
That my life is so nearly done
It gives me comfort to dwell upon
Remembered friends who are dead and gone
And the jokes we had and the fun.

How happy they are I cannot know
But happy am I who loved them so.

Sir Noël Coward

ON THIS DAY:

Sir Noël Coward (1899–1973), playwright and composer, died.

Robert Frost (1874–1963), poet, was born.

Walt Whitman (1819–1892), poet, died.

Cecil Rhodes (1853–1902), businessman and statesman, died.

Tennessee Williams (1911–1983), playwright and author of *The Glass Menagerie*, was born.

David Lloyd George (1863–1945), Prime Minister from 1916 to 1922, died.

March 27

Easter Day

The silver trumpets rang across the Dome:
   The people knelt upon the ground with awe:
   And borne upon the necks of men I saw,
Like some great God, the Holy Lord of Rome.
Priest-like, he wore a robe more white than foam,
   And, king-like, swathed himself in royal red,
   Three crowns of gold rose high upon his head:
In splendour and in light the Pope passed home.
My heart stole back across wide wastes of years
   To One who wandered by a lonely sea,
   And sought in vain for any place of rest:
'Foxes have holes, and every bird its nest.
I, only I, must wander wearily,
And bruise my feet, and drink wine salt with tears.'

Oscar Wilde

ON THIS DAY:

In 1625, James I died. He was succeeded by his son, Charles, who became Charles I of Great Britain and Ireland.

Sir Henry Royce (1863–1933) was born.

James Callaghan, Lord Callaghan of Cardiff (1912–2005), Labour Prime Minster from 1976 to 1979, was born. He was followed as Prime Minister by the Conservative leader Margaret Thatcher (b.1925), the first woman to hold the office.

March 28

Groundsmen

The pile of cuttings puts on dreadful weight,
swelters in the season, and leaks treacle.
Beside it, the tractor and the cutters drip oil
into the earth floor, in a shed where cobwebs
link the roof to the wired window and the oil drums.
The twisted blades and the spiked roller
rest from the nibbling and pricking of the pitch;
and in the corner a white liner, clogged white
round the wheels, darkens towards the handles.
The quiet men whose stuff this is
have the next shed along. Their door shuts
neatly to, unlike the tractor shed
where the door drags and billows against the bricks.
It was a secret kingdom for a boy.
I envied them their work; lending out bats,
lowering the posts, the twirl of the cutter
at the end of a straight run; and their shed
at the edge of the known world.

David Scott

ON THIS DAY:

The Women's Army Auxiliary Corps (WAAC) was founded in 1917.

Dirk Bogarde (1921–1999), Sir Derek Niven van den Bogaerde, actor and writer, was born.

General Franco (1892–1975) entered Madrid in 1939, ending the Spanish Civil War.

The Cenotaph

Not yet will those measureless fields be green again
Where only yesterday the wild, sweet, blood of wonderful youth was shed;
There is a grave whose earth must hold too long, too deep a stain,
Though for ever over it we may speak as proudly as we may tread.
But here, where the watchers by lonely hearths from the thrust of an inward
      sword have more slowly bled,
We shall build the Cenotaph: Victory, winged, with Peace, winged too, at
      the column's head.
And over the stairway, at the foot – oh! here, leave desolate, passionate hands
      to spread
Violets, roses, and laurel, with the small, sweet, twinkling country things
Speaking so wistfully of other Springs,
From the little gardens of little places where son or sweetheart was born
      and bred.

In splendid sleep, with a thousand brothers
    To lovers – to mothers
    Here, too, lies he:
Under the purple, the green, the red,
It is all young life: it must break some women's hearts to see
Such a brave, gay coverlet to such a bed!
Only when all is done and said,
God is not mocked and neither are the dead.

For this will stand in our Market-place–
    Who'll sell, who'll buy
    (Will you or I
Lie each to each with the better grace)?
While looking into every busy whore's and huckster's face
As they drive their bargains, is the Face
Of God: and some young, piteous, murdered face.

Charlotte Mew

ON THIS DAY:

Sir Edwin Lutyens (1869–1944), architect, and designer of the Cenotaph memorial in Whitehall, was born.

On Palm Sunday 1461, the Yorkist forces defeated the Lancastrians at the battle of Towton, near York. The bloody encounter took place during a heavy snowstorm.

Good Friday, 1613. Riding Westward

Let man's soul be a sphere, and then, in this,
Th'intelligence that moves, devotion is,
And as the other spheres, by being grown
Subject to foreign motions, lose their own,
And being by others hurried every day,
Scarce in a year their natural form obey;
Pleasure or business, so, our souls admit
For their first mover, and are whirled by it.
Hence is 't, that I am carried towards the West
This day, when my soul's form bends towards the East.
There I should see a Sun, by rising, set,
And by that setting endless day beget:
But that Christ on this cross did rise and fall,
Sin had eternally benighted all.
Yet dare I'almost be glad I do not see
That spectacle, of too much weight for me.
Who sees God's face, that is self-life, must die;
What a death were it then to see God die?
It made his own lieutenant, Nature, shrink;
It made his footstool crack, and the sun wink.
Could I behold those hands which span the poles,
And tune all spheres at once, pierced with those holes?
Could I behold that endless height which is
Zenith to us, and to'our antipodes,
Humbled below us? Or that blood which is
The seat of all our souls, if not of His,
Makes dirt of dust, or that flesh which was worn
By God, for his apparel, ragg'd and torn?
If on these things I durst not look, durst I
Upon his miserable mother cast mine eye,
Who was God's partner here, and furnished thus
Half of that sacrifice which ransomed us?
Though these things, as I ride, be from mine eye,
They're present yet unto my memory,
For that looks towards them; and Thou look'st towards me,

O Saviour, as Thou hang'st upon the tree.
I turn my back to Thee but to receive
Corrections, till Thy mercies bid Thee leave.
O think me worth Thine anger; punish me;
Burn off my rusts and my deformity;
Restore Thine image so much, by Thy grace,
That Thou may'st know me, and I'll turn my face.

John Donne

ON THIS DAY:

In 1856 the Treaty of Paris brought the Crimean War to an end.

In 1842 anaesthetic was used for the first time in an operation, performed in Georgia, USA.

Vincent Van Gogh (1853–1890), artist, was born.

Julian Grenfell (1888–1915), poet and soldier, was born.

The Relic

When my grave is broke up again
Some second guest to entertain,
(For graves have learned that woman-head
To be to more than one a bed)
    And he that digs it, spies
A bracelet of bright hair about the bone,
    Will he not let us alone,
And think that there a loving couple lies,
Who thought that this device might be some way
To make their souls, at the last busy day,
Meet at this grave, and make a little stay?

If this fall in a time, or land,
Where mis-devotion doth command,
Then, he that digs us up, will bring
Us, to the Bishop, and the King,
    To make us relics; then
Thou shalt be a Mary Magdalen, and I
    A something else thereby;
All women shall adore us, and some men;
And since at such time, miracles are sought,
I would have that age by this paper taught
What miracles we harmless lovers wrought.

First, we loved well and faithfully,
Yet knew not what we loved, nor why,
Difference of sex no mo&re we knew,
Than our guardian angels do;
    Coming and going, we
Perchance might kiss, but not between those meals;
    Our hands ne'er touched the seals,
Which nature, injured by late law, sets free:
These miracles we did; but now alas,
All measure, and all language, I should pass,
Should I tell what a miracle she was.

John Donne

ON THIS DAY:
John Donne (1572–1631), poet and Dean of St Paul's Cathedral, died.

APRIL

April 1

Lie in the Dark and Listen

Lie in the dark and listen,
It's clear tonight so they're flying high
Hundreds of them, thousands perhaps,
Riding the icy, moonlight sky.
Men, material, bombs and maps
Altimeters and guns and charts
Coffee, sandwiches, fleece-lined boots
Bones and muscles and minds and hearts
English saplings with English roots
Deep in the earth they've left below
Lie in the dark and let them go
Lie in the dark and listen.

Lie in the dark and listen
They're going over in waves and waves
High above villages, hills and streams
Country churches and little graves
And little citizen's worried dreams.
Very soon they'll have reached the sea
And far below them will lie the bays
And coves and sands where they used to be
Taken for summer holidays.
Lie in the dark and let them go
Lie in the dark and listen.

Lie in the dark and listen
City magnates and steel contractors,
Factory workers and politicians
Soft, hysterical little actors
Ballet dancers, 'Reserved' musicians,
Safe in your warm, civilian beds.
Count your profits and count your sheep
Life is flying above your heads
Just turn over and try to sleep.
Lie in the dark and let them go
Theirs is a world you'll never know
Lie in the dark and listen.

Sir Noël Coward

ON THIS DAY:

The Royal Air Force was founded in 1918.

Battle of the Baltic

Of Nelson and the North
Sing the glorious day's renown,
When to battle fierce came forth
All the might of Denmark's crown,
And her arms along the deep proudly shone;
By each gun the lighted brand
In a bold determined hand,
And the Prince of all the land
Led them on.

Like leviathans afloat
Lay their bulwarks on the brine;
While the sign of battle flew
On the lofty British line:
It was ten of April morn by the chime:
As they drifted on their path
There was silence deep as death;
And the boldest held his breath
For a time.

But the might of England flush'd
To anticipate the scene;
And her van the fleeter rush'd
O'er the deadly space between.
'Hearts of oak!' our captains cried, when each gun
From its adamantine lips
Spread a death-shade round the ships,
Like the hurricane eclipse
Of the sun.

Again! again! again!
And the havoc did not slack,
Till a feeble cheer the Dane
To our cheering sent us back;–

Their shots along the deep slowly boom: –
Then ceased–and all is wail,
As they strike the shatter'd sail;
Or in conflagration pale
Light the gloom.

Out spoke the victor then
As he hail'd them o'er the wave,
'Ye are brothers! ye are men!
And we conquer but to save:–
So peace instead of death let us bring:
But yield, proud foe, thy fleet
With the crews, at England's feet,
And make submission meet
To our King.'

Then Denmark blest our chief
That he gave her wounds repose;
And the sounds of joy and grief
From her people wildly rose,
As death withdrew his shades from the day:
While the sun look'd smiling bright
O'er a wide and woful sight,
Where the fires of funeral light
Died away.

Now joy, old England, raise!
For the tidings of thy might,
By the festal cities' blaze,
Whilst the wine-cup shines in light;
And yet amidst that joy and uproar,
Let us think of them that sleep
Full many a fathom deep
By thy wild and stormy steep,
Elsinore!

Brave hearts! to Britain's pride
Once so faithful and so true,
On the deck of fame they died
With the gallant good Riou:
Soft sigh the winds of Heaven o'er their grave!
While the billow mournful rolls
And the mermaid's song condoles
Singing glory to the souls
Of the brave!

Thomas Campbell

ON THIS DAY:

The British fleet commanded by Sir Hyde Parker, whose second in command was Horatio Nelson (1758–1805), defeated the Danish at the battle of Copenhagen in 1801. Nelson had been ordered to withdraw, but chose to disregard these orders, subsequently securing victory.

Charlemagne, King of the Franks (771–814) and Holy Roman Emperor (800–814), was born in 742.

In 1860 the first Italian Parliament was convened in Turin.

Samuel Morse (1791–1872), inventor of the telegraphic code, died.

April 3

I am the Very Model of a Modern Major-General

I am the very model of a modern Major-General,
I've information vegetable, animal, and mineral,
I know the kings of England, and I quote the fights historical,
From Marathon to Waterloo, in order categorical;
I'm very well acquainted too with matters mathematical,
I understand equations, both the simple and quadratical,
About binomial theorem I'm teeming with a lot o' news –
With many cheerful facts about the square of the hypotenuse.

All   With many cheerful facts about the square of the hypotenuse.

Gen.   I'm very good at integral and differential calculus,
I know the scientific names of being animalculous;
In short, in matters vegetable, animal, and mineral,
I am the very model of a modern Major-General.

All   In short, in matters vegetable, animal, and mineral,
He is the very model of a modern Major-General.

Gen.   I know our mythic history, King Arthur's and Sir Caradoc's,
I answer hard acrostics, I've a pretty taste for paradox,
I quote in elegiacs all the crimes of the Heliogabalus,
In conics I can floor peculiarities parabolous.

I can tell undoubted Raphaels from Gerard Dows and Zoffanies,
I know the croaking chorus from the *Frogs* of Aristophanes,
Then I can hum a fugue of which I've heard the music's dinafore,
And whistle all the airs from that infernal nonsense *Pinafore*.

All   And whistle all the airs from that infernal nonsense *Pinafore*.

Gen.   Then I can write a washing bill in Babylonic cuneiform,
And tell you every detail of Caractacus's uniform;
In short, in matters vegetable, animal, and mineral,
I am the very model of a modern Major-General.

All   In short, in matters vegetable, animal, and mineral,
        He is the very model of a modern Major-General.

Gen.   In fact, when I know what is meant by 'mamelon' and 'ravelin,'
        When I can tell at sight a chassepôt rifle from a javelin,
        When such affairs as sorties and surprises I'm more wary at,
        And when I know precisely what is meant by 'commissariat',
        When I have learnt what progress has been made in modern
        gunnery,
        When I know more of tactics than a novice in a nunnery:
        In short, when I've a smattering of elemental strategy,
        You'll say a better Major-Gener*al* has never *sat* a gee –

All   You'll say a better Major-Gener*al* has never *sat* a gee –

Gen.   For my military knowledge, though I'm plucky and adventury,
        Has only been brought down to the beginning of the century;
        But still in matters vegetable, animal, and mineral,
        I am the very model of a modern Major-General.

All   But still in matters vegetable, animal, and mineral,
        He is the very model of a modern Major-General.

W. S. Gilbert

ON THIS DAY:

Gilbert and Sullivan's *The Pirates of Penzance* opened in London in 1880.

George Herbert (1593–1633), poet, was born.

The 100th boat race between Oxford and Cambridge took place on this day in 1954. Oxford won.

Graham Greene (1904–1991), writer, died.

April 4

In Memoriam (Easter, 1915)

The flowers left thick at nightfall in the wood
This Eastertide call into mind the men,
Now far from home, who, with their sweethearts, should
Have gathered them and will do never again.

Edward Thomas

ON THIS DAY:
The first Easter of the First World War fell on this day in 1915.
The North Atlantic Treaty Organisation (NATO) was founded in 1949.
Martin Luther King (1929–1968) was assassinated.

The Arrest of Oscar Wilde at the Cadogan Hotel

He sipped at a weak hock and seltzer
    As he gazed at the London skies
Through the Nottingham lace of the curtains
    Or was it his bees-winged eyes?

To the right and before him Pont Street
    Did tower in her new built red,
As hard as the morning gaslight
    That shone on his unmade bed,

'I want some more hock in my seltzer,
    And Robbie, please give me your hand –
Is this the end or beginning?
    How can I understand?

'So you've brought me the latest *Yellow Book*:
    And Buchan has got in it now:
Approval of what is approved of
    Is as false as a well-kept vow.

'More hock, Robbie – where is the seltzer?
    Dear boy, pull again at the bell!
They are all little better than *cretins*,
    Though this *is* the Cadogan Hotel.

'One astrakhan coat is at Willis's –
    Another one's at the Savoy:
Do fetch my morocco portmanteau,
    And bring them on later, dear boy.'

A thump, and a murmur of voices –
    ('O why must they make such a din?')
As the door of the bedroom swung open
    And TWO PLAIN CLOTHES POLICEMEN came in:

'Mr Woilde, we 'ave come for tew take yew
  Where felons and criminals dwell:
We must ask yew tew leave with us quoietly
  For this *is* the Cadogan Hotel.'

He rose, and he put down *The Yellow Book*.
  He staggered – and, terrible-eyed,
He brushed past the palms on the staircase
  And was helped to a hansom outside.

Sir John Betjeman

ON THIS DAY:

In 1895 Oscar Wilde (1854–1900) was arrested while at the Cadogan Hotel, London.

Thomas Hobbes (1588–1679), philosopher, was born.

Sir Thomas Masterman Hardy (1769–1839), flag-captain to Lord Nelson at the battle of Trafalgar, was born.

Joseph Lister (1827–1912), surgeon who pioneered the use of antiseptic, was born.

Algernon Charles Swinburne (1837–1901), poet, was born.

April 6

Shiloh: A Requiem

Skimming lightly, wheeling still,
   The swallows fly low
Over the field in clouded days,
   The forest-field of Shiloh—
Over the field where April rain
Solaced the parched one stretched in pain
Through the pause of night
That followed the Sunday fight
   Around the church of Shiloh—
The church so lone, the log-built one,
That echoed to many a parting groan
     And natural prayer
Of dying foemen mingled there—
Foemen at morn, but friends at eve—
   Fame or country least their care:
(What like a bullet can undeceive!)
   But now they lie low,
While over them the swallows skim,
   And all is hushed at Shiloh.

Herman Melville

ON THIS DAY:

In 1862 the battle at Shiloh Church, Tennessee, began. It was the second serious encounter of the American Civil War and one of the bloodiest.

Sir John Betjeman (1906–1984), Poet Laureate, died.

In 1917 the United States of America entered the First World War by officially declaring war on Germany.

April 7

I wandered lonely as a cloud

I wandered lonely as a cloud
    That floats on high o'er vales, and hills,
When all at once I saw a crowd,
    A host, of golden daffodils;
Beside the lake, beneath the trees,
Fluttering and dancing in the breeze.

Continuous as the stars that shine
    And twinkle on the Milky Way,
They stretched in never-ending line
    Along the margin of a bay:
Ten thousand saw I at a glance,
Tossing their heads in sprightly dance.

The waves beside them danced, but they
    Out-did the sparkling waves in glee:
A poet could not but be gay,
    In such a jocund company:
I gazed – and gazed – but little thought
What wealth the show to me had brought:

For oft, when on my couch I lie
    In vacant or in pensive mood,
They flash upon that inward eye
    Which is the bliss of solitude;
And then my heart with pleasure fills,
And dances with the daffodils.

William Wordsworth

ON THIS DAY:

William Wordsworth (1770–1850), poet and Poet Laureate from 1843 (after the death of Robert Southey), was born.

April 8

Stepping Westward

'What, you are stepping westward?' – 'Yea.'
– 'Twould be a *wildish* destiny,
If we, who thus together roam
In a strange Land, and far from home,
Were in this place the guests of Chance:
Yet who would stop, or fear to advance,
Though home or shelter he had none,
With such a sky to lead him on?

The dewy ground was dark and cold;
Behind, all gloomy to behold;
And stepping westward seemed to be
A kind of *heavenly* destiny:
I liked the greeting; 'twas a sound
Of something without place or bound;
And seemed to give me spiritual right
To travel through that region bright.

The voice was soft, and she who spake
Was walking by her native lake:
The salutation had to me
The very sound of courtesy:
Its power was felt; and while my eye
Was fixed upon the glowing Sky,
The echo of the voice enwrought
A human sweetness with the thought
Of travelling through the world that lay
Before me in my endless way.

William Wordsworth

ON THIS DAY:

In 1838 the SS *Great Western* began her maiden voyage from Bristol to New York. Designed by Isambard Kingdom Brunel (1806–1859), the ship provided the first regular transatlantic steamship service for passengers. The trip took fifteen days.

In 1904 the Entente Cordiale was signed between Britain and France.

April 9

Lights Out

I have come to the borders of sleep,
The unfathomable deep
Forest where all must lose
Their way, however straight,
Or winding, soon or late;
They cannot choose.

Many a road and track
That, since the dawn's first crack,
Up to the forest brink,
Deceived the travellers,
Suddenly now blurs,
And in they sink.

Here love ends,
Despair, ambition ends;
All pleasure and all trouble,
Although most sweet or bitter,
Here ends in sleep that is sweeter
Than tasks most noble.

There is not any book
Or face of dearest look
That I would not turn from now
To go into the unknown
I must enter, and leave, alone,
I know not how.

The tall forest towers;
Its cloudy foliage lowers
Ahead, shelf above shelf;
Its silence I hear and obey
That I may lose my way
And myself.

Edward Thomas

ON THIS DAY:
Edward Thomas (1878–1917), poet and solider, died in France at the battle of Arras.

April 10

Spring Offensive

Halted against the shade of a last hill,
They fed, and lying easy, were at ease
And, finding comfortable chests and knees,
Carelessly slept. But many there stood still
To face the stark, blank sky beyond the ridge,
Knowing their feet had come to the end of the world.

Marvelling they stood, and watched the long grass swirled
By the May breeze, murmurous with wasp and midge,
For though the summer oozed into their veins
Like an injected drug for their bodies' pains,
Sharp on their souls hung the imminent line of grass,
Fearfully flashed the sky's mysterious glass.

Hour after hour they ponder the warm field—
And the far valley behind, where the buttercup
Had blessed with gold their slow boots coming up,
Where even the little brambles would not yield,
But clutched and clung to them like sorrowing hands;
They breathe like trees unstirred.

Till like a cold gust thrills the little word
At which each body and its soul begird
And tighten them for battle. No alarms
Of bugles, no high flags, no clamorous haste—
Only a lift and flare of eyes that faced
The sun, like a friend with whom their love is done.
O larger shone that smile against the sun,—
Mightier than his whose bounty these have spurned.

So, soon they topped the hill, and raced together
Over an open stretch of herb and heather
Exposed. And instantly the whole sky burned
With fury against them; earth set sudden cups
In thousands for their blood; and the green slope
Chasmed and steepened sheer to infinite space.

Of them who running on that last high place
Leapt to swift unseen bullets, or went up
On the hot blast and fury of hell's upsurge,
Or plunged and fell away past this world's verge,
Some say God caught them even before they fell.

But what say such as from existence' brink
Ventured but drave too swift to sink,
The few who rushed in the body to enter hell,
And there out-fiending all its fiends and flames
With superhuman inhumanities,
Long-famous glories, immemorial shames—
And crawling slowly back, have by degrees
Regained cool peaceful air in wonder—
Why speak not they of comrades that went under?

Wilfred Owen

ON THIS DAY:

John Wilmot, second Earl of Rochester (1647–1680), poet, was born.

Algernon Charles Swinburne (1837–1909), poet, died.

In 1912 the White Star liner RMS *Titanic* departed from Southampton on her fateful maiden voyage.

Evelyn Waugh (1903–1966), author of *Brideshead Revisited*, died.

April 11

Mist in the Meadows

The evening oer the meadow seems to stoop
More distant lessens the diminished spire
Mist in the hollows reaks and curdles up
Like fallen clouds that spread – and things retire
Less seen and less – the shepherd passes near
And little distant most grotesquely shades
As walking without legs – lost to his knees
As through the rawky creeping smoke he wades
Now half way up the arches dissappear
And small the bits of sky that glimmer through
Then trees loose all but tops – I meet the fields
And now the indistinctness passes bye
The shepherd all his length is seen again
And further on the village meets the eye

John Clare

ON THIS DAY:

Sir Archibald McIndoe (1900–1960), pioneering plastic surgeon who helped seriously injured Second World War soldiers and airmen, died.

Bob Dylan (b.1941) made his New York debut in 1961, supporting John Lee Hooker.

Apollo 13 was launched from Cape Kennedy in 1970. Its mission was to explore a section of the moon but it was unable to land due to technical difficulties, and the astronauts were forced to orbit the moon instead, finally returning to earth.

Primo Levi (1919–1987), poet and writer, died. Levi had been imprisoned in Auschwitz during the Second World War and wrote of his experiences at that time in his book *If this is a Man*.

April 12

Philomela

The Nightingale, as soon as April bringeth
  Unto her rested sense a perfect waking,
While late-bare Earth, proud of new clothing, springeth,
  Sings out her woes, a thorn her song-book making;
      And mournfully bewailing,
      Her throat in tunes expresseth
      What grief her breast oppresseth,
For Tereus' force on her chaste will prevailing.

    O Philomela fair, O take some gladness
    That here is juster cause of plaintful sadness!
      Thine earth now springs, mine fadeth;
    Thy thorn without, my thorn my heart invadeth.

Alas! she hath no other cause of anguish
  But Tereus' love, on her by strong hand wroken;
Wherein she suffering, all her spirits languish,
  Full womanlike complains her will was broken.
      But I, who, daily craving,
      Cannot have to content me,
      Have more cause to lament me,
Since wanting is more woe than too much having.

    O Philomela fair, O take some gladness
    That here is juster cause of plaintful sadness!
      Thine earth now springs, mine fadeth;
    Thy thorn without, my thorn my heart invadeth.

Sir Philip Sidney

ON THIS DAY:

Franklin D. Roosevelt (1882–1945), President of the United States of America, who served a record four terms in office, died. He had first been elected to office in 1932. He oversaw a period of great recovery in America, and during his first 'hundred days' introduced a programme that helped businesses and unemployed alike. He favoured dialogue with Russia and devoted much time to the concept of the United Nations. Following the Japanese attack on Pearl Harbor in 1941 he mobilised the nation for participation in the Second World War.

Spring

To what purpose, April, do you return again?
Beauty is not enough.
You can no longer quiet me with the redness
Of little leaves opening stickily.
I know what I know.
The sun is hot on my neck as I observe
The spikes of the crocus.
The smell of the earth is good.
It is apparent that there is no death.
But what does that signify?
Not only under ground are the brains of men
Eaten by maggots.
Life in itself
Is nothing,
An empty cup, a flight of uncarpeted stairs.
It is not enough that yearly, down this hill,
April
Comes like an idiot, babbling and strewing flowers.

Edna St Vincent Millay

ON THIS DAY:

Sir Robert Watson-Watt (1892–1973), the inventor of radar, was born.

Air Chief Marshal Sir Arthur Harris (1892–1984), commander-in-chief of Bomber Command, was born.

Samuel Beckett (1906–1989), winner of the Nobel Prize for literature in 1969, was born.

The Convergence of the Twain

In a solitude of the sea
Deep from human vanity,
And the Pride of Life that planned her, stilly couches she.

Steel chambers, late the pyres
Of her salamandrine fires,
Cold currents thrid, and turn to rhythmic tidal lyres.

Over the mirrors meant
To glass the opulent
The sea-worm crawls—grotesque, slimed, dumb, indifferent.

Jewels in joy designed
To ravish the sensuous mind
Lie lightless, all their sparkles bleared and black and blind.

Dim moon-eyed fishes near
Gaze at the gilded gear
And query: 'What does this vaingloriousness down here?'…

Well: while was fashioning
This creature of cleaving wing,
The Immanent Will that stirs and urges everything

Prepared a sinister mate
For her—so gaily great—
A Shape of Ice, for the time far and dissociate.

And as the smart ship grew
In stature, grace, and hue,
In shadowy silent distance grew the Iceberg too.

Alien they seemed to be:
No mortal eye could see
The intimate welding of their later history,

Or sign that they were bent
By paths coincident
On being anon twin halves of one august event,

Till the Spinner of the Years
Said 'Now!' And each one hears,
And consummation comes, and jars two hemispheres.

Thomas Hardy

ON THIS DAY:

In 1912 RMS *Titantic*, which had departed from Liverpool a few days earlier, hit an iceberg on 14th April and a few hours later, on 15th April, sank.

George Frederick Handel (1685–1759), composer, died.

Sir John Gielgud (1904–2000), actor, was born.

Growing Old

What is it to grow old?
Is it to lose the glory of the form,
The lustre of the eye?
Is it for beauty to forego her wreath?
— Yes, but not this alone.

Is it to feel our strength—
Not our bloom only, but our strength—decay?
Is it to feel each limb
Grow stiffer, every function less exact,
Each nerve more loosely strung?

Yes, this, and more; but not
Ah, 'tis not what in youth we dream'd 'twould be!
'Tis not to have our life
Mellow'd and soften'd as with sunset-glow,
A golden day's decline.

'Tis not to see the world
As from a height, with rapt prophetic eyes,
And heart profoundly stirr'd;
And weep, and feel the fulness of the past,
The years that are no more.

It is to spend long days
And not once feel that we were ever young;
It is to add, immured
In the hot prison of the present, month
To month with weary pain.

It is to suffer this,
And feel but half, and feebly, what we feel.
Deep in our hidden heart
Festers the full remembrance of a change,
But no emotion—none.

It is—last stage of all—
When we are frozen up within, and quite
The phantom of ourselves,
To hear the world applaud the hollow ghost
Which blamed the living man.

Matthew Arnold

ON THIS DAY:

Matthew Arnold (1822–1888), poet, died.

Leonardo da Vinci (1452–1519), artist and inventor, was born.

Sir William Empson (1906–1984), poet, died.

Jean-Paul Sartre (1905–1980), existentialist philosopher and writer, died. Sartre declined the Nobel Prize for literature in 1964.

April 16

Lament for Culloden

The lovely lass o' Inverness,
Nae joy nor pleasure can she see;
For e'en and morn she cries, Alas!
And ay the saut tear blin's her e'e:
Drumossie moor—Drumossie day—
A waefu' day it was to me!
For there I lost my father dear,
My father dear, and brethren three.
Their winding-sheet the bluidy clay,
Their graves are growing green to see:
And by them lies the dearest lad
That ever blest a woman's e'e!
Now wae to thee, thou cruel lord,
A bluidy man I trow thou be;
For mony a heart thou hast made sair
That ne'er did wrong to thine or thee.

Robert Burns

ON THIS DAY:

The battle of Culloden was fought in 1746. The Young Pretender, Bonnie Prince Charlie, and his forces, who were devoted to returning the Stuarts to the throne of England and Scotland, were heavily defeated by the English.

Aphra Behn (1640–1689), playwright and author of *The Rover*, died.

Sir Charles Chaplin (1889–1977), actor, was born.

The Royal Yacht *Britannia* was launched in 1953.

Sudden Light

I have been here before,
But when or how I cannot tell:
I know the grass beyond the door,
The sweet, keen smell,
The sighing sound, the lights around the shore.

You have been mine before, –
How long ago I may not know:
But just when at that swallow's soar
Your neck turned so,
Some veil did fall, – I knew it all of yore.

Has this been thus before?
And shall not thus time's eddying flight
Still with our lives our love restore
In death's despite,
And day and night yield one delight once more?

Dante Gabriel Rossetti

ON THIS DAY:

Benjamin Franklin (1709–1790), inventor and statesman, died.

In 1951 the British submarine HMS *Affray* failed to resurface after submerging off the Isle of Wight. The entire crew of 75 was lost.

In 1984, WPC Yvonne Fletcher, 25, was shot outside the Libyan embassy and died soon afterwards at Westminster Hospital.

April 18

The Scientists are Wrong

They're wrong, the scientists. The universe wasn't created
billions of years ago.
The universe is created every day.

The scientists are wrong to claim
the universe was created from one primordial
substance.
The world is created every day
from various substances with nothing in common.

Only the relative proportion of their masses,
like the elements of sorrow and hope,
make them companions
and curbstones. I'm sorry

I have to get up, in all modesty, and disagree
with what is so sure and recognized by experts:
that there's no speed faster than the speed of light,
when I and my lighted flesh
just noticed something else right here –

whose speed is even greater than the speed of light
and which also returns,
though not in a straight line, because of the curve of the universe
or because of the innocence of God.

And if we connect all this to an equation, according to the rules, maybe
it will make sense that I refuse to believe that her voice
and everything I always cherished
and everything so real and suddenly
lost,
is actually lost forever.

Abba Kovner

ON THIS DAY:

Joan of Arc (1412–1431) was beatified by Pope Pius X in 1909.

Sir John Ambrose Fleming (1849–1945), pioneer of the telephone, electric lighting and the electron tube, died.

In 1968 London Bridge was sold to a US oil company. It was dismantled and rebuilt in America.

Albert Einstein (1879–1955), physicist who was appointed Nobel Laureate (1921), died.

April 19

Concord Hymn

Sung at the completion of the Battle Monument, 4th July 1837, which commemorated the battles of Lexington and Concord on 19th April 1775

By the rude bridge that arched the flood,
    Their flag to April's breeze unfurled,
Here once the embattled farmers stood
    And fired the shot heard round the world.

The foe long since in silence slept;
    Alike the conqueror silent sleeps;
And Time the ruined bridge has swept
    Down the dark stream which seaward creeps.

On this green bank, by this soft stream,
    We set to-day a votive stone;
That memory may their deed redeem,
    When, like our sires, our sons are gone.

Spirit, that made those heroes dare
    To die, and leave their children free,
Bid Time and Nature gently spare
    The shaft we raise to them and thee.

Ralph Waldo Emerson

ON THIS DAY:

The American War of Independence began in 1775. The British forces were defeated in the first battles at Concord and Lexington.

George Gordon, Lord Byron (1788–1824) died.

Benjamin Disraeli, first Earl of Beaconsfield (1804–1881), former Prime Minister, died.

Charles Darwin (1809–1882), naturalist, died.

At St Paul's, April 20, 1917

Not since Wren's Dome has whispered with man's prayer
    Have angels leaned to wonder out of Heaven
    At such uprush of intercession given,
Here where to-day one soul two nations share,
And with accord send up thro' trembling air
    Their vows to strive as Honour ne'er has striven
    Till back to hell the Lords of hell are driven,
And Life and Peace again shall flourish fair.

This is the day of conscience high-enthroned,
    The day when East is West and West is East
    To strike for human Love and Freedom's word
Against foul wrong that cannot be atoned;
    To-day is hope of brotherhood's bond increased,
    And Christ, not Odin, is acclaimed the Lord

Hardwicke Drummond Rawnsley

ON THIS DAY:

Marcus Aurelius (121–180), Roman Emperor, was born.

Oliver Cromwell (1599–1658) dissolved the Rump Parliament in 1653.

Harold Lloyd (1893–1971), silent film comedian, was born.

The Flower

How fresh, O Lord, how sweet and clean
Are thy returns! even as the flowers in spring,
   To which, besides their own demean,
The late-past frosts tributes of pleasure bring,
         Grief melts away
         Like snow in May,
   As if there were no such cold thing.

Who would have thought my shrivelled heart
Could have recovered greenness? It was gone
   Quite underground; as flowers depart
To see their mother-root, when they have blown;
         Where they together
         All the hard weather,
Dead to the world, keep house unknown.

These are thy wonders, Lord of power,
Killing and quickening, bringing down to hell
   And up to heaven in an hour;
Making a chiming of a passing-bell.
         We say amiss,
         This or that is.
Thy word is all, if we could spell.

O that I once past changing were,
Fast in thy Paradise, where no flower can wither!
   Many a spring I shoot up fair,
Offering at heaven, growing and groaning thither:
         Nor doth my flower
         Want a spring shower,
My sins and I joining together.

But while I grow in a straight line,
Still upwards bent, as if heaven were mine own,
   Thy anger comes and I decline:
What frost to that? what pole is not the zone,
         Where all things burn,
         When thou dost turn,
And the least frown of thine is shown?

   And now in age I bud again,
After so many deaths I live and write;
   I once more smell the dew and rain,
And relish versing: O my only light,
         It cannot be
         That I am he
On whom thy tempests fell all night.

   These are thy wonders, Lord of love,
To make us see we are but flowers that glide;
   Which when we once can find and prove,
Thou hast a garden for us, where to bide.
         Who would be more,
         Swelling through store,
Forfeit their Paradise by their pride.

George Herbert

ON THIS DAY:

Charlotte Brontë (1816–1855), author of *Jane Eyre* and the eldest of the three literary Brontë sisters, was born.

Dr Richard Beeching (1913–1985), chairman of British Railways 1963–1965, was born.

The West Wind

It's a warm wind, the west wind, full of birds' cries;
I never hear the west wind but tears are in my eyes.
For it comes from the west lands, the old brown hills,
And April's in the west wind, and daffodils.

It's a fine land, the west land, for hearts as tired as mine,
Apple orchards blossom there, and the air's like wine.
There is cool green grass there, where men may lie at rest,
And the thrushes are in song there, fluting from the nest.

'Will ye not come home, brother? ye have been long away,
It's April, and blossom time, and white is the may;
And bright is the sun, brother, and warm is the rain, –
Will ye not come home, brother, home to us again?

'The young corn is green, brother, where the rabbits run,
It's blue sky, and white clouds, and warm rain and sun.
It's song to a man's soul, brother, fire to a man's brain,
To hear the wild bees and see the merry spring again.

'Larks are singing in the west, brother, above the green wheat,
So will ye not come home, brother, and rest your tired feet?
I've a balm for bruised hearts, brother, sleep for aching eyes,'
Says the warm wind, the west wind, full of birds' cries.

It's the white road westwards is the road I must tread
To the green grass, the cool grass, and rest for heart and head,
To the violets and the warm hearts and the thrushes' song,
In the fine land, the west land, the land where I belong.

John Masefield

ON THIS DAY:

In 1838 the *Sirius* made the first transatlantic crossing using only steam power. Setting off from Cork the *Sirius* reached New York in eighteen days and ten hours.

Lenin (1870–1924), first leader of the Soviet Union, was born.

J. Robert Oppenheimer (1904–1967), theoretical physicist, was born. His studies contributed to the development of the atomic bombs dropped on Hiroshima and Nagasaki, Japan in August 1945.

April 23

Written in the Church Yard at Middleton in Sussex

Pressed by the moon, mute arbitress of tides,
　　While the loud equinox its power combines,
　　The sea no more its swelling surge confines,
But o'er the shrinking land sublimely rides.
The wild blast, rising from the western cave,
　　Drives the huge billows from their heaving bed,
　　Tears from their grassy tombs the village dead,
And breaks the silent sabbath of the grave!
With shells and sea-weed mingled, on the shore
　　Lo! their bones whiten in the frequent wave;
　　But vain to them the winds and waters rave;
They hear the warring elements no more:
While I am doomed – by life's long storm oppressed,
To gaze with envy on their gloomy rest.

Charlotte Smith

ON THIS DAY:

Today is the feast day of St George, the patron saint of England.

In 1849 the new church at Middleton was dedicated after the previous structure had been washed away by sea.

William Shakespeare (1564–1616), playwright, was born and died.

Joseph Mallord William Turner (1775–1851), painter, was born.

William Wordsworth (1770–1850), Poet Laureate, died.

Rupert Brooke (1887–1915), soldier and poet, died while en route to the Dardanelles.

April 24

The Eve of St Mark

Stroke the small silk with your whispering hands,
godmother; nod and nod from the half-gloom;
broochlight intermittent between the fronds,
the owl immortal in its crystal dome.

Along the mantelpiece veined lustres trill,
the clock discounts us with a telling chime.
Familiar ministrants, clerks-of-appeal,
burnish upon the threshold of the dream:

churchwardens in wing-collars bearing scrolls
of copyhold well-tinctured and well-tied.
Your photo-albums loved by the boy-king

preserve in sepia waterglass the souls
of distant cousins, virgin till they died,
and the lost delicate suitors who could sing.

Geoffrey Hill

ON THIS DAY:

In 1800 the Library of Congress was established by an Act of Congress, when President John Adams signed a Bill concerning the transfer of the seat of government to Washington, DC from Philadelphia. The Library was originally housed in the new Capitol building, until invading British troops destroyed it in 1814. The present Library of Congress building was opened on 1st November 1897.

In 1916 the Easter Rising began in Dublin, Ireland.

In 1953 Winston Churchill (1874–1965) was knighted.

To the Memory of My Beloved, the Author
Mr. William Shakespeare (and what he hath left us)

To draw no envy, Shakespeare, on thy name,
Am I thus ample to thy book and fame,
While I confess thy writings to be such
As neither man nor Muse can praise too much.
'Tis true, and all men's suffrage. But these ways
Were not the paths I meant unto thy praise:
For silliest ignorance on these may light,
Which, when it sounds at best, but echoes right;
Or blind affection, which doth ne'er advance
The truth, but gropes, and urgeth all by chance;
Or crafty malice might pretend this praise,
And think to ruin where it seemed to raise.
These are as some infamous bawd or whore
Should praise a matron. What could hurt her more?
But thou art proof against them, and, indeed,
Above th' ill fortune of them, or the need.
I therefore will begin. Soul of the age!
The applause! delight! the wonder of our stage!
My Shakespeare, rise; I will not lodge thee by
Chaucer or Spenser, or bid Beaumont lie
A little further to make thee a room:
Thou art a monument without a tomb,
And art alive still while thy book doth live,
And we have wits to read and praise to give.
That I not mix thee so, my brain excuses,
I mean with great, but disproportioned Muses;
For, if I thought my judgment were of years,
I should commit thee surely with thy peers,
And tell how far thou didst our Lyly outshine,
Or sporting Kyd, or Marlowe's mighty line.
And though thou hadst small Latin and less Greek,
From thence to honour thee I would not seek
For names, but call forth thund'ring Aeschylus,

Euripides, and Sophocles to us,
Pacuvius, Accius, him of Cordova dead,
To life again, to hear thy buskin tread
And shake a stage; or, when thy socks were on,
Leave thee alone for the comparison
Of all that insolent Greece or haughty Rome
Sent forth, or since did from their ashes come.
Triumph, my Britain; thou hast one to show
To whom all scenes of Europe homage owe.
He was not of an age, but for all time!
And all the Muses still were in their prime
When like Apollo he came forth to warm
Our ears, or like a Mercury to charm.
Nature herself was proud of his designs,
And joyed to wear the dressing of his lines,
Which were so richly spun, and woven so fit,
As, since, she will vouchsafe no other wit:
The merry Greek, tart Aristophanes,
Neat Terence, witty Plautus now not please,
But antiquated and deserted lie,
As they were not of Nature's family.
Yet must I not give Nature all; thy Art,
My gentle Shakespeare, must enjoy a part.
For though the poet's matter Nature be,
His Art doth give the fashion; and that he
Who casts to write a living line must sweat
(Such as thine are) and strike the second heat
Upon the muses' anvil; turn the same,
And himself with it, that he thinks to frame,
Or for the laurel he may gain a scorn;
For a good poet's made as well as born.
And such wert thou! Look how the father's face
Lives in his issue, even so the race
Of Shakespeare's mind and manners brightly shines
In his well-turnèd and true-filèd lines,
In each of which he seems to shake a lance,
As brandished at the eyes of ignorance.

Sweet swan of Avon, what a sight it were
To see thee in our waters yet appear,
And make those flights upon the banks of Thames
That so did take Eliza and our James!
But stay; I see thee in the hemisphere
Advanced and made a constellation there!
Shine forth, thou star of poets, and with rage
Or influence chide or cheer the drooping stage,
Which, since thy flight from hence, hath mourned like night,
And despairs day, but for thy volume's light.

Ben Jonson

ON THIS DAY:

William Shakespeare (1564–1616) buried in Holy Trinity Church, Stratford-upon-Avon.

John Keble (1792–1866), clergyman and poet, was born.

Walter de la Mare (1873–1956), poet, was born.

William Cowper (1731–1800), poet, died.

Home Thoughts from Abroad

Oh, to be in England
Now that April's there,
And whoever wakes in England
Sees, some morning, unaware,
That the lowest boughs and the brushwood sheaf
Round the elm-tree bole are in tiny leaf,
While the chaffinch sings on the orchard bough
In England—now!

And after April, when May follows,
And the whitethroat builds, and all the swallows!
Hark, where my blossomed pear-tree in the hedge
Leans to the field and scatters on the clover
Blossoms and dewdrops—at the bent spray's edge—
That's the wise thrush; he sings each song twice over,
Lest you should think he never could recapture
The first fine careless rapture!
And though the fields look rough with hoary dew
All will be gay when noontide wakes anew
The buttercups, the little children's dower
—Far brighter than this gaudy melon-flower!

Robert Browning

ON THIS DAY:

Charles Richter (1900–1985), professor of seismology who developed the Richter scale as a means of measuring the strength of earthquakes, was born.

Lady Elizabeth Bowes-Lyon married the Duke of York (the future king George VI) at Westminster Abbey in 1923.

In 1992 the Russian Orthodox Easter was celebrated in Moscow for the first time in seventy-four years.

In 1994 South Africa's first all-race elections were held, following which Nelson Mandela (b.1918) became President.

April 27

Morse

Tuckett. Bill Tuckett. Telegraph operator, Hall's Creek,
which is way out back of the Outback, but he stuck it,
quite likely liked it, despite heat, glare, dust and the lack
of diversion or doctors. Come disaster you trusted to luck,
ingenuity and pluck. This was back when nice people said pluck,
the sleevelink and green eyeshade epoch.
　　　　　　　Faced, though, like Bill Tuckett
with a man needing surgery right on the spot, a lot
would have done their dashes. It looked hopeless (dot dot dot)
Lift him up on the table, said Tuckett, running the key hot
till Head Office turned up a doctor who coolly instructed
up a thousand miles of wire, as Tuckett advanced slit by slit
with a safety razor blade, pioneering on into the wet,
copper-wiring the rivers off, in the first operation conducted
along dotted lines, with rum drinkers gripping the patient:
d-d-dash it, take care, Tuck!
　　　　　　　And the vital spark stayed unshorted.
Yallah! breathed the camelmen. Tuckett, you did it, you did it!
cried the spattered la-de-dah jodhpur-wearing Inspector of Stock.
We imagine, some weeks later, a properly laconic
convalescent averring Without you, I'd have kicked the bucket…

From Chungking to Burrenjuck, morse keys have mostly gone silent
and only old men meet now to chit-chat in their electric
bygone dialect. The last letter many will forget
is dit-dit-dit-dah, V for Victory. The coders' hero had speed,
resource and a touch. So ditditdit daah for Bill Tuckett.

Les Murray

ON THIS DAY:

Samuel Morse (1791–1872), the American inventor of Morse code, was born.

In 1828 London Zoo, Regent's Park was opened.

Ralph Waldo Emerson (1803–1882), poet, died.

C. Day Lewis (1904–1972), poet, was born.

April 1885

Wanton with long delay the gay spring leaping cometh;
The blackthorn starreth now his bough on the eve of May:
All day in the sweet box-tree the bee for pleasure hummeth:
The cuckoo sends afloat his note on the air all day.

Now dewy nights again and rain in gentle shower
At root of tree and flower have quenched the winter's drouth:
On high the hot sun smiles, and banks of cloud uptower
In bulging heads that crowd for miles the dazzling south.

Robert Bridges

ON THIS DAY:

Elizabeth I's funeral took place in London in 1603. Many thousands of people crowded the streets to witness the event.

Mike Brearley, cricketer and England cricket captain, was born in 1942.

Sir Alf Ramsey (1920–1999), footballer and football manager, died.

At the British War Cemetery, Bayeux

I walked where in their talking graves
And shirts of earth five thousand lay,
When history with ten feasts of fire
Had eaten the red air away.

'I am Christ's boy,' I cried. 'I bear
In iron hands the bread, the fishes.
I hang with honey and with rose
This tidy wreck of all your wishes.

'On your geometry of sleep
The chestnut and the fir-tree fly,
And lavender and marguerite
Forge with their flowers an English sky.

'Turn now towards the belling town
Your jigsaws of impossible bone,
And rising read your rank of snow
Accurate as death upon the stone.'

About your easy head my prayers
I said with syllables of clay.
'What gift,' I asked, 'shall I bring now
Before I weep and walk away?'

Take, they replied, *the oak and laurel.*
Take our fortune of tears and live
Like a spendthrift lover. All we ask
Is the one gift you cannot give.

Charles Causley

ON THIS DAY:

Sir Fabian Ware (1869–1949), founder of the Imperial, now Commonwealth, War Graves Commission
(founded by Royal Charter in 1917), died.

Emperor Hirohito (1901–1989), was born. He became Emperor of Japan in 1926.

Sir Alfred Hitchcock (1899–1980), film director whose films include *The Birds, North by Northwest*
and *Marnie*, died.

April 30

Loveliest of Trees, the Cherry Now

Loveliest of trees, the cherry now
Is hung with bloom along the bough,
And stands about the woodland ride
Wearing white for Eastertide.

Now, of my threescore years and ten,
Twenty will not come again,
And take from seventy springs a score,
It only leaves me fifty more.

And since to look at things in bloom
Fifty springs are little room,
About the woodlands I will go
To see the cherry hung with snow.

A. E. Housman

ON THIS DAY:

A. E. Housman (1859–1936), poet, died.

In 1789 George Washington (1732–1799) was sworn in as the first President of the United States of America.

Édouard Manet (1832–1883), painter, died.

MAY

May 1

Corinna's Going-a-Maying

Get up! get up for shame! the blooming morn
Upon her wings presents the god unshorn.
    See how Aurora throws her fair
    Fresh-quilted colours through the air:
    Get up, sweet slug-a-bed, and see
    The dew-bespangling herb and tree.
Each flower has wept, and bow'd toward the east
Above an hour since, yet you not dressed,
    Nay, not so much as out of bed?
    When all the birds have matins said,
    And sung their thankful hymns, 'tis sin,
    Nay, profanation to keep in,
Whenas a thousand virgins on this day
Spring, sooner than the lark, to fetch in May.

Rise, and put on your foliage, and be seen
To come forth, like the springtime, fresh and green,
    And sweet as Flora. Take no care
    For jewels for your gown or hair;
    Fear not; the leaves will strew
    Gems in abundance upon you;
Besides, the childhood of the day has kept,
Against you come, some orient pearls unwept;
    Come and receive them while the light
    Hangs on the dew-locks of the night,
    And Titan on the eastern hill
    Retires himself, or else stands still
Till you come forth. Wash, dress, be brief in praying:
Few beads are best when once we go a-Maying.

Come, my Corinna, come; and coming mark
How each field turns a street, each street a park
    Made green and trimmed with trees; see how
    Devotion gives each house a bough
    Or branch: each porch, each door, ere this,
    An ark, a tabernacle is,
Made up of whitethorn neatly interwove,
As if here were those cooler shades of love.

Can such delights be in the street
And open fields, and we not see't?
Come, we'll abroad; and let's obey
The proclamation made for May,
And sin no more, as we have done, by staying;
But, my Corinna, come, let's go a-Maying.

There's not a budding boy or girl this day
But is got up and gone to bring in May;
A deal of youth, ere this, is come
Back, and with whitethorn laden home.
Some have dispatched their cakes and cream
Before that we have left to dream;
And some have wept and wooed, and plighted troth,
And chose their priest, ere we can cast off sloth:
Many a green-gown has been given,
Many a kiss, both odd and even,
Many a glance too has been sent
From out the eye, love's firmament;
Many a jest told of the keys betraying
This night, and locks picked: yet we're not a-Maying.

Come, let us go while we are in our prime,
And take the harmless folly of the time
We shall grow old apace, and die
Before we know our liberty.
Our life is short, and our days run
As fast away as does the sun;
And as a vapour or a drop of rain
Once lost, can ne'er be found again;
So when or you or I are made
A fable, song, or fleeting shade,
All love, all liking, all delight
Lies drowned with us in endless night.
Then while time serves, and we are but decaying,
Come, my Corinna, come, let's go a-Maying.

Robert Herrick

ON THIS DAY:
People traditionally went 'a-maying', collecting flowers and hawthorn to decorate their houses.

May 2

The Merry Ploughman

As I was a-wand'ring ae morning in spring,
I heard a young ploughman sae sweetly to sing;
And as he was singin', thir words he did say—
There's nae life like the ploughman's in the month o' sweet May.

The lav'rock in the morning she'll rise frae her nest,
And mount i' the air wi' the dew on her breast;
And wi' the merry ploughman she'll whistle and sing,
And at night she'll return to her nest back again.

Robert Burns

ON THIS DAY:

John Cabot (c.1450–c.1499) embarked from Bristol in 1497, in an attempt to seek a route to Asia.
He sighted land on 24th June and thus claimed North America for England.

The Hudson Bay Company was founded in 1670.

Alfred de Musset (1810–1857), playwright and poet, died.

I Remember, I Remember

I remember, I remember,
    The house where I was born,
The little window where the sun
    Came peeping in at morn;
He never came a wink too soon,
    Nor brought too long a day,
But now, I often wish the night
    Had borne my breath away!

I remember, I remember,
    The roses, red and white,
The violets, and the lily-cups,
    Those flowers made of light!
The lilacs where the robin built,
    And where my brother set
The laburnum on this birthday, –
    The tree is living yet!

I remember, I remember,
    Where I was used to swing,
And thought the air must rush as fresh
    To swallows on the wing;
My spirit flew in feathers then,
    That is so heavy now,
And summer pools could hardly cool
    The fever on my brow!

I remember, I remember,
    The fir trees dark and high;
I used to think their slender tops
    Were close against the sky:
It was a childish ignorance,
    But now 'tis little joy
To know I'm farther off from heaven
    Than when I was a boy.

Thomas Hood

ON THIS DAY:
Thomas Hood (1799–1845), poet, died.

Composed at Rydal on May Morning, 1838

If with old love of you, dear Hills! I share
New love of many a rival image brought
From far, forgive the wanderings of my thought:
Nor art thou wronged, sweet May! when I compare
Thy present birth-morn with thy last, so fair,
So rich to me in favours. For my lot
Then was, within the famed Egerian Grot
To sit and muse, fanned by its dewy air
Mingling with thy soft breath! That morning too,
Warblers I heard their joy unbosoming
Amid the sunny, shadowy, Coloseum;
Heard them, unchecked by aught of saddening hue,
For victories there won by flower-crowned Spring,
Chant in full choir their innocent Te Deum.

William Wordsworth

ON THIS DAY:

The Derby was first run at Epsom Downs in 1780. The winning horse was called Diomed.

The Yorkist forces defeated the Lancastrians at the battle of Tewkesbury in 1471.

Joseph Whitaker (1820–1895), bookseller, publisher and founder of *Whitaker's Almanack*, first published in 1868, was born.

John Hanning Speke (1827–1864), explorer who discovered Lake Victoria and the source of the Nile, was born.

The Yellowhammer

When shall I see the white thorn leaves agen
And Yellowhammers gath'ring the dry bents
By the Dyke side on stilly moor or fen
Feathered wi love and natures good intents
Rude is the nest this Architect invents
Rural the place wi cart ruts by dyke side
Dead grass, horse hair and downy headed bents
Tied to dead thistles she doth well provide
Close to a hill o' ants where cowslips bloom
And shed o'er meadows far their sweet perfume
In early Spring when winds blow chilly cold
The yellow hammer trailing grass will come
To fix a place and choose an early home
With yellow breast and head of solid gold

John Clare

ON THIS DAY:

Karl Marx (1818–1883) was born.

Napoleon I (1769–1821), Emperor of France, died.

In 1980 the SAS stormed the terrorist-occupied Iranian embassy in London, rescuing nineteen surviving hostages and killing all but one of the terrorists.

May 6

A World Where News Travelled Slowly

It could take from Monday to Thursday
and three horses. The ink was unstable,
the characters cramped, the paper tore where it creased.
Stained with the leather and sweat of its journey,
the envelope absorbed each climatic shift,
as well as the salt and grease of the rider
who handed it over with a four-day chance
that by now things were different and while the head
had to listen, the heart could wait.

Semaphore was invented at a time of revolution;
the judgement of swing in a vertical arm.
News travelled letter by letter, along a chain of towers,
each built within telescopic distance of the next.
The clattering mechanics of the six-shutter telegraph
still took three men with all their variables
added to those of light and weather,
to read, record and pass the message on.

Now words are faster, smaller, harder
... *we're almost talking in one another's arms.*
Coded and squeezed, what chance has my voice
to reach your voice unaltered and to leave no trace?
Nets tighten across the sky and the sea bed.
When London made contact with New York,
there were such fireworks, City Hall caught light.
It could have burned to the ground.

Lavinia Greenlaw

ON THIS DAY:

In 1840 the first postage stamp, known as the Penny Black, was issued.

Rudolph Valentino (1895–1926), star of the silent screen, was born.

In 1954 Roger Bannister (b.1929) succeeded in running the first sub-four-minute mile in Oxford.

The Channel Tunnel, linking England and France by railway routes for passengers, cars and freight, was officially opened in 1994.

Midnight: May 7th, 1945

Thunder gathers all the sky,
Tomorrow night a war will end,
Men their natural deaths may die
And Cain shall be his brother's friend.

From the lethal clouds of lead
Thickening hatred shall descend
In fruitful rain upon the head:
Tomorrow night a war will end.

Thunder, mock not Abel's cry:
Let this symbolic storm expend
The sum of man's malignity!
– And Cain shall be his brother's friend.

There are no words to be said:
Let the future recommend
The living to the luckless dead.
Tomorrow night a war will end.

Patric Dickinson

ON THIS DAY:

Robert Browning (1812–1889), poet, was born.

Archibald MacLeish (1892–1982), poet and politician, was born.

The Cunard liner *Lusitania* was torpedoed by a German submarine in 1915 off the coast of Ireland. Over 2,000 people lost their lives, including many Americans. The loss of the *Lusitania* is widely considered to have influenced the United States of America to join the Allies during the First World War.

May 8

Old Photograph

It is VE night, Tobermory.
Cottages blaze and shimmer in the mirror of the bay.
Light is necklaced everywhere,
on the cross-trees of destroyers,
on the hulls of every cockleshell and scalloper afloat,
even on the gutted snout of a U-boat,
but there are shadows, to imagine
the black and frozen water
and the land, lonely of men,
from Sunart to Mers el Kébir.

Daisy chained by sailors, three WAAFs
pose for a photograph.
Her friends are grinning, wide-eyed,
but my mother's smile is dying
and she's turned away
to the sound of the waves,
as if she could sense my father,
whose war would never cease,
limping inexorably back to her
across the oil scarred sea.

Hugh McMillan

ON THIS DAY:

The War in Europe ended on 8th May 1945, now known as VE (Victory in Europe) day, followed three months later by Japan's surrender and VJ (Victory in Japan) day (15th August 1945).

Never the Time and the Place

Never the time and the place
    And the loved one all together!
This path – how soft to pace!
    This May – what magic weather!
Where is the loved one's face?
In a dream that loved one's face meets mine,
   But the house is narrow, the place is bleak
Where, outside, rain and wind combine
   With a furtive ear, if I strive to speak,
   With a hostile eye at my flushing cheek,
With a malice that marks each word, each sign!
O enemy sly and serpentine,
   Uncoil thee from the waking man!
    Do I hold the Past
    Thus firm and fast
   Yet doubt if the Future hold I can?
This path so soft to pace shall lead
Through the magic of May to herself indeed!
Or narrow if needs the house must be,
Outside are the storms and strangers: we –
Oh, close, safe, warm sleep I and she,
– I and she!

Robert Browning

ON THIS DAY:

Sir J. M. Barrie (1860–1937), author of *Peter Pan*, was born.

Howard Carter (1874 –1939), Egyptologist, was born.

Sherpa Tenzing (1914–1986) died. Tenzing and Sir Edmund Hillary (b.1919) became the first men to climb Mount Everest in 1953.

Your Logic Frightens Me, Mandela

Your logic frightens me, Mandela
Your logic frightens me. Those years
Of dreams, of time accelerated in
Visionary hopes, of savouring the task anew,
The call, the tempo primed
To burst in supernovae round a 'brave new world'!
Then stillness. Silence. The world closes round
Your sole reality; the rest is … dreams?

Your logic frightens me.
How coldly you disdain legerdemains!
'Open Sesame' and – two decades' rust on hinges
Peels at the touch of a conjurer's wand?
White magic, ivory-topped black magic wand,
One moment wand, one moment riot club
Electric cattle prod and whip or *sjambok*
Tearing flesh and spilling blood and brain?

This bag of tricks, whose silk streamers
Turn knotted cords to crush dark temples?
A rabbit punch sneaked beneath the rabbit?
Doves metamorphosed in milk-white talons?
Not for you the olive branch that sprouts
Gun muzzles, barbed-wire garlands, tangled thorns
To wreathe the brows of black, unwilling Christs.

Your patience grows inhuman, Mandela.
Do you grow food? Do you make friends
Of mice and lizards? Measure the growth of grass
For time's unhurried pace?
Are you now the crossword puzzle expert?
Chess? Ah, no! Subversion lurks among
Chess pieces. Structured clash of black and white,
Equal ranged and paced? An equal board? No!
Not on Robben Island. Checkers? Bad to worse.
That game has no respect for class or king-serf
Ordered universe. So, scrabble?

Monopoly? Now, that…! You know
The game's modalities, so do they.
Come collection time, the cards read 'White Only'
In the Community Chest. Like a gambler's coin
Both sides heads or tails, the 'Chance' cards read:
Go to jail. Go straight to jail. Do not pass 'GO'.
Do not collect a hundredth rand. Fishes feast,
I think, on those who sought to by-pass 'GO'
On Robben Island.

Your logic frightens me, Mandela, your logic
Humbles me. Do you tame geckos?
Do grasshoppers break your silences?
Bats' radar pips pinpoint your statuesque
Gaze transcending distances at will?
Do moths break wing
Against a light bulb's fitful glow
That brings no searing illumination?
Your sight shifts from moth to bulb,
Rests on its pulse-glow fluctuations –
Are kin feelings roused by a broken arc
Of tungsten trapped in vacuum?

Your pulse, I know, has slowed with earth's
Phlegmatic turns. I know your blood
Sagely warms and cools with seasons,
Responds to the lightest breeze
Yet scorns to race with winds (or hurricanes)
That threaten change on tortoise pads.

Is our world light-years away, Mandela?
Lost in visions of that dare supreme
Against a dire supremacy of race,
What brings you back to earth? The night guard's
Inhuman tramp? A sodden eye transgressing through
The Judas hole? Tell me Mandela,
That guard, is he *your* prisoner?

Your bounty threatens me, Mandela, that taut
Drumskin of your heart on which our millions
Dance. I fear we latch, fat leeches
On your veins. Our daily imprecisions
Dull keen edges of your will.
Compromises deplete your act's repletion –
Feeding will-voided stomachs of a continent,
What will be left of you, Mandela?

Wole Soyinka

ON THIS DAY:

In 1994 Nelson Mandela was installed as President of South Africa.

In 1857 the Indian Mutiny began with a rising at Meerut.

Fred Astaire (1899–1987), dancer and star, with Ginger Rogers, of many films in the 1930s and 1940s, including *Top Hat*, was born.

The Noble Nature

It is not growing like a tree
In bulk, doth make Man better be;
Or standing long an oak, three hundred year,
To fall a log at last, dry, bald, and sere:

A lily of a day
Is fairer far in May,
Although it fall and die that night –
It was the plant and flower of Light.
In small proportions we just beauties see:
And in short measures life may perfect be.

Ben Jonson

ON THIS DAY:

William Pitt the Elder (1708–1778), politician and Prime Minister from 1766 to 1768, died.

Irving Berlin (1888–1989), songwriter, was born.

The Tate Modern gallery (housed in a former power station on the southern bank of the river Thames) was opened in 2000.

May 12

Easter 1916

I have met them at close of day
Coming with vivid faces
From counter or desk among grey
Eighteenth-century houses.
I have passed with a nod of the head
Or polite meaningless words,
Or have lingered awhile and said
Polite meaningless words,
And thought before I had done
Of a mocking tale or a gibe
To please a companion
Around the fire at the club,
Being certain that they and I
But lived where motley is worn:
All changed, changed utterly:
A terrible beauty is born.

That woman's days were spent
In ignorant good-will,
Her nights in argument
Until her voice grew shrill.
What voice more sweet than hers
When, young and beautiful,
She rode to harriers?
This man had kept a school
And rode our wingèd horse;
This other his helper and friend
Was coming into his force;
He might have won fame in the end,
So sensitive his nature seemed,
So daring and sweet his thought.
This other man I had dreamed
A drunken, vainglorious lout.
He had done most bitter wrong
To some who are near my heart,

Yet I number him in the song;
He, too, has resigned his part
In the casual comedy;
He, too, has been changed in his turn,
Transformed utterly:
A terrible beauty is born.

Hearts with one purpose alone
Through summer and winter seem
Enchanted to a stone
To trouble the living stream.
The horse that comes from the road,
The rider, the birds that range
From cloud to tumbling cloud,
Minute by minute they change;
A shadow of cloud on the stream
Changes minute by minute;
A horse-hoof slides on the brim,
And a horse plashes within it;
The long-legged moor-hens dive,
And hens to moor-cocks call;
Minute by minute they live:
The stone's in the midst of all.

Too long a sacrifice
Can make a stone of the heart.
O when may it suffice?
That is Heaven's part, our part
To murmur name upon name,
As a mother names her child
When sleep at last has come
On limbs that had run wild.
What is it but nightfall?
No, no, not night but death;
Was it needless death after all?
For England may keep faith
For all that is done and said.

We know their dream; enough
To know they dreamed and are dead;
And what if excess of love
Bewildered them till they died?
I write it out in a verse –
MacDonagh and MacBride
And Connolly and Pearse
Now and in time to be,
Wherever green is worn,
Are changed, changed utterly:
A terrible beauty is born.

W. B. Yeats

ON THIS DAY:

The Easter Rising conspirators were hanged in 1916.

Lord Grimthorpe (1816–1905), horologist and designer of Big Ben tower clock, was born.

Florence Nightingale (1820–1910), nurse who treated injured soldiers during the Crimean War, was born.

George VI was crowned at Westminster Abbey in 1937. His was the first coronation to be televised.

The Green Linnet

Beneath these fruit-tree boughs that shed
Their snow-white blossoms on my head,
With brightest sunshine round me spread
Of Spring's unclouded weather,
In this sequester'd nook how sweet
To sit upon my orchard-seat!
And flowers and birds once more to greet,
My last year's friends together.

One have I mark'd, the happiest guest
In all this covert of the blest:
Hail to Thee, far above the rest
In joy of voice and pinion!
Thou, Linnet! in thy green array
Presiding Spirit here today
Dost lead the revels of the May,
And this is thy dominion.

While birds, and butterflies, and flowers,
Make all one band of paramours,
Thou, ranging up and down the bowers,
Art sole in thy employment;
A Life, a Presence like the air,
Scattering thy gladness without care,
Too blest with any one to pair,
Thyself thy own enjoyment.

Amid yon tuft of hazel trees
That twinkle to the gusty breeze,
Behold him perch'd in ecstasies
Yet seeming still to hover;
There, where the flutter of his wings
Upon his back and body flings
Shadows and sunny glimmerings,
That cover him all over.

My dazzled sight he oft deceives –
A brother of the dancing leaves;
Then flits, and from the cottage-eaves
Pours forth his song in gushes,
As if by that exulting strain
He mock'd and treated with disdain
The voiceless Form he chose to feign,
While fluttering in the bushes.

William Wordsworth

ON THIS DAY:

Arthur Sullivan (1842–1900), composer, was born.

Dame Daphne Du Maurier (1907–1989), novelist whose works included *Jamaica Inn* and *Rebecca*, was born.

In 1981 Pope John Paul II (1920–2005) was shot in St Peter's Square, Rome.

May 14

Come Live with Me

Come live with me and be my Love,
And we will all the pleasures prove
That hills and valleys, dale and field,
And all the craggy mountains yield.

There will we sit upon the rocks
And see the shepherds feed their flocks,
By shallow rivers, to whose falls
Melodious birds sing madrigals.

There will I make thee beds of roses
And a thousand fragrant posies,
A cap of flowers, and a kirtle
Embroider'd all with leaves of myrtle.

A gown made of the finest wool,
Which from our pretty lambs we pull,
Fair linèd slippers for the cold,
With buckles of the purest gold.

A belt of straw and ivy buds
With coral clasps and amber studs:
And if these pleasures may thee move,
Come live with me and be my Love.

Thy silver dishes for thy meat
As precious as the gods do eat,
Shall on an ivory table be
Prepared each day for thee and me.

The shepherd swains shall dance and sing
For thy delight each May-morning:
If these delights thy mind may move,
Then live with me and be my Love.

Christopher Marlowe

ON THIS DAY:

In 1264 Simon de Montfort defeated Henry III's (1207–1272, reigned 1216–1272) forces at the battle of Lewes.

May 15

Edith Cavell

She was binding the wounds of her enemies when they came –
  The lint in her hand unrolled.
They battered the door with their rifle-butts, crashed it in:
  She faced them gentle and bold.

The haled her before the judges where they sat
  In their places, helmet on head.
With question and menace the judges assailed her,
  'Yes, I have broken your law,' she said.

'I have tended the hurt and hidden the hunted, have done
  As a sister does to a brother,
Because of a law that is greater than that you have made,
  Because I could do none other.

'Deal as you will with me. This is my choice to the end,
  To live in the life I vowed,'
'She is self-confessed,' they cried: 'she is self-condemned.
  She shall die, that the rest may be cowed.'

In the terrible hour of the dawn, when the veins are cold,
  They led her forth to the wall.
'I have loved my land,' she said, 'but it is not enough:
  Love requires of me all.'

'I will empty my heart of the bitterness, hating none.'
  And sweetness filled her brave
With a vision of understanding beyond the hour
  That knelled to the waiting grave.

They bound her eyes, but she stood as if she shone.
  The rifles it was that shook
When the hoarse command rang out. They could not endure
  That last, that defenceless look.

And the officer strode and pistolled her surely, ashamed
  That men, seasoned in blood,
Should quail at a woman, only a woman, –
  As a flower stamped in the mud.

And now that the deed was securely done, in the night
　　When none had known her fate,
They answered those that had striven for her, day by day:
　　'It is over, you come too late.'

And with many words and sorrowful-phrased excuse
　　Argued their German right
To kill, most legally; hard though the duty be,
　　The law must assert its might.

Only a woman! yet she had pity on them,
　　The victim offered slain
To the gods of fear that they worship. Leave them there,
　　Red hands, to clutch their gain!

She bewailed not herself, and we will bewail her not,
　　But with tears of pride rejoice
That an English soul was found so crystal-clear
　　To be the triumphant voice.

Of the human heart that dares adventure all
　　But live to itself untrue,
And beyond all laws sees love as the light in the night,
　　As the star it must answer to.

The hurts she healed, the thousands comforted – these
　　Make a fragrance of her fame.
But because she stepped to her star right on through death
　　It is Victory speaks her name.

Laurence Binyon

ON THIS DAY:

The remains of Edith Cavell (1865–1915) were returned to England and buried at Norwich Cathedral in 1919 (she had been executed by the Germans on 12th October 1915).

In 1918 the first airmail service was instituted by the US Post Office, between New York and Washington, DC.

Emily Dickinson (1830–1886), poet, died.

Edwin Muir (1887–1959), poet, was born.

Edward Hopper (1882–1967), painter, died.

May 16

The Ploughman's Song

In the merry month of May,
In a morn by break of day,
Forth I walked by the wood side,
Whereas May was in his pride.
There I spied all alone
Phyllida and Corydon.
Much ado there was, Got wot,
He would love and she would not.
She said, never man was true;
He said, none was false to you.
He said, he had loved her long;
She said, love should have no wrong.
Corydon would kiss her then;
She said, maids must kiss no men,
Till they did for good and all.
Then she made the shepherd call
All the heavens to witness truth,
Never loved a truer youth.
Thus with many a pretty oath,
Yea and nay, and faith and troth,
Such as silly shepherds use,
When they will not love abuse,
Love, which had been long deluded,
Was with kisses sweet concluded:
And Phyllida with garlands gay
Was made the Lady of the May.

Nicholas Breton

ON THIS DAY:

Felicia Dorothea Hemans (1793–1835), poet, died.

H. E. Bates (1905–1974), writer and creator of the character Pop Larkin, was born.

The first Academy Awards (Oscars) were presented in 1929.

May 17

London Snow

When men were all asleep the snow came flying,
In large white flakes falling on the city brown,
Stealthily and perpetually settling and loosely lying,
   Hushing the latest traffic of the drowsy town;
Deadening, muffling, stifling its murmurs failing;
Lazily and incessantly floating down and down:
   Silently sifting and veiling road, roof and railing;
Hiding difference, making unevenness even,
Into angles and crevices softly drifting and sailing.
   All night it fell, and when full inches seven
It lay in the depth of its uncompacted lightness,
The clouds blew off from a high and frosty heaven;
   And all woke earlier for the unaccustomed brightness
Of the winter dawning, the strange unheavenly glare:
The eye marvelled—marvelled at the dazzling whiteness;
   The ear hearkened to the stillness of the solemn air;
No sound of wheel rumbling nor of foot falling,
And the busy morning cries came thin and spare.
   Then boys I heard, as they went to school, calling,
They gathered up the crystal manna to freeze
Their tongues with tasting, their hands with snowballing;
   Or rioted in a drift, plunging up to the knees;
Or peering up from under the white-mossed wonder,
'O look at the trees!' they cried, 'O look at the trees!'
   With lessened load a few carts creak and blunder,
Following along the white deserted way,
A country company long dispersed asunder:
   When now already the sun, in pale display
Standing by Paul's high dome, spread forth below
His sparkling beams, and awoke the stir of the day.
   For now doors open, and war is waged with the snow;
And trains of sombre men, past tale of number,
Tread long brown paths, as toward their toil they go:

184

But even for them awhile no cares encumber
Their minds diverted; the daily word is unspoken,
The daily thoughts of labour and sorrow slumber
At the sight of the beauty that greets them, for the
charm they have broken.

Robert Bridges

ON THIS DAY:

On the night of 16th/17th May 1955 the heaviest May snowfall for almost a century fell in London.

Edward Jenner (1749–1823), doctor who developed the smallpox vaccine, was born.

In 1900 the British Garrison in Mafeking was relieved after a 217-day siege.

The 'dambusters' raid began on this night in 1943, led by Wing Commander Guy Gibson, VC (1918–1944).

God's Grandeur

The world is charged with the grandeur of God.
    It will flame out, like shining from shook foil;
    It gathers to a greatness, like the ooze of oil
Crushed. Why do men then now not reck his rod?
Generations have trod, have trod, have trod;
    And all is seared with trade; bleared, smeared with toil;
    And wears man's smudge and shares man's smell: the soil
Is bare now, nor can foot feel, being shod.

And for all this, nature is never spent;
    There lives the dearest freshness deep down things;
And though the last lights off the black West went
    Oh, morning, at the brown brink eastward, springs—
Because the Holy Ghost over the bent
    World broods with warm breast and with ah! bright wings.

Gerard Manley Hopkins

ON THIS DAY:

Tsar Nicholas II (1868–1918), the last Tsar of Russia, was born.

Fred Perry (1909–1995), tennis player and the first player to win all four of the major tennis titles, was born.

Pope John Paul II (Karol Wojtyla, 1920–2005), was born in Poland.

The Simplon Pass

Brook and road
Were fellow-travellers in this gloomy Pass,
And with them did we journey several hours
At a slow step. The immeasurable height
Of woods decaying, never to be decayed,
The stationary blasts of waterfalls,
And in the narrow rent, at every turn,
Winds thwarting winds bewildered and forlorn,
The torrents shooting from the clear blue sky,
The rocks that muttered close upon our ears,
Black drizzling crags that spake by the wayside
As if a voice were in them, the sick sight
And giddy prospect of the raving stream,
The unfettered clouds and region of the heavens,
Tumult and peace, the darkness and the light—
Were all like workings of one mind, the features
Of the same face, blossoms upon one tree,
Characters of the great Apocalypse,
The types and symbols of Eternity,
Of first, and last, and midst, and without end.

William Wordsworth

ON THIS DAY:

In 1906 the Simplon Tunnel was opened linking Italy and Switzerland through the Alps.

W. E. Gladstone (1809–1898), Prime Minister from 1868 to 1874, 1880 to 1885, briefly in 1886 and finally in 1892 until 1894, died.

Sir John Betjeman (1906–1984), poet and author, died.

May 20

Nightingales

Beautiful must be the mountains whence ye come,
And bright in the fruitful valleys the streams, wherefrom
Ye learn your song:
Where are those starry woods? O might I wander there,
Among the flowers, which in that heavenly air
Bloom the year long!

Nay, barren are those mountains and spent the streams:
Our song is the voice of desire, that haunts our dreams,
A throe of the heart,
Whose pining visions dim, forbidden hopes profound,
No dying cadence nor long sigh can sound,
For all our art.

Alone, aloud in the raptured ear of men
We pour our dark nocturnal secret; and then,
As night is withdrawn
From these sweet-springing meads and bursting boughs of May,
Dream, while the innumerable choir of day
Welcome the dawn.

Robert Bridges

ON THIS DAY:

The Chelsea Flower Show was held at the Royal Hospital, Chelsea (designed by Sir Christopher Wren) for the first time in 1913. The event had originally been known as the Great Spring Show, and was first held in Kensington in 1862.

Margery Allingham (1904–1966), writer of detective stories, was born.

Within King's College Chapel, Cambridge

Tax not the royal Saint with vain expense,
With ill-matched aims the Architect who planned—
Albeit labouring for a scanty band
Of white-robed Scholars only – this immense
And glorious Work of fine intelligence!
Give all thou canst; high Heaven rejects the lore
Of nicely-calculated less or more;
So deemed the man who fashioned for the sense
These lofty pillars, spread that branching roof
Self-poised, and scooped into ten thousand cells,
Where light and shade repose, where music dwells
Lingering – and wandering on as loth to die;
Like thoughts whose very sweetness yieldeth proof
That they were born for immortality.

William Wordsworth

ON THIS DAY:

In 1471 Henry VI was murdered, whilst at prayer, in the Tower of London. The founder of Eton College in 1440, he later founded King's College at Cambridge University, the foundation stone for which was laid on 25th July 1441. The architect was Reginald of Ely. William Wordsworth's younger brother, Christopher, served as Master of King's College.

In 1894 Queen Victoria opened the Manchester Ship Canal.

By the Ninth Green, St Enodoc

Dark of primaeval pine encircles me
With distant thunder of an angry sea
While wrack and resin scent alternately
   The air I breathe.

On slate compounded before man was made
The ocean ramparts roll their light and shade
Up to Bray Hill and, leaping to invade,
   Fall back and seethe.

A million years of unrelenting tide
Have smoothed the strata of the steep cliffside:
How long ago did rock with rock collide
   To shape these hills?

One day the mayfly's life, three weeks the cleg's,
The woodworm's four-year cycle bursts its eggs,
The flattened centipede lets loose its legs
   And stings and kills.

Hot life pulsating in this foreshore dry,
Damp life upshooting from the reed-beds high,
Under those barrows, dark against the sky,
   The Iron Age dead—

Why is it that a sunlit second sticks?
What force collects all this and seeks to fix
This fourth March morning nineteen sixty-six
   Deep in my head?

Sir John Betjeman

ON THIS DAY:

Sir John Betjeman (1906–1984) was buried at St Enodoc Church, Cornwall.

Ceylon became the Republic of Sri Lanka in 1972.

Sir Arthur Conan Doyle (1859–1930), creator of the fictional detective Sherlock Holmes, was born.

May the Twenty-third

There never was a finer day,
And never will be while May is May, –
The third, and not the last of its kind;
But though fair and clear the two behind
Seemed pursued by tempests overpast;
And the morrow with fear that it could not last
Was spoiled. To-day ere the stones were warm
Five minutes of thunderstorm
Dashed it with rain, as if to secure,
By one tear, its beauty the luck to endure.

At mid-day then along the lane
Old Jack Noman appeared again,
Jaunty and old, crooked and tall,
And stopped and grinned at me over the wall,
With a cowslip bunch in his button-hole
And one in his cap. Who could say if his roll
Came from flints in the road, the weather, or ale?
He was welcome as the nightingale.
Not an hour of the sun had been wasted on Jack.
'I've got my Indian complexion back,'
Said he. He was tanned like a harvester,
Like his short clay pipe, like the leaf and bur
That clung to his coat from last night's bed,
Like the ploughland crumbling red.
Fairer flowers were none on the earth
Than his cowslips wet with the dew of their birth,
Or fresher leaves than the cress in his basket.
'Where did they come from, Jack?' 'Don't ask it,
And you'll be told no lies.' 'Very well:
Then I can't buy.' 'I don't want to sell.
Take them and these flowers, too, free.
Perhaps you have something to give me?
Wait till next time. The better the day ...
The Lord couldn't make a better, I say;

If he could, he never has done.'
So off went Jack with his roll-walk-run,
Leaving his cresses from Oakshott rill
And his cowslips from Wheatham hill.

'Twas the first day that the midges bit;
But though they bit me, I was glad of it:
Of the dust in my face, too, I was glad.
Spring could do nothing to make me sad.
Bluebells hid all the ruts in the copse,
The elm seeds lay in the road like hops,
That fine day, May the twenty-third,
The day Jack Noman disappeared.

Edward Thomas

ON THIS DAY:

Joan of Arc was captured by the French and sold to the English in 1430. She was burnt at the stake in May 1431.

Girolamo Savonarola (1452–1498), religious reformer, burnt at the stake in Florence.

Carolus Linnaeus (1707–1778), botanist who developed the binomial system for naming animals and plants, was born.

Thomas Hood (1799–1845), poet, was born.

May 24

The Railway Children

When we climbed the slopes of the cutting
We were eye-level with the white cups
Of the telegraph poles and the sizzling wires.

Like lovely freehand they curved for miles
East and miles west beyond us, sagging
Under their burden of swallows.

We were small and thought we knew nothing
Worth knowing. We thought words travelled the wires
In the shiny pouches of raindrops,

Each one seeded full with the light
Of the sky, the gleam of the lines, and ourselves
So infinitesimally scaled

We could stream through the eye of a needle.

Seamus Heaney

ON THIS DAY:

The Ashmolean Museum in Oxford was opened in 1683.

Samuel Morse (1791–1872) sent the first telegraph message, from Washington, DC to Baltimore, in 1844.

The University of Bristol was granted a Royal Charter in 1909.

May 1915

Let us remember Spring will come again
To the scorched, blackened woods, where the wounded trees
Wait, with their wise old patience for the heavenly rain,
Sure of the sky: sure of the sea to send its healing breeze,
    Sure of the sun. And even as to these
      Surely the Spring, when God shall please,
    Will come again like a divine surprise
To those who sit today with their great Dead, hands in their hands, eyes
      in their eyes,
At one with love, at one with Grief: blind to the scattered things and
changing skies.

Charlotte Mew

ON THIS DAY:

The Second Battle of Ypres ended in 1915.

Igor Sikorsky (1889–1972), engineer and designer of aircraft whose helicopter was first used during the Second World War, was born.

Sir Ian McKellen, actor who in 2005 fulfilled a long-held ambition to appear in Coronation Street, was born in 1939.

The Worship of Nature

The harp at Nature's advent strung
　　Has never ceased to play;
The song the stars of morning sung
　　Has never died away.

And prayer is made, and praise is given,
　　By all things near and far;
The ocean looketh up to heaven,
　　And mirrors every star.

Its waves are kneeling on the strand,
　　As kneels the human knee,
Their white locks bowing to the sand,
　　The priesthood of the sea!

They pour their glittering treasures forth,
　　Their gifts of pearl they bring,
And all the listening hills of earth
　　Take up the song they sing.

The green earth sends its incense up
　　From many a mountain shrine;
From folded leaf and dewy cup
　　She pours her sacred wine.

The mists above the morning rills
　　Rise white as wings of prayer;
The altar-curtains of the hills
　　Are sunset's purple air.

The winds with hymns of praise are loud,
　　Or low with sobs of pain, –
The thunder-organ of the cloud,
　　The dropping tears of rain.

With drooping head and branches crossed
    The twilight forest grieves,
Or speaks with tongues of Pentecost
    From all its sunlit leaves.

The blue sky is the temple's arch,
    Its transept earth and air,
The music of its starry march
    The chorus of a prayer.

So Nature keeps the reverent frame
    With which her years began,
And all her signs and voices shame
    The prayerless heart of man.

John Greenleaf Whittier

ON THIS DAY:

In 1865 the American Civil War ended when the Confederates surrendered at Shreveport, New Orleans.

Samuel Pepys (1633–1703), diarist, died.

Julian Grenfell (1888–1915), poet, killed in action at Ypres during the first year of the First World War .

The Mighty Task is Done

At last the mighty task is done;
Resplendent in the western sun
The bridge looms mountain high;
Its titan piers grip ocean floor,
Its great steel arms link shore with shore,
Its towers pierce the sky.

On its broad decks in rightful pride,
The world in swift parade shall ride,
Throughout all time to be;
Beneath, fleet ships from every port,
Vast landlocked bay, historic fort,
And dwarfing all – the sea.

To north, the Redwood Empire's gates;
To south, a happy playground waits,
In Rapturous appeal;
Here nature, free since time began,
Yields to the restless moods of man,
Accepts his bonds of steel.

Launched midst a thousand hopes and fears,
Damned by a thousand hostile sneers,
Yet ne'er its course was stayed,
But ask of those who met the foe,
Who stood alone when faith was low,
Ask them the price they paid.

Ask of the steel, each strut and wire,
Ask of the searching, purging fire,
That marked their natal hour;
Ask of the mind, the hand, the heart,
Ask of each single, stalwart part,
What gave it force and power.

An honoured cause and nobly fought
And that which they so bravely wrought,
Now glorifies their deed,
No selfish urge shall stain its life,
Nor envy, greed, intrigue, nor strife,
Nor false, ignoble creed.

High overhead its lights shall gleam,
Far, far below life's restless stream,
Unceasingly shall flow;
For this was spun its lithe fine form,
To fear not war, nor time, nor storm,
For Fate had meant it so.

Joseph B. Strauss

ON THIS DAY:

The Golden Gate Bridge in San Francisco opened in 1937. Joseph Strauss (1870–1938) was the Chief Engineer. At 4,200 feet the Golden Gate was then the longest suspension bridge in the world.

John Calvin (1509–1564), theologian and reformer, died.

Pandit Jawaharlal Nehru (1889–1964), first prime minister of India, died.

Into Battle

The naked earth is warm with Spring,
   And with green grass and bursting trees
Leans to the sun's gaze glorying,
   And quivers in the sunny breeze;

And life is colour and warmth and light,
   And a striving for evermore for these;
And he is dead who will not fight;
   And who dies fighting has increase.

The fighting man shall from the sun
   Take warmth, and life from the glowing earth;
Speed with the light-foot winds to run,
   And with the trees to newer birth;
And find, when fighting shall be done,
   Great rest, and fullness after dearth.

All the bright company of Heaven
   Hold him in their high comradeship,
The Dog-Star, and the Sisters Seven,
   Orion's Belt and sworded hip.

The woodland trees that stand together,
   They stand to him each one a friend;
They gently speak in the windy weather;
   They guide to valley and ridge's end.

The kestrel hovering by day,
   And the little owls that call by night,
Bid him be swift and keen as they,
   As keen of ear, as swift of sight.

The blackbird sings to him, 'Brother, brother,
   If this is the last song you shall sing,
Sing well, for you may not sing another;
   Brother, sing.'

In dreary, doubtful waiting hours,
    Before the brazen frenzy starts,
The horses show him nobler powers;
    O patient eyes, courageous hearts!

And when the burning moment breaks,
    And all things else are out of mind,
And only joy of battle takes
    Him by the throat, and makes him blind,

Through joy and blindness he shall know,
    Not caring much to know, that still
Nor lead nor steel shall reach him, so
    That it be not the Destined Will.

The thundering line of battle stands,
    And in the air Death moans and sings;
But Day shall clasp him with strong hands,
    And Night shall fold him in soft wings.

Julian Grenfell

ON THIS DAY:

Julian Grenfell's (1888–1915) poem was published for the first time in *The Times* on this day. He had been killed two days earlier while fighting in France.

William Pitt the Younger (1759–1806) was born. In 1783, aged twenty-four he became the youngest British Prime Minister and the first son of a former Prime Minister to hold the office.

Sir Stephen Spender (1909–1995), poet, died.

A Year and a Day

Slow days have passed that make a year,
    Slow hours that make a day,
Since I could take my first dear love
    And kiss him the old way;
Yet the green leaves touch me on the cheek,
    Dear Christ, this month of May.

I lie among the tall green grass
    That bends above my head
And covers up my wasted face
    And folds me in its bed
Tenderly and lovingly
    Like grass above the dead.

Dim phantoms of an unknown ill
    Float through my tired brain;
The unformed visions of my life
    Pass by in ghostly train;
Some pause to touch me on the cheek,
    Some scatter tears like rain.

A shadow falls along the grass
    And lingers at my feet;
A new face lies between my hands –
    Dear Christ, if I could weep
Tears to shut out the summer leaves
    When this new face I greet.

Still it is but the memory
    Of something I have seen
In the dreamy summer weather
    When the green leaves came between:
The shadow of my dear love's face –
    So far and strange it seems.

The river ever running down
   Between its grassy bed,
The voices of a thousand birds
   That clang above my head,
Shall bring to me a sadder dream,
   When this sad dream is dead.

A silence falls upon my heart
   And hushes all its pain.
I stretch my hands in the long grass
   And fall to sleep again,
There to lie empty of all love
   Like beaten corn of grain.

Elizabeth Siddall

ON THIS DAY:

John F. Kennedy (1917–1963), the youngest man to be elected President of the United States of America, was born.

G. K. Chesterton (1874–1936), writer, was born.

In 1953 Mount Everest was conquered by Sherpa Tenzing and Sir Edmund Hillary.

May 30

Happy the man...

Happy the man, whose wish and care
A few paternal acres bound,
Content to breathe his native air
        In his own ground.

Whose herds with milk, whose fields with bread,
Whose flocks supply him with attire;
Whose trees in summer yield him shade,
        In winter, fire.

Blest, who can unconcern'dly find
Hours, days, and years, slide soft away
In health of body, peace of mind,
        Quiet by day,

Sound sleep by night; study and ease
Together mix'd; sweet recreation,
And innocence, which most does please
        With meditation.

Thus let me live, unseen, unknown;
Thus unlamented let me die;
Steal from the world, and not a stone
        Tell where I lie.

Alexander Pope

ON THIS DAY:
Alexander Pope (1688–1744) died.
Joan of Arc (1412–1431) was burnt at the stake by the English.

The End of May

How the wind howls this morn
About the end of May,
And drives June on apace
To mock the world forlorn
And the world's joy passed away
And my unlonged-for face!
The world's joy passed away;
For no more may I deem
That any folk are glad
To see the dawn of day
Sunder the tangled dream
Wherein no grief they had.
Ah, through the tangled dream
Where others have no grief
Ever it fares with me
That fears and treasons stream
And dumb sleep slays belief
Whatso therein may be.
Sleep slayeth all belief
Until the hopeless light
Wakes at the birth of June
More lying tales to weave,
More love in woe's despite,
More hope to perish soon.

William Morris

ON THIS DAY:

The bell known as Big Ben rang out for the first time in 1859. It was named after Sir Benjamin Hall (1802–1867), Minister of Works.

The Second Anglo-Boer War ended with the signing of the Peace of Vereeniging, at Pretoria in South Africa in 1902.

JUNE

An Horation Ode upon
Cromwell's return from Ireland, 1650

The forward youth that would appear
Must now forsake his Muses dear,
    Nor in the shadows sing
    His numbers languishing.

'Tis time to leave the books in dust,
And oil the unusèd armour's rust,
    Removing from the wall
    The corslet of the hall.

So restless Cromwell could not cease
In the inglorious arts of peace,
    But through adventurous war
    Urgèd his active star:

And like the three-forked lightning, first
Breaking the clouds where it was nurst,
    Did thorough his own side
    His fiery way divide:

For 'tis all one to courage high,
The emulous, or enemy;
    And with such, to enclose
    Is more than to oppose.

Then burning through the air he went
And palaces and temples rent;
    And Caesar's head at last
    Did through his laurels blast.

'Tis madness to resist or blame
The force of angry Heaven's flame;
    And if we would speak true,
    Much to the man is due,

Who, from his private gardens, where
He lived reservèd and austere
    (As if his highest plot
    To plant the bergamot),

Could by industrious valour climb
To ruin the great work of time,
    And cast the Kingdom old
    Into another mould.

Though Justice against Fate complain,
And plead the ancient rights in vain –
    But those do hold or break
    As men are strong or weak –

Nature, that hateth emptiness,
Allows of penetration less,
    And therefore must make room
    Where greater spirits come.

What field of all the civil wars
Where his were not the deepest scars?
    And Hampton shows what part
    He had of wiser art;

Where, twining subtle fears with hope,
He wove a net of such a scope
    That Charles himself might chase
    To Car'sbrook's narrow case;

That thence the Royal Actor borne
The tragic scaffold might adorn:
    While round the armèd bands
    Did clap their bloody hands.

He nothing common did or mean
Upon that memorable scene,
    But with his keener eye
    The axe's edge did try;

Nor called the Gods, with vulgar spite,
To vindicate his helpless right;
 But bowed his comely head
 Down, as upon a bed.

This was that memorable hour
Which first assured the forcèd power:
 So when they did design
 The Capitol's first line,

A bleeding head, where they begun,
Did fright the architects to run;
 And yet in that the State
 Foresaw its happy fate!

And now the Irish are ashamed
To see themselves in one year tamed:
 So much one man can do
 That does both act and know.

They can affirm his praises best,
And have, though overcome, confest
 How good he is, how just
 And fit for highest trust;

Nor yet grown stiffer with command,
But still in the Republic's hand–
 How fit he is to sway
 That can so well obey!

He to the Commons' feet presents
A Kingdom for his first year's rents,
 And, what he may, forbears
 His fame, to make it theirs:

And has his sword and spoils ungirt
To lay them at the public's skirt.
 So when the falcon high
 Falls heavy from the sky,

She, having killed, no more does search
But on the next green bough to perch,
    Where, when he first does lure,
    The falconer has her sure.

What may not then our Isle presume
While victory his crest does plume?
    What may not others fear,
    If thus he crown each year?

A Caesar he, ere long, to Gaul,
To Italy an Hannibal,
    And to all States not free
    Shall climacteric be.

The Pict no shelter now shall find
Within his particoloured mind,
    But from this valour sad
    Shrink underneath the plaid,

Happy, if in the tufted brake
The English hunter him mistake,
    Nor lay his hounds in near
    The Caledonian deer.

But thou, the War's and Fortune's son,
March indefatigably on;
    And for the last effect,
    Still keep thy sword erect:

Besides the force it has to fright
The spirits of the shady night,
    The same arts that did gain
    A power, must it maintain.

Andrew Marvell

ON THIS DAY:

In 1650 Oliver Cromwell (1599–1658) arrived back in London. He had been summoned to return to the city at the beginning of the year but refused to do so until his work in Ireland was completed.

John Masefield (1878–1967), poet and Poet Laureate from 1930 until his death, was born.

June 2

He Never Expected Much (or) A Consideration
(A reflection) on my eighty-sixth birthday

Well, World, you have kept faith with me,
    Kept faith with me;
Upon the whole you have proved to be
    Much as you said you were.
Since as a child I used to lie
Upon the leaze and watch the sky,
Never, I own, expected I
    That life would all be fair.

'Twas then you said, and since have said,
    Times since have said,
In that mysterious voice you shed
    From clouds and hills around:
'Many have loved me desperately,
Many with smooth serenity,
While some have shown contempt of me
    Till they dropped underground.

'I do not promise overmuch,
    Child; overmuch;
Just neutral-tinted haps and such,'
    You said to minds like mine.
Wise warning for your credit's sake!
Which I for one failed not to take,
And hence could stem such strain and ache
    As each year might assign.

Thomas Hardy

ON THIS DAY:

Thomas Hardy (1840–1928), poet and novelist, was born.

In 1953 the coronation of HM Queen Elizabeth II took place at Westminster Abbey, London. The news of the conquest of Everest on 29th May arrived on this day.

Vita Sackville-West (1892–1962), poet and novelist, died.

June 3

Recipe for a Salad

To make this condiment your poet begs
The pounded yellow of two hard-boiled eggs;
Two boiled potatoes, passed through kitchen sieve,
Smoothness and softness to the salad give.
Let onion atoms lurk within the bowl
And, half-suspected, animate the whole.
Of mordant mustard add a single spoon,
Distrust the condiment that bites so soon;
But deem it not, thou man of herbs, a fault
To add a double quantity of salt;
Four times the spoon with oil of Lucca crown,
And twice with vinegar procured from town;
And lastly o'er the flavoured compound toss
A magic *soupçon* of anchovy sauce.
Oh, green and glorious! Oh herbaceous treat!
'Twould tempt the dying anchorite to eat;
Back to the world he'd turn his fleeting soul,
And plunge his fingers in the salad-bowl!
Serenely full, the epicure would say,
'Fate cannot harm me, I have dined today.'

Sydney Smith

ON THIS DAY:

Sydney Smith (1771–1845), cleric and gourmet, was born.

George V was born in 1865. The second son of Edward VII (1841–1910, reigned 1901–1910) and Queen Alexandra, he became next in line to the throne after his father, following the death of his elder brother in 1892. George V had a reputation for punctuality, and he created one of the finest philatelic collections in the world.

In 1935 the French liner *Normandie* captured the Blue Riband for the fastest Atlantic crossing.

In 1956, 'Third' class rail tickets were renamed 'Second' class.

June 4

Midnight on the Great Western

In the third-class seat sat the journeying boy,
    And the roof-lamp's oily flame
Played down on his listless form and face,
Bewrapt past knowing to what he was going,
    Or whence he came.

In the band of his hat the journeying boy
    Had a ticket stuck; and a string
Around his neck bore the key of his box,
That twinkled gleams of the lamp's sad beams
    Like a living thing.

What past can be yours, O journeying boy
    Towards a world unknown,
Who calmly, as if incurious quite
On all at stake, can undertake
    This plunge alone?

Knows your soul a sphere, O journeying boy
    Our rude realms far above,
Whence with spacious vision you mark and mete
This region of sin that you find you in
    But are not of?

Thomas Hardy

ON THIS DAY:

The public opening of the Great Western Railway (GWR) from Paddington Station, London took place in 1838. Eton College chartered the train for pupils travelling to and from the school.

In 1805 the first Trooping the Colour ceremony took place on Horse Guards Parade, London.

George III (1738–1820, reigned 1760–1820) was born. He acceded to the throne following the death of his father, George II (1683–1760, reigned 1727–1760).

The architect Sir James Pennethorne (1801–1871) was born. He designed a number of government buildings including the former Public Record Office in Chancery Lane, the Duchy of Cornwall Offices in Buckingham Gate and the ballroom at Buckingham Palace.

In a Wood

Pale beech and pine so blue,
   Set in one clay,
Bough to bough cannot you
   Live out your day?
When the rains skim and skip,
Why mar sweet comradeship,
Blighting with poison-drip
   Neighbourly spray?

Heart-halt and spirit-lame,
   City-opprest,
Unto this wood I came
   As to a nest;
Dreaming that sylvan peace
Offered the harrowed ease –
Nature a soft release
   From men's unrest.

But, having entered in,
   Great growths and small
Show them to men akin –
   Combatants all!
Sycamore shoulders oak,
Bines the slim sapling yoke,
Ivy-spun halters choke
   Elms stout and tall.

Touches from ash, O wych,
   Sting you like scorn!
You, too, brave hollies, twitch
   Sidelong from thorn.
Even the rank poplars bear
Lothly a rival's air,
Cankering in black despair
   If overborne.

Since, then, no grace I find
    Taught me of trees,
Turn I back to my kind,
    Worthy as these.
There at least smiles abound,
There discourse trills around,
There, now and then, are found
    Life-loyalties.

Thomas Hardy

ON THIS DAY:

In 1972 the United Nations established World Environment Day.

Adam Smith (1723–1790), economist and author of *An Enquiry into the Nature and Causes of the Wealth of Nations* (published 1776), was born.

John Maynard Keynes (1883–1946), economist, was born.

June 6

Warm Summer Sun

Warm summer sun,
Shine kindly here,
Warm southern wind,
Blow softly here.
Green sod above,
Lie light, lie light.
Good night, dear heart,
Good night, good night.

Mark Twain

ON THIS DAY:

Olivia Langdon, the wife of the author Mark Twain (1835–1910), died on this day in 1904. They had married in 1870. He wrote 'Warm Summer Sun' as her epitaph.

In 1944, Allied forces landed on the French coast between Cherbourg and Le Havre to begin the liberation of Europe from Nazi occupation.

Sir Henry Newbolt (1862–1938), poet and naval historian, was born.

Captain Robert Falcon Scott (1868–1912), polar explorer, was born. Scott and four companions were the first Englishmen to reach the South Pole in January 1912.

June 7

Summer

Come we to the summer, to the summer we will come,
For the woods are full of bluebells and the hedges full of bloom,
And the crow is on the oak a-building of her nest,
And love is burning diamonds in my true lover's breast;
She sits beneath the whitethorn a-plaiting of her hair,
And I will to my true lover with a fond request repair;
I will look upon her face, I will in her beauty rest,
And lay my aching weariness upon her lovely breast.

The clock-a-clay is creeping on the open bloom of May,
The merry bee is trampling the pinky threads all day,
And the chaffinch it is brooding on its grey mossy nest
In the whitethorn bush where I will lean upon my lover's breast;
I'll lean upon her breast and I'll whisper in her ear
That I cannot get a wink o'sleep for thinking of my dear;
I hunger at my meat and I daily fade away
Like the hedge rose that is broken in the heat of the day.

John Clare

ON THIS DAY:

Paul Gauguin (1848–1903), artist who spent the majority of his life in Tahiti, was born.

The Cunard liner *Lusitania* was launched in 1906.

E. M. Forster (1879–1970), author of *A Room with a View* and *A Passage to India*, died.

June 8

Sea Love

Tide be runnin' the great world over:
    T'was only last June month I mind that we
Was thinkin' the toss and the call in the breast of the lover
    So everlastin' as the sea.

Heer's the same little fishes that sputter and swim,
    Wi' the moon's old glim on the grey, wet sand;
An' him no more to me nor me to him
    Than the wind goin' over my hand.

Charlotte Mew

ON THIS DAY:

John Smeaton (1724–1792), engineer who constructed the third Eddystone lighthouse, was born.

Robert Stevenson (1772–1850), engineer and constructor of the Bell Rock lighthouse, was born.

Sir John Everett Millais (1829–1896), artist and member of the Pre-Raphaelite group, was born.

Thomas Paine (1737–1809), author of *Common Sense*, died.

Sir Joseph Paxton (1803–1865), designer of the grounds at Chatsworth House, and head gardener for thirty years, died.

Frank Lloyd Wright (1869–1959), architect, was born.

June 9

On a Return from Egypt

To stand here in the wings of Europe
disheartened, I have come away
from the sick land where in the sun lay
the gentle sloe-eyed murderers
of themselves, exquisites under a curse;
here to exercise my depleted fury.

For the heart is a coal, growing colder
when jewelled cerulean seas change
into grey rocks, grey water-fringe,
sea and sky altering like a cloth
till colour and sheen are gone both:
cold is an opiate of the soldier.

And all my endeavours are unlucky explorers
come back, abandoning the expedition;
the specimens, the lilies of ambition
still spring in their climate, still unpicked:
but time, time is all I lacked
to find them, as the great collectors before me.

The next month, then, is a window
and with a crash I'll split the glass.
Behind it stands one I must kiss,
person of love or death
a person or a wraith,
I fear what I shall find.

Keith Douglas

ON THIS DAY:

Keith Douglas (1920–1944), soldier and poet, died. He had been in Egypt briefly before being posted to Normandy, and died there after participating in the D-Day assaults three days earlier.

The Book of Common Prayer was first used during Church of England services (on Pentecost Sunday) in 1549.

George Stephenson (1781–1848), railway engineer who built the *Rocket*, was born in Wylam.

June 10

Winter will follow

The heaving roses of the hedge are stirred
By the sweet breath of summer, and the bird
Makes from within his jocund voice be heard.

The winds that kiss the roses sweep the sea
Of uncut grass, whose billows rolling free
Half drown the hedges which part lea from lea.

But soon shall look the wondering roses down
Upon an empty field cut close and brown,
That lifts no more its height against their own.

And in a little while those roses bright,
Leaf after leaf, shall flutter from their height,
And on the reaped field lie pink and white.

And yet again the bird that sings so high
Shall ask the snow for alms with piteous cry,
Take fright in his bewildering bower, and die.

Richard Watson Dixon

ON THIS DAY:

The first boat race between the universities of Oxford and Cambridge took place at Henley-on-Thames in 1829. Oxford University won. The longest breaks between races occurred between 1829 and 1836, 1914 and 1920 and 1939 and 1946. Cambridge's lead as winner of the greatest number of races is under threat following a further win by Oxford in 2005.

Sir Terence Rattigan (1911–1977), playwright, was born.

The architect Antonio Gaudí y Cornet (1852–1926), architect who worked in and around Barcelona for much of his life, died.

Frederick Delius (1862–1934), composer, died.

Amoretti LXXV
One Day I Wrote her Name

One day I wrote her name upon the strand,
    But came the waves and washèd it away;
    Again I wrote it with a second hand,
    But came the tide, and made my pains his prey.
'Vain man,' said she, 'that dost in vain assay
    A mortal thing so to immortalize;
    For I myself shall like to this decay,
    And eke my name be wipèd out likewise'.
'Not so', quod I 'let baser things devise
    To die in dust, but you shall live by fame:
    My verse your virtues rare shall eternize,
    And in the heavens write your glorious name
Where, whenas death shall all the world subdue,
Our love shall live, and later life renew.'

Edmund Spenser

ON THIS DAY:

In 1509 Henry VIII married his first wife, Catherine of Aragon (mother of Mary I).

Ben Jonson (1572–1637), poet and dramatist, was born.

John Constable (1776–1837), painter, was born.

R. J. Mitchell (1895–1937), designer of the Spitfire fighter aeroplane, died a little over a year after the Spitfire completed its maiden flight.

June 12

Young and Old

When all the world is young, lad,
    And all the trees are green;
And every goose a swan, lad,
    And every lass a queen;
Then hey for boot and horse, lad,
    And round the world away!
Young blood must have its course, lad,
    And every dog his day.

When all the world is old, lad,
    And all the trees are brown;
And all the sport is stale, lad,
    And all the wheels run down;
Creep home, and take your place there,
    The spent and maimed among:
God grant you find one face there,
    You loved when all was young.

Charles Kingsley

ON THIS DAY:

Charles Kingsley (1819–1875), author of the novel *The Water Babies*, was born.

Anthony Eden (1897–1977), Prime Minister from 1955 to 1957 and later Lord Avon, was born.

Anne Frank (1929–1945) was born. Frank's diary, describing her experiences hiding from the Nazis in occupied Holland, has become one of the most widely read descriptions of wartime life.

June 13

Move eastward, happy earth

Move eastward, happy earth, and leave
    Yon orange sunset waning slow:
From fringes of the faded eve,
    O, happy planet, eastward go;
Till over thy dark shoulder glow
    Thy silver sister-world, and rise
    To glass herself in dewy eyes
That watch me from the glen below.

Ah, bear me with thee, smoothly borne,
    Dip forward under starry light,
And move me to my marriage-morn,
    And round again to happy night.

Alfred, Lord Tennyson

ON THIS DAY:

Alfred, Lord Tennyson (1809–1892) married Emily Sellwood on 13th June 1850.

Harriet Beecher Stowe (1811–1896), author of *Uncle Tom's Cabin*, was born.

W. B. Yeats (1865–1939), poet and winner of the Nobel Prize for literature in 1923, was born.

The first flying bomb – the V-1 – was used against Britain by Germany in 1944.

June 14

The Battle of Naseby

By Obadiah, Bind-their-Kings-in-Chains-
and-their-Nobles-with-Links-of-Iron,
Serjeant in Ireton's Regiment

Oh! wherefore come ye forth, in triumph from the North,
    With your hands, and your feet, and your railment all red?
And wherefore doth your rout send forth a joyous shout?
    And whence be the grapes of the wine-press which ye tread?

Oh evil was the root, and bitter was the fruit,
    And crimson was the juice of the vintage that we trod;
For we trampled on the throng of the haughty and the strong,
    Who sate in the high places and slew the saints of God.

It was about the noon of a glorious day of June
    That we saw their banners dance and their cuirasses shine,
And the Man of Blood was there, with his long essenced hair,
    And Astley, and Sir Marmaduke, and Rupert of the Rhine.

Like a servant of the Lord, with his Bible and his sword,
    The General rode along us to form us for the fight,
When a murmuring sound broke out, and swelled into a shout,
    Among the godless horsemen upon the tyrant's right.

And hark! like the roar of the billows on the shore,
    The cry of battle rises along their charging line!
For God! for the Cause! for the Church! for the Laws!
    For Charles King of England, and Rupert of the Rhine!

The furious German comes, with his clarions and his drums,
    His bravoes of Alsatia and pages of Whitehall;
They are bursting on our flanks. Grasp your pikes:—close your ranks:—
    For Rupert never comes but to conquer or to fall.

They are here:—they rush on.—We are broken:—we are gone:—
    Our left is borne before them like stubble on the blast.
O Lord, put forth thy might! O Lord, defend the right!
    Stand back to back, in God's name, and fight it to the last.

Stout Skippon hath a wound:—the centre hath given ground:—
    Hark! hark!—What means the trampling of horsemen on our rear?
Whose banner do I see, boys? 'Tis he, thank God, 'tis he, boys.
    Bear up another minute. Brave Oliver is here.

Their heads all stooping low, their points all in a row,
    Like a whirlwind on the trees, like a deluge on the dykes,
Our cuirassiers have burst on the ranks of the Accurst,
    And at a shock have scattered the forest of his pikes.

Fast, fast, the gallants ride, in some safe nook to hide
    Their coward heads, predestined to rot on Temple-Bar,
And he—he turns, he flies,—shame on those cruel eyes
    That bore to look on torture, and dare not look on war.

Ho! comrades, scour the plain: and, ere ye strip the slain,
    First give another stab to make your quest secure,
Then shake from sleeves and pockets their broadpieces and lockets,
    The tokens of the wanton, the plunder of the poor.

Fools, your doublets shone with gold, and your hearts were gay and bold,
    When you kissed your lily hands to your lemans to-day;
And to-morrow shall the fox, from her chambers in the rocks,
    Lead forth her tawny cubs to howl above the prey.

Where be your tongues that late mocked at heaven and hell and fate,
    And the fingers that once were so busy with your blades,
Your perfumed satin clothes, your catches and your oaths,
    Your stage-plays and your sonnets, your diamonds and your spades?

Down, down, for ever down with the mitre and the crown,
  With the Belial of the court, and the Mammon of the Pope;
There is woe in Oxford Halls: there is wail in Durham's Stalls:
  The Jesuit smites his bosom: the Bishop rends his cope.

And She of the seven hills shall mourn her children's ills,
  And tremble when she thinks on the edge of England's sword;
And the Kings of earth in fear, shall shudder when they hear
  What the hand of God hath wrought for the Houses and the Word.

Thomas Babington Macaulay, Lord Macaulay

ON THIS DAY:

In 1645 Oliver Cromwell's Parliamentarian forces (Roundheads) met the Royalist forces (Cavaliers) under Charles I at Naseby, and defeated them in one of the most significant battles of the Civil War.

G. K. Chesterton (1874–1936), writer and poet, died.

For a Column at Runnymede

Thou, who the verdant plain dost traverse here
While Thames among his willows from thy view
Retires; O stranger, stay thee, and the scene
Around contemplate well. This is the place
Where England's ancient barons, clad in arms
And stern with conquest, from their tyrant king
(Then render'd tame) did challenge and secure
The charter of thy freedom. Pass not on
Till thou hast bless'd their memory, and paid
Those thanks which God appointed the reward
Of public virtue. And if chance thy home
Salute thee with a father's honour'd name,
Go, call thy sons: instruct them what a debt
They owe their ancestors; and make them swear
To pay it, by transmitting down entire
Those sacred rights to which themselves were born.

Mark Akenside

ON THIS DAY:

In 1215 a gathering of English barons demanded that King John (1167–1216, reigned 1199–1216) accept a declaration that is now known as Magna Carta. The document detailed his duties and rights, together with the political rights and liberties of his subjects.

Edward III's eldest son, Edward (1330–1376), was born. Known as the Black Prince, he died a year before his father and his son Richard thus became king on Edward III's death.

Wat Tyler (?–1381), the leader of the Peasants' Revolt against Richard II, was beheaded.

In 1825 the foundation stone of the new London Bridge was laid by the Lord Mayor of London.

June 16

A Satirical Elegy.
On the Death of a Late Famous General

His Grace! impossible! what dead!
Of old age too, and in his bed!
And could that Mighty Warrior fall?
And so inglorious, after all!
Well, since he's gone, no matter how,
The last loud trump must wake him now:
And, trust me, as the noise grows stronger,
He'd wish to sleep a little longer.
And could he be indeed so old
As by the news-papers we're told?
Threescore, I think, is pretty high;
'Twas time in conscience he should die.
This world he cumber'd long enough;
He burnt his candle to the snuff;
And that's the reason, some folks think,
He left behind *so great a stink.*
Behold his funeral appears,
Nor widow's sighs, nor orphan's tears,
Wont at such times each heart to pierce,
Attend the progress of his herse.
But what of that, his friends may say,
He had those honours in his day.
True to his profit and his pride,
He made them weep before he dy'd.
   Come hither, all ye empty things,
Ye bubbles rais'd by breath of Kings;
Who float upon the tide of state,
Come hither, and behold your fate.
Let pride be taught by this rebuke,
How very mean a thing's a Duke;
From all his ill-got honours flung,
Turn'd to that dirt from whence he sprung.

Jonathan Swift

ON THIS DAY:

John Churchill, first Duke of Marlborough (1650–1722), died. He was a successful soldier and was close to the King but towards the end of his life fell from favour.

June 17

The Eve of Waterloo

There was a sound of revelry by night,
 And Belgium's Capital had gathered then
 Her Beauty and her Chivalry, and bright
 The lamps shone o'er fair women and brave men;
 A thousand hearts beat happily; and when
 Music arose with its voluptuous swell,
 Soft eyes looked love to eyes which spake again,
 And all went merry as a marriage bell;
But hush! hark! a deep sounds strikes like a rising knell!

Did ye not hear it?—No; 'twas but the wind,
 Or the car rattling o'er the stony street;
 On with the dance! let joy be unconfined;
 No sleep till morn, when Youth and Pleasure meet
 To chase the glowing Hours with flying feet—
 But hark!—that heavy sound breaks in once more,
 As if the clouds its echo would repeat;
 And nearer, clearer, deadlier than before!
Arm! Arm! it is—it is—the cannon's opening roar!

Within a windowed niche of that high hall
 Sate Brunswick's fated chieftain; he did hear
 That sound the first amidst the festival,
 And caught its tone with Death's prophetic ear;
 And when they smiled because he deemed it near,
 His heart more truly knew that peal too well
 Which stretched his father on a bloody bier,
 And roused the vengeance blood alone could quell;
He rushed into the field, and, foremost fighting, fell.

Ah! then and there was hurrying to and fro,
 And gathering tears, and tremblings of distress,
 And cheeks all pale, which but an hour ago
 Blushed at the praise of their own loveliness;
 And there were sudden partings, such as press

The life from out young hearts, and choking sighs
Which ne'er might be repeated; who could guess
If ever more should meet those mutual eyes,
Since upon night so sweet such awful morn could rise!

And there was mounting in hot haste: the steed,
The mustering squadron, and the clattering car,
Went pouring forward with impetuous speed,
And swiftly forming in the ranks of war;
And the deep thunder peal on peal afar;
And near, the beat of the alarming drum
Roused up the soldier ere the morning star;
While thronged the citizens with terror dumb,
Or whispering, with white lips—'The foe! They come!
    they come!'

And wild and high the 'Cameron's Gathering' rose!
The war-note of Lochiel, which Albyn's hills
Have heard, and heard, too, have her Saxon foes:—
How in the noon of night that pibroch thrills,
Savage and shrill! But with the breath which fills
Their mountain-pipe, so fill the mountaineers
With the fierce native daring which instils
The stirring memory of a thousand years,
And Evan's, Donald's fame rings in each clansman's ears!

And Ardennes waves above them her green leaves,
Dewy with nature's tear-drops, as they pass,
Grieving, if aught inanimate e'er grieves,
Over the unreturning brave, —alas!
Ere evening to be trodden like the grass
Which now beneath them, but above shall grow
In its next verdure, when this fiery mass
Of living valour, rolling on the foe
And burning with high hope, shall moulder cold and low.

Last noon beheld them full of lusty life,
    Last eve in Beauty's circle proudly gay,
    The midnight brought the signal-sound of strife,
    The morn the marshalling in arms,—the day
    Battle's magnificently-stern array!
    The thunder-clouds close o'er it, which when rent
    The earth is covered thick with other clay
    Which her own clay shall cover, heaped and pent,
Rider and horse, —friend, foe,—in one red burial blent!

George Gordon, Lord Byron

ON THIS DAY:

Sir Fabian Ware (1869–1949), founder of the Imperial (now Commonwealth) War Graves Commission, was born.

Sir Edward Burne-Jones (1833–1898), Pre-Raphaelite artist, died.

In 1972 five men were arrested in Washington, DC while attempting to break into the Democratic Party National Committee's headquarters in the Watergate building. The ensuing scandal led to the resignation of President Nixon (1913–1994) in 1974.

June 18

Memorials of a Tour on the Continent
V
After Visiting the Field of Waterloo

A wingèd Goddess – clothed in vesture wrought
Of rainbow colours; One whose port was bold,
Whose overburthened hand could scarcely hold
The glittering crowns and garlands which it brought —
Hovered in air above the far-famed Spot.
She vanished; leaving prospect blank and cold
Of wind-swept corn that wide around us rolled
In dreary billows, wood, and meagre cot,
And monuments that soon must disappear:
Yet a dread local recompence we found;
While glory seemed betrayed, while patriot-zeal
Sank in our hearts, we felt as men *should* feel
With such vast hoards of hidden carnage near,
And horror breathing from the silent ground!

William Wordsworth

ON THIS DAY:

In 1815 Napoleon I (1769–1821), having launched an attack against the British, was defeated by the Duke of Wellington's (1769–1852) and von Blücher's forces at the battle of Waterloo. Napoleon's brief resurgence of power was cut short and he was exiled to St Helena where he died.

In 1155 Frederick I 'Barbarossa' (1123–1190) was crowned Holy Roman Emperor.

June 19

To the Bartholdi Statue

O Liberty, God-gifted–
    Young and immortal maid–
In your high hand uplifted,
    The torch declares your trade.

Its crimson menace, flaming
    Upon the sea and shore,
Is, trumpet-like, proclaiming
    That Law shall be no more.

Austere incendiary,
    We're blinking in the light;
Where is your customary
    Grenade of dynamite?

Where are your staves and switches
    For men of gentle birth?
Your mask and dirk for riches?
    Your chains for wit and worth?

Perhaps, you've brought the halters
    You used in the old days,
When round religion's altars
    You stabled Cromwell's bays?

Behind you, unsuspected,
    Have you the axe, fair wench,
Wherewith you once collected
    A poll-tax for the French?

America salutes you–
    Preparing to 'disgorge.'
Take everything that suits you,
    And marry Henry George.

Ambrose Bierce

ON THIS DAY:

In 1885 the sections that comprised the Statue of Liberty arrived in New York City's harbour. It was designed by the French sculptor Frederic Auguste Bartholdi (1834–1904). It was reassembled and dedicated in October 1886.

In 1997 William Hague (b.1961) became the youngest leader of the Conservative Party since William Pitt the Younger in 1783. In 2004 Hague published a widely acclaimed biography of his predecessor.

A Rhyme of the Sun-Dial

The dial is dark, 'tis but half-past one:
But the crow is abroad, and the day's begun.

The dial is dim, 'tis but half-past two:
Fit the small foot with its neat first shoe.

The light gains fast, it is half-past three:
Now the blossom appears all over the tree.

The gnomon tells it is but half-past four:
Shut upon him the old school-door.

The sun is strong, it is half-past five:
Through this and through that let him hustle and strive.

Ha, thunder and rain! it is half-past six:
Hither and thither, go, wander and fix.

The shadows are sharp, it is half-past seven:
The Titan dares to scale even heaven!

The rain soon dries, it is half-past eight:
Time faster flies, but it is not late!

The sky now is clear, it is half-past nine:
Draw all the threads and make them entwine.

Clearer and calmer, 'tis half-past ten:
Count we the gains? not yet: try again.

The shadows lengthen, half-past eleven:
He looks back, alas! let the man be shriven!

The mist falls cold, it is half-past twelve:
Hark, the bell tolls! up, sexton and delve!

William Bell Scott

ON THIS DAY:

In 1837 Princess Victoria acceded to the throne as Queen Victoria on the death of her uncle, William IV (1765–1837, reigned 1830–1837).

June 21

Mad Dogs and Englishmen

In tropical climes there are certain times of day
When all the citizens retire
To tear their clothes off and perspire.
It's one of those rules that the greatest fools obey,
Because the sun is much too sultry
And one must avoid its ultry-violet ray.

The natives grieve when the white men leave their huts,
Because they're obviously definitely nuts!

Mad dogs and Englishmen
Go out in the midday sun,
The Japanese don't care to.
The Chinese wouldn't dare to,
Hindoos and Argentines sleep firmly from twelve to one.
But Englishmen detest a siesta.
In the Philippines
there are lovely screens
To protect you from the glare.
In the Malay States
There are hats like plates
Which the Britishers won't wear.
At twelve noon
The natives swoon
And no further work is done.
But mad dogs and Englishmen
Go out in the midday sun.

It's such a surprise for the Eastern eyes to see
That though the English are effete
They're quite impervious to heat,
When the white man rides every native hides in glee,
Because the simple creatures hope he
Will impale his solar topee on a tree.

It seems such a shame
When the English claim
The earth
That they give rise to such hilarity and mirth.

Mad dogs and Englishmen
Go out in the midday sun.
The toughest Burmese bandit
Can never understand it.
In Rangoon the heat of noon
Is just what the natives shun.
They put their Scotch or Rye down
And lie down.
In a jungle town
Where the sun beats down
To the rage of man and beast
The English garb
Of the English sahib
Merely gets a bit more creased.
In Bangkok
At twelve o'clock
They foam at the mouth and run,
But mad dogs and Englishmen
Go out in the midday sun.

Mad dogs and Englishmen
Go out in the midday sun.
The smallest Malay rabbit
Deplores this foolish habit.
In Hongkong
They strike a gong
And fire off a noonday gun
To reprimand each inmate
Who's in late.
In the mangrove swamps
Where the python romps
There is peace from twelve till two.

Even caribous
Lie around and snooze;
For there's nothing else to do.
In Bengal
To move at all
Is seldom, if ever done,
But mad dogs and Englishmen
Go out in the midday sun.

Sir Noël Coward

ON THIS DAY:

June 21st marks the summer solstice, the longest day of the year.

In 1675 the foundation stone for the new St Paul's Cathedral was laid. Designed by Sir Christopher Wren (1632–1723) the new cathedral replaced the building that had been destroyed in the Great Fire of London.

The West Indies beat Australia by 17 runs at Lord's in 1975, winning cricket's first World Cup.

June 22

At Lord's

It is little I repair to the matches of the Southron folk,
  Though my own red roses there may blow;
It is little I repair to the matches of the Southron folk,
  Though the red roses crest the caps, I know.
For the field is full of shades as I near the shadowy coast,
And a ghostly batsman plays to the bowling of a ghost,
And I look through my tears on a soundless-clapping host
  As the run-stealers flicker to and fro,
    To and fro:
  Oh my Hornby and my Barlow long ago!

It is Glo'ster coming North, the irresistible,
  The Shire of Graces, long ago!
It is Gloucestershire up North, the irresistible,
  And new-risen Lancashire the foe!
A Shire so young that has scarce impressed its traces,
Ah, how shall it stand before all-resistless Graces?
Oh little red rose, their bats are as maces
  To beat thee down, this summer long ago!

This day of seventy-eight they are come up North against thee,
  This day of seventy-eight, long ago!
The champion of the centuries, he cometh up against thee,
  With his brethren, every one a famous foe!
The long-whiskered Doctor, that laugheth rules to scorn,
While the bowler, pitched against him, bans the day that he was born;
And G.F. with his science makes the fairest length forlorn;
  They are come from the West to work thee woe!

It is little I repair to the matches of the Southron folk,
  Though my own red roses there may blow;
It is little I repair to the matches of the Southron folk,
  Though the red roses crest the caps, I know.

For the field is full of shades as I near the shadowy coast,
And a ghostly batsman plays to the bowling of a ghost,
And I look through my tears on a soundless-clapping host
 As the run-stealers flicker to and fro,
  To and fro:
Oh my Hornby and my Barlow long ago!

Francis Thompson

ON THIS DAY:

In 1814 the first cricket match was played at the present Lord's cricket ground, between Marylebone Cricket Club and Hertfordshire.

In 1653 Galileo (1564–1642) was forced to renounce his scientific beliefs by the Inquisition.

Billy Wilder (1906–2002), Austrian-born film director whose films include *Double Indemnity* and *Sunset Boulevard*, was born.

In 1941 Germany invaded the USSR.

June 23

To Sir Len Hutton

There was no violence in him, rather
The quiet mathematician
Given over to geometrics
And the study of angles,
Arcs,
Perimeters and perpendiculars,
Curves and dividing lines,
But rarely, rarely
The parabola.

And the mystery of it all
Was the mastery of it all.

Colin Shakespeare

ON THIS DAY:

Sir Leonard Hutton (1916–1990), cricketer and the first professional player to captain his country in the modern era, was born.

Today is known as Midsummer Eve or Midsummer Night.

Jean Anouilh (1910–1987), playwright and author of *Antigone*, was born.

June 24

Robert Bruce's March to Bannockburn

Scots, wha hae wi' Wallace bled,
Scots, wham Bruce has aften led,
Welcome to your gory bed,
    Or to victory!

Now's the day, and now's the hour;
See the front o' battle lour,
See approach proud Edward's power –
    Chains and slavery!

Wha will be a traitor knave?
Wha can fill a coward's grave?
Wha sae base as be a slave? –
    Let him turn, and flee!

Wha for Scotland's King and Law
Freedom's sword will strongly draw,
Freeman stand or freeman fa',
    Let him follow me!

By Oppression's woes and pains,
By your sons in servile chains,
We will drain our dearest veins,
    But they shall be free!

Lay the proud usurpers low!
Tyrants fall in every foe!
Liberty's in every blow!
    Let us do, or die!

Robert Burns

ON THIS DAY:

In 1314 the Scots, whose forces, led by Robert the Bruce (1274–1329), were outnumbered by the English under Edward II, defeated them at Bannockburn.

John Churchill, first Duke of Marlborough (1650–1722), was born.

Earl Kitchener (1850–1916), whose face appeared on a First World War recruiting poster, was born.

Ambrose Bierce (1842–?1913), journalist and writer, who disappeared in Mexico in 1913, was born.

June 25

The British Museum Reading Room

Under the hive-like dome the stooping haunted readers
Go up and down the alleys, tap the cells of knowledge –
   Honey and wax, the accumulation of years –
Some on commission, some for the love of learning,
Some because they have nothing better to do
Or because they hope these walls of books will deaden
   The drumming of the demon in their ears.

Cranks, hacks, poverty-stricken scholars,
In pince-nez, period hats or romantic beards
   And cherishing their hobby or their doom
Some are too much alive and some are asleep
Hanging like bats in a world of inverted values,
Folded up in themselves in a world which is safe and silent:
   This is the British Museum Reading Room.

Out on the steps in the sun the pigeons are courting,
Puffing their ruffs and sweeping their tails or taking
   A sun-bath at their ease
And under the totem poles – the ancient terror –
Between the enormous fluted Ionic columns
There seeps from heavily jowled or hawk-like foreign faces
   The guttural sorrow of the refugees.

Louis MacNeice

ON THIS DAY:

HM Queen Elizabeth II opened the new British Library at St Pancras in 1998.

The patent for barbed wire was registered by Lucien B. Smith in 1867.

George Orwell (1903–1950), writer, was born.

June 26

High Summer

I never wholly feel that summer is high,
However green the trees, or loud the birds,
However movelessly eye-winking herds
Stand in field ponds, or under large trees lie,
Till I do climb all cultured pastures by,
That hedged by hedgerows studiously fretted trim,
Smile like a lady's face with lace laced prim,
And on some moor or hill that seeks the sky
Lonely and nakedly, – utterly lie down,
And feel the sunshine throbbing on body and limb,
My drowsy brain in pleasant drunkenness swim,
Each rising thought sink back and dreamily drown,
Smiles creep o'er my face, and smother my lips, and cloy,
Each muscle sink to itself, and separately enjoy.

Ebenezer Jones

ON THIS DAY:

Richard III (1452–1485, reigned 1483–1485) acceded to the throne in 1483.

In 1843 Hong Kong became a colony of the British crown.

The United Nations Charter was signed in the United States of America in 1945 by representatives from fifty countries.

June 27

Lausanne, in Gibbon's Old Garden: 11–12pm

*(The 110th anniversary of the completion of the
'Decline and Fall' at the same hour and place)*

A spirit seems to pass,
Formal in pose, but grave withal and grand :
He contemplates a volume in his hand,
And far lamps fleck him through the thin acacias.

Anon the book is closed,
With 'It is finished!' And at the alley's end
He turns, and when on me his glances bend
As from the Past comes speech – small, muted, yet composed.

'How fares the Truth now? – Ill?
– Do pens but slily further her advance?
May one not speed her but in phrase askance?
Do scribes aver the Comic to be Reverend still?

'Still rule those minds on earth
At whom sage Milton's wormwood words were hurled:
*"Truth like a bastard comes into the world
Never without ill-fame to him who gives her birth"?'*

Thomas Hardy

ON THIS DAY:

In 1787 Edward Gibbon (1737–1794) completed his epic work *The Decline and Fall of the Roman Empire.*

In 1961 Michael Ramsey (1904–1988) was enthroned at Canterbury Cathedral as the 100th Archbishop of Canterbury.

June 28

from History of the Twentieth Century
1914

Nineteen-fourteen! Oh, nineteen-fourteen!
Ah, some years shouldn't be let out of quarantine!
Well, this is one of them. Things get raw:
In Paris, the editor of *Figaro*
is shot dead by the wife of the French finance
minister, for printing this lady's – *sans*
merci, should we add? – steamy letters to
– ah, who cares!... And apparently it's *c'est tout*
also for a socialist and pacifist
of all times, Jean Jaurès. He who shook his fist
at the Parliament urging hot heads to cool it,
dies, as he dines, by some bigot's bullet
in a cafe. Ah, those early, single
shots of Nineteen-fourteen! ah, the index finger
of an assassin! ah white puffs in the blue acrylic!...
There is something pastoral, nay! idyllic
about these murders. About that Irish enema
the Brits suffer in Dublin again. And about Panama
Canal's grand opening. Or about that doc
and his open heart surgery on his dog...
Well, to make these things disappear forever,
the Archduke is arriving at Sarajevo;
and there is in the crowd that unshaven, timid
youth, with his handgun... (*To be continued*)

Joseph Brodsky

ON THIS DAY:

In 1914 Austrian Archduke Franz Ferdinand was assassinated in Sarajevo by Gavrilo Princip. The shooting led to war between Austria and Serbia, which escalated into the First World War.

Queen Victoria was crowned in 1838.

The Treaty of Versailles was signed in 1919 by Germany and the Allies.

A Sonnet upon the Pittifull Burning
of the Globe Playhouse in London

Now sitt thee downe, Melpomene,
Wrapt in a sea-coal robe,
And tell the dolefull tragedie,
That late was play'd at Globe;
For noe man that can singe and saye
But was scar'd on St Peter's Daye.
Oh sorrow, pittifull sorrow, and yett all this is true.

All yow that please to understand,
Come listen to my storye,
To see Death with his rakeing brand
'Mongst such an auditorye;
Regarding neither Cardinalls might,
Nor yett the rugged face of Henry the Eight.
Oh sorrow, pittifull sorrow, and yett all this is true.

This fearfull fire beganne above,
A wonder strange and true,
And to the stage-howse did remove,
As round as taylors clewe;
And burnt downe both beame and snagg,
And did not spare the silken flagg.
Oh sorrow, pittifull sorrow, and yett all this is true.

Out runne the knightes, out runne the lordes,
And there was great adoe;
Some lost their hattes and some their swordes;
Then out runne Burbidge too;
The reprobates, though druncke on Munday,
Pray'd for the Foole and Henry Condye.
Oh sorrow, pittifull sorrow, and yett all this is true.

The perrywigges and drumme-heades frye,
Like to a butter firkin;
A woefull burneing did betide
To many a good buffe jerkin.

Then with swolne eyes, like druncken Flemminges,
Distressed stood old stuttering Heminges.
Oh sorrow, pittifull sorrow, and yett all this is true.

No shower his raine did there downe force
In all that Sunn-shine weather,
To save that great renowned howse;
Nor thou, O ale-howse, neither.
Had itt begunne belowe, sans doubte,
Their wives for feare had pissed itt out.
Oh sorrow, pittifull sorrow, and yett all this is true.

Bee warned, yow stage strutters all,
Least yow againe be catched,
And such a burneing doe befall,
As to them whose howse was thatched;
Forbeare your whoreing, breeding biles,
And laye up that expence for tiles.
Oh sorrow, pittifull sorrow, and yett all this is true.

Goe drawe yow a petition,
And doe yow not abhor itt,
And gett, with low submission,
A licence to begg for itt
In churches, sans churchwardens checkes,
In Surrey and Middlesex,
Oh sorrow, pittifull sorrow, and yett all this is true.

Anonymous

ON THIS DAY:

In 1613 the Globe Theatre burned down during a performance of *Henry VIII* by William Shakespeare.
Today is the feast day of St Peter and St Paul.
Elizabeth Barrett Browning (1806–1861), poet and wife of Robert Browning (1812–1889), died.
Joseph Hansom (1803–1882), architect and designer of the Hansom Cab, died.

Perp. Revival i' the North

O, I wad gang tae Harrogate
    Tae a kirk by Temple Moore,
Wi' a tall choir and a lang nave
    And rush mats on the floor;
And Percy Dearmer chasubles
    And nae pews but chairs,
And there we'll sing the Sarum rite
    Tae English Hymnal airs.

It's a far cry frae Harrogate
    And mony a heathery mile
Tae a stane kirk wi' a wee spire
    And a verra wee south aisle.
The rhododendrons bloom wi'oot
    On ilka Simmer's day,
And it's there the Airl o' Feversham
    Wad hae his tenants pray;
For there's something in the painted roof
    And the mouldings round the door,
The braw bench and the plain font
    That tells o' Temple Moore.

Sir John Betjeman

ON THIS DAY:

Temple Moore (1856–1920), architect of St Wilfrid's Harrogate, died. The church was completed by his son-in-law, Leslie Moore.

London's Tower Bridge was opened in 1894.

JULY

July 1

She Walks in Beauty

She walks in beauty, like the night
    Of cloudless climes and starry skies;
And all that's best of dark and bright
    Meet in her aspect and her eyes:
Thus mellowed to that tender light
    Which heaven to gaudy day denies.

One shade the more, one ray the less,
    Had half impaired the nameless grace
Which waves in every raven tress,
    Or softly lightens o'er her face;
Where thoughts serenely sweet express
    How pure, how dear their dwelling-place.

And on that cheek, and o'er that brow,
    So soft, so calm, yet eloquent,
The smiles that win, the tints that glow,
    But tell of days in goodness spent,
A mind at peace with all below,
    A heart whose love is innocent.

George Gordon, Lord Byron

ON THIS DAY:

The battle of Gettysburg (American Civil War) began in 1863.

Louis Blériot (1872–1936), the first man to fly across the English Channel (in 1909), was born.

Charles Laughton (1899–1962), actor who collaborated with Bertolt Brecht (1898–1956) on a production of Brecht's play *Galileo*, was born.

The battle of the Somme began on this day in 1916, and on the first day of fighting the fatalities totalled 21,000 men.

Peter Barnes (1931–2004), dramatist, died.

July 2

Why are the Clergy...?

Why are the clergy of the Church of England
Always changing the words of the prayers in the Prayer Book?
Cranmer's touch was surer than theirs, do they not respect him?
For instance last night in church I heard
(I italicise the interpolation)
'The Lord bless you and keep you *and all who are dear unto you*'
As the blessing is a congregational blessing and meant to be
This is questionable on theological grounds
But is it not offensive to the ear and also ludicrous?
That 'unto' is a particularly ripe piece of idiocy
Oh how offensive it is. I suppose we shall have next
'Lighten our darkness we beseech thee O Lord
    and also the darkness of all those who are dear unto us'
It seems a pity. Does Charity object to the objection?
Then I cry, and not for the first time to that smooth face
Charity, have pity.

Stevie Smith

ON THIS DAY:

Thomas Cranmer (1489–1556), Archbishop of Canterbury during the reigns of Henry VIII and Edward VI and author of the Book of Common Prayer, was born. The most recent amendments to the liturgy of the Church of England were published in the Alternative Service Book and Common Worship.

In 1937 Amelia Earhart (1898–1937) disappeared during her attempt to fly around the world.

July 3

Summer is y-comen in

Summer is y-comen in,
  Loude sing, cuckoo!
Groweth seed and bloweth meed
  And spring'th the woode now–
    Sing cuckoo!

Ewe bleateth after lamb,
  Low'th after calfe cow;
Bullock starteth, bucke farteth.
  Merry sing, cuckoo!

  Cuckoo, cuckoo!
Well sing'st thou, cuckoo:
  Ne swike thou never now!

Sing cuckoo, now! Sing, cuckoo!
Sing cuckoo! Sing, cuckoo, now!

Anonymous

ON THIS DAY:

Franz Kafka (1843–1924), novelist, was born.

In 1938, the *Mallard* set a new world record for steam locomotives of 126 mph near Peterborough. The *Mallard* is a Gresley A4 Pacific and its designer, Sir Nigel Gresley (1876–1941), was on board the train to record the speed.

In 1954 the end of food rationing in Britain was announced by the government. Rationing had lasted for fourteen years. Ration books were ceremoniously burned in Trafalgar Square.

July 4

I have a Rendezvous with Death

I have a rendezvous with Death
At some disputed barricade,
When Spring comes back with rustling shade
And apple blossoms fill the air –
I have a rendezvous with Death
When Spring brings back blue days and fair.

It may be he shall take my hand,
And lead me into his dark land,
And close my eyes and quench my breath –
It may be I shall pass him still.
I have a rendezvous with Death
On some scarred slope of battered hill,
When Spring comes round again this year
And the first meadow flowers appear.

God knows 'twere better to be deep
Pillowed in silk and scented down,
Where Love throbs out in blissful sleep,
Pulse nigh to pulse, and breath to breath,
Where hushed awakenings are dear ...
But I've a rendezvous with Death
At midnight in some flaming town,
When Spring trips north again this year;
And I to my pledged word am true,
I shall not fail that rendezvous.

Alan Seeger

ON THIS DAY:

Alan Seeger (1888–1916), poet and soldier, died.

In 1776 the Declaration of Independence of thirteen North American Colonies from Great Britain was formally adopted. Two former presidents of the United States died on this day: Thomas Jefferson (1743–1826, President 1801–1809) had succeeded John Adams (1735–1826, President 1797–1801) as the third President. Both men died within a few hours of each other on 4th July, 1826. The day is now celebrated as Independence Day in the United States of America.

Sir George Everest (1790–1866), surveyor-general of India, and after whom Mount Everest is named, was born.

The Triple Fool

I am two fools, I know,
For loving, and for saying so
   In whining poetry;
But where's that wiseman, that would not be I,
   If she would not deny?
Then as th'earth's inward narrow crooked lanes
Do purge sea water's fretful salt away,
   I thought, if I could draw my pains
Through rhyme's vexation, I should them allay.
Grief brought to numbers cannot be so fierce,
For, he tames it, that fetters it in verse.

But when I have done so,
Some man, his art and voice to show,
   Doth set and sing my pain,
And, by delighting many, frees again
   Grief, which verse did restrain.
To love and grief tribute of verse belongs,
But not of such as pleases when 'tis read,
   Both are increased by such songs:
For both their triumphs so are published,
And I, which was two fools, do so grow three;
Who are a little wise, the best fools be.

John Donne

ON THIS DAY:

Luke Hansard (1752–1828), printer whose name was given to the official reports of daily debates and readings in the House of Commons, was born.

In 1841 Thomas Cook (1808–1892) arranged a railway excursion for 500 people, and from this humble beginning built up a successful travel agency.

The Blossom

Little think'st thou, poor flower,
   Whom I have watched six or seven days,
And seen thy birth, and seen what every hour
Gave to thy growth, thee to this height to raise,
And now dost laugh and triumph on this bough,
     Little think'st thou
That it will freeze anon, and that I shall
Tomorrow find thee fall'n, or not at all.

Little think'st thou, poor heart
   That labour'st yet to nestle thee,
And think'st by hovering here to get a part
In a forbidden or forbidding tree,
And hop'st her stiffness by long siege to bow:
     Little think'st thou,
That thou tomorrow, ere that sun doth wake,
Must with this sun, and me a journey take.

But thou which lov'st to be
   Subtle to plague thyself, wilt say,
Alas, if you must go, what's that to me?
Here lies my business, and here I will stay:
You go to friends, whose love and means present
     Various content
To your eyes, ears, and tongue, and every part.
If then your body go, what need you a heart?

Well then, stay here; but know,
   When thou hast stayed and done thy most;
A naked thinking heart, that makes no show,
Is to a woman, but a kind of ghost;
How shall she know my heart; or having none,
     Know thee for one?
Practice may make her know some other part,
But take my word, she doth not know a heart.

Meet me at London, then,
　Twenty days hence, and thou shalt see
Me fresher, and more fat, by being with men,
Than if I had stayed still with her and thee.
For God's sake, if you can, be you so too:
　　I would give you
There, to another friend, whom we shall find
As glad to have my body, as my mind.

John Donne

ON THIS DAY:

Jan Huss (1369–1415), religious reformer, was burnt at the stake.

Sir Thomas More (1478–1535) was executed for high treason.

Alexander Wilson (1766–1813), Scottish naturalist and author of *American Ornithology*, was born.

July 7

In Front of Chagall's 'America Windows'

Eyes rest, dissolve into a deep
Lucid blue, like a lead-lined
Mosaic of the sea at nightfall.

Eyes play on a primitive mouth
At a trumpet, a lifted gold megaphone
Out of a riot of blue.

A child of America stumbles at the tripwire.
For an instant the arc of her balance
Crosses Chagall's cascading light,

Points to the field-grey of the courtyard.
Leaded blue and luminous violet tumble together,
Buckle the upraised torch of liberty.

The child and the masterpiece are saved
By an arresting hand. The arc remains,
Printed on us as possibility.

Christopher Southgate

ON THIS DAY:

Marc Chagall (1887–1985), artist, was born. Chagall created *America Windows* in 1976 to commemorate the bicentennial of American Independence. The windows were dedicated on 15th May 1977 at the Art Institute of Chicago.

Sir Winston Churchill (1874–1965) made his final appearance in the House of Commons in 1964.

Sir Allen Lane (1902–1970), founder of Penguin Books, died.

Rome: at the Pyramid of Cestius, near the Graves of Shelley and Keats

Who, then, was Cestius,
And what is he to me? –
Amid thick thoughts and memories multitudinous
One thought alone brings he.

I can recall no word
Of anything he did;
For me he is a man who died and was interred
To leave a pyramid

Whose purpose was exprest
Not with its first design,
Nor till, far down in Time, beside it found their rest
Two countrymen of mine.

Cestius in life, maybe,
Slew, breathed out threatening;
I know not. This I know: in death all silently
He does a finer thing,

In beckoning pilgrim feet
With marble finger high
To where, by shadowy wall and history-haunted street,
Those matchless singers lie…

– Say, then, he lived and died
That stones which bear his name
Should mark, through Time, where two immortal Shades abide;
It is an ample fame.

Thomas Hardy

ON THIS DAY:

Percy Bysshe Shelley (1792–1822), poet, drowned when his boat sank in the Bay of Spezia.

Count Ferdinand von Zeppelin (1838–1917), designer of airships, was born. Zeppelins were widely used in the early part of the 20th century until the *Hindenburg* disaster in May 1937.

The *Wall Street Journal* was published for the first time in 1889.

The Jewish Cemetery at Newport

How strange it seems! These Hebrews in their graves,
   Close by the street of this fair seaport town,
Silent beside the never-silent waves,
   At rest in all this moving up and down!

The trees are white with dust, that o'er their sleep
   Wave their broad curtains in the southwind's breath,
While underneath these leafy tents they keep
   The long, mysterious Exodus of Death.

And these sepulchral stones, so old and brown,
   That pave with level flags their burial-place,
Seem like the tablets of the Law, thrown down
   And broken by Moses at the mountain's base.

The very names recorded here are strange,
   Of foreign accent, and of different climes;
Alvares and Rivera interchange
   With Abraham and Jacob of old times.

'Blessed be God! for he created Death!'
   The mourners said, 'and Death is rest and peace;'
Then added, in the certainty of faith,
   'And giveth Life that nevermore shall cease.'

Closed are the portals of their Synagogue,
   No Psalms of David now the silence break,
No Rabbi reads the ancient Decalogue
   In the grand dialect the Prophets spake.

Gone are the living, but the dead remain,
   And not neglected; for a hand unseen,
Scattering its bounty, like a summer rain,
   Still keeps their graves and their remembrance green.

How came they here? What burst of Christian hate,
    What persecution, merciless and blind,
Drove o'er the sea – that desert desolate –
    These Ishmaels and Hagars of mankind?

They lived in narrow streets and lanes obscure,
    Ghetto and Judenstrass, in mirk and mire;
Taught in the school of patience to endure
    The life of anguish and the death of fire.

All their lives long, with the unleavened bread
    And bitter herbs of exile and its fears,
The wasting famine of the heart they fed,
    And slaked its thirst with marah of their tears.

Anathema maranatha! was the cry
    That rang from town to town, from street to street;
At every gate the accursed Mordecai
    Was mocked and jeered, and spurned by Christian feet.

Pride and humiliation hand in hand
    Walked with them through the world where'er they went;
Trampled and beaten were they as the sand,
    And yet unshaken as the continent.

For in the background figures vague and vast
    Of patriarchs and of prophets rose sublime,
And all the great traditions of the Past
    They saw reflected in the coming time.

And thus forever with reverted look
    The mystic volume of the world they read,
Spelling it backward, like a Hebrew books,
    Till life became a Legend of the Dead.

But ah! what once has been shall be no more!
The groaning earth in travail and in pain
Brings forth its races, but does not restore,
And the dead nations never rise again.

Henry Wadsworth Longfellow

In 1877 the first Wimbledon Lawn Tennis Championships were held.

Sir Edward Heath (1916–2005), statesman and Prime Minister from 1970 to 1974, was born.

In 1984 a fire broke out in the Gothic cathedral of York Minster and severely damaged many areas of the building, particularly the north transept and the Rose Window.

Pete Sampras (b.1971) won his seventh Men's Singles title at Wimbledon in 2000. He beat the Australian Pat Rafter (b.1972).

In 2005 HM Queen Elizabeth II unveiled a memorial in London to all women who served during the Second World War.

July 10

The Cross of Snow

In the long, sleepless watches of the night,
    A gentle face – the face of one long dead –
    Looks at me from the wall, where round its head
    The night-lamp casts a halo of pale light.
Here in this room she died; and soul more white
    Never through martyrdom of fire was led
    To its repose; nor can in books be read
    The legend of a life more benedight.
There is a mountain in the distant West
    That, sun-defying, in its deep ravines
    Displays a cross of snow upon its side.
Such is the cross I wear upon my breast
    These eighteen years, through all the changing scenes
    And seasons, changeless since the day she died.

Henry Wadsworth Longfellow

ON THIS DAY:

Henry Wadsworth Longfellow (1807–1882) wrote this poem in memory of his wife Fanny, who died in a fire on this day in 1861.

John Calvin (1509–1564), theologian and reformer, was born.

Marcel Proust (1871–1922), novelist and author of the epic *Remembrance of Things Past*, was born.

Arthur Ashe (1943–1993), tennis champion and winner of the Men's Singles title at Wimbledon in 1975, was born.

On the Departure Platform

We kissed at the barrier; and passing through
She left me, and moment by moment got
Smaller and smaller, until to my view
    She was but a spot;

A wee white spot of muslin fluff
That down the diminishing platform bore
Through hustling crowds of gentle and rough
    To the carriage door.

Under the lamplight's fitful glowers
Behind dark groups from far and near,
Whose interests were apart from ours,
    She would disappear,

Then show again, till I ceased to see
That flexible form, that nebulous white;
And she who was more than my life to me
    Had vanished quite.

We have penned new plans since that fair fond day,
And in season she will appear again—
Perhaps in the same soft white array—
    But never as then!

—'And why, young man, must eternally fly
A joy you'll repeat, if you love her well?'
—O friend, nought happens twice thus; why,
    I cannot tell!

Thomas Hardy

ON THIS DAY:

Robert the Bruce (1274–1329), Scottish king who defeated the English at the battle of Bannockburn, was born.

John Quincy Adams (1767–1848), sixth President of the United States (1825–1829), was born. Adams was the first son of a former President (John Adams, 1735–1826, President 1797–1801) to be elected to the office.

The original London Waterloo station opened in 1848.

In 1986 British newspapers were banned from publishing any extracts or serialisations of sections from the book *Spycatcher* by Peter Wright (1916–1995).

July 12

Inscription for a Fountain on a Heath

This Sycamore, oft musical with bees,—
Such tents the Patriarchs loved! O long unharmed
May all its agèd boughs o'er-canopy
The small round basin, which this jutting stone
Keeps pure from falling leaves! Long may the Spring,
Quietly as a sleeping infant's breath,
Send up cold waters to the traveller
With soft and even pulse! Nor ever cease
Yon tiny cone of sand its soundless dance,
Which at the bottom, like a Fairy's Page,
As merry and no taller, dances still,
Nor wrinkles the smooth surface of the Fount.
Here Twilight is and Coolness: here is moss,
A soft seat, and a deep and ample shade.
Thou may'st toil far and find no second tree.
Drink, Pilgrim, here; Here rest! and if thy heart
Be innocent, here too shalt thou refresh
Thy spirit, listening to some gentle sound,
Or passing gale or hum of murmuring bees!

Samuel Taylor Coleridge

ON THIS DAY:

Lord Nelson (1758–1805) lost his right eye at the siege of Calvi, Corsica in 1794.

Charles Rolls (1877–1910) died in an aeroplane accident. He was the first man to fly in both directions across the English Channel.

George Eastman (1854–1932), who devised a roll-film camera and founded Kodak, was born.

Lost Poems

I think sometimes of poems I have lost –
Maybe their loss it was that saved the world – still
They do get lost, and I recall them only
When a fragment levitates behind
Discarded invoices, the black-rimmed notice
Of a last goodbye, a birth, a wedding invitation
And other milestones of a lesser kind.

The moment torments – why? Beyond
An instant's passion, dubious flash –
Satori in a bar, taxi or restaurant, an airport
Waiting lounge – that births the scribble
On a stained napkin, what cast of the ephemeral
Once resonates, then spurns the mind
The morning after? All that survives

Mimics a wrinkled petal pressed
Between pages of long-discarded books.
A falling leaf trapped briefly by the passing sun
It flashes, a mere shard of memory
But filled with wistful accusations
Of abandonment. Too late,

No life to it. The book is closed
The moment's exultation or despair
Drowned in wine rivers, shrivelled
In suns of greater wars. I turn
These scrapbooks of a moment's truth
To cinders, their curlings curse in smoke –
Once more fugitive beyond recall
Of usurper's summons by
The morning after.

I think of voices I have lost, and touches,
The fleeting brush of eyes that burrows
Deep within the heart of need, the pledge
Unspoken, the more than acts of faith
That forge an instant world in silent pact
With strangers – deeper, deeper bonds
Than the dearest love's embrace.

Wole Soyinka

ON THIS DAY:

Wole Soyinka, poet, writer and Nobel Prize winner, was born in 1934.

Queen Victoria became the first monarch to live in Buckingham Palace in 1837.

Kenneth Clark, Baron Clark (1903–1983), art historian and presenter of the BBC television series *Civilisation*, was born.

Zermatt: to the Matterhorn
(June–July 1897)

Thirty-two years since, up against the sun,
Seven shapes, thin atomies to lower sight,
Labouringly leapt and gained thy gabled height,
And four lives paid for what the seven had won.

They were the first by whom the deed was done,
And when I look at thee, my mind takes flight
To that day's tragic feat of manly might,
As though, till then, of history thou hadst none.

Yet ages ere men topped thee, late and soon
Thou didst behold the planets lift and lower;
Saw'st, maybe, Joshua's pausing sun and moon,
And the betokening sky when Caesar's power
Approached its bloody end; yea, even that Noon
When darkness filled the earth till the ninth hour.

Thomas Hardy

ON THIS DAY:

In 1865 the first successful ascent of the Matterhorn was made. The party of seven men was led by Edward Whymper (1840–1911). Only three of the party returned from the summit safely. Michel Croz, Lord Francis Douglas, Robert Hadow and the Reverend Charles Hudson all died during the descent.

Bastille Day is celebrated in France with processions and fireworks. The event marks the storming of the Bastille prison by the people of Paris in 1789, widely considered the start of the French Revolution.

July 15

The Water-Seller's Song in the Rain

I sell water. Who will taste it?
— Who would want to in this weather?
All my labour has been wasted
Fetching these few pints together.
I stand shouting Buy my water!
And nobody thinks it
Worth stopping and buying
Or greedily drinks it.
(Buy water, you devils!)

O to stop the leaky heaven
Hoard what stock I've got remaining:
Recently I dreamt that seven
Years went by without it raining.
How they'd all shout Give me water!
How they'd fight for my good graces
And I'd make their further treatment
Go by how I liked their faces.
(Stay thirsty, you devils!)

Wretched weeds, you're through with thirsting
Heaven must have heard you praying.
You can drink until you're bursting
Never bother about paying.
I'm left shouting Buy my water!
And nobody thinks it
Worth stopping and buying
Or greedily drinks it.
(Buy water, you devils!)

Bertolt Brecht

ON THIS DAY:

The translation of the relics of St Swithun (Bishop of Winchester 852–862) is celebrated. There is an ancient legend that if rain falls on St Swithun's Day it will continue for forty days and forty nights.

Inigo Jones (1573–1652), architect, was born. As Surveyor of the King's Works, Jones built the Banqueting House, Whitehall and the Queen's Chapel, St James's Palace.

Iris Murdoch (1919–1999), novelist, was born.

July 16

At the Bomb Testing Site

At noon in the desert a panting lizard
waited for history, its elbows tense,
watching the curve of a particular road
as if something might happen.

It was looking at something farther off
than people could see, an important scene
acted in stone for little selves
at the flute end of consequences.

There was just a continent without much on it
under a sky that never cared less.
Ready for a change, the elbows waited.
The hands gripped hard on the desert.

William Stafford

ON THIS DAY:

In 1945 the first nuclear device was tested at the Trinity Test Site, south eastern New Mexico (the operation was codenamed 'Trinity'). A few weeks later an atomic bomb was dropped on the Japanese city of Hiroshima (6th August 1945).

Pope Innocent III (c.1160–1216, Pope 1198–1216) died at Perugia, Italy.

Sir Joshua Reynolds (1723–1792), President of the Royal Academy of Arts, was born.

Hilaire Belloc (1870–1953), author and former Member of Parliament for Salford, died.

July 17

The Duck's Egg

(Written on the shell of a duck's egg and found on the cricket field of Amersham Hall, on 17th July 1866, after a match)

Two balls I survived,
  But the third one came straight,
For the bowler contrived
(Seeing what I survived)
To bowl at a rate
  I did not contemplate.
Two balls I survived,
  But the third one came straight.

Anonymous

July 18

Grace at Gloucester

I saw the 'Old Man' once
When he was old as I
Was young. He did not score,
So far as I recall, a heap of runs,
Nor even hit a four.
But still he lives before my schoolboy eye
A giant among pygmies. In his hand
The bat looked like a toy. I saw him stand
Firm set on legs as massive as the piers
Of the Norman nave at Gloucester; and the cheers
Which greeted him on the 'Spa' were heard
As far as the Cathedral. When he stirred
The ground shook, and the crazy old
Pavilion creaked and groaned. I saw him field
– At point. When 'Father' Roberts bowled
And the batsman, now forgotten, from the group
Around the wicket cut a fast one square
Along the ground, the Doctor saw it there
A moment ere it was concealed
By his great bulk. He did not deign to stoop,
But let it pass. He bowled a few
Himself, slow lumbering to the crease. The batsmen knew
By then his simple bluff, and did not care.

Upon the Spa no county players pace;
The great ones of to-day it does not know.
I deem it better so,
Leaving the elm-girt field its dreams of Grace.

Oscar Lloyd

ON THIS DAY:

William Gilbert 'W. G.' Grace (1848–1915), cricketer, was born.

Gilbert White (1720–1793), author and naturalist, was born.

Nelson Mandela, the first President of post-apartheid South Africa, was born in 1918.

July 19

Roman Fountain

Up from the bronze, I saw
Water without a flaw
Rush to its rest in air,
Reach to its rest, and fall.

Bronze of the blackest shade,
An element man-made,
Shaping upright the bare
Clear gouts of water in air.

O, as with arm and hammer,
Still it is good to strive
To beat out the image whole,
To echo the shout and stammer
When full-gushed waters, alive,
Strike on the fountain's bowl
After the air of summer.

Louise Bogan

July 20

Moon-Man

Stranded on the moon,
a librium dreamer in a lunar landscape,
the tabloids were full of your blurred, blown-up face,
the neat curled head, the secret animal eyes,
immolated forever in the Sea of Tranquility.

I keep getting messages from outer space,
'Meet me at Cape Canaveral, Houston, Tullamarine.'
A telegram came through at dawn to the Dead Heart Tracking Station.
I wait on winter mornings in hangars
dwarfed by grounded crates like giant moths
          furred with frost.

Moon-pictures – you dance clumsily on the screen,
phosphorescent, domed, dehumanised,
          floating above the dust,
your robot voice hollow as bells.

The crowds queue for the late edition,
scan headlines avidly, their necks permanently awry,
looking for a sign, a scapegoat, a priest, a king:
the circulation is rising.

They say you have been knighted in your absence,
but those who swear they know you best,
assert you are still too radical to accept the honour.

They have sent several missions,
but at lift-off three astronauts fried,
          strapped in their webbing.
Plane-spotters on penthouse roofs
have sighted more UFOs.

Sometimes I go out at night
    to stare at the galaxies.
Is that your shadow, weightless,
    magnified in light,
man's flesh enclosed in armour,
suffering eyes in perspex looking down,
sacred and murderous from your sanctuary?

Dorothy Hewett

ON THIS DAY:

In 1969 Neil Armstrong (b.1930) and Dr Edwin E. 'Buzz' Aldrin (b.1930) landed on the moon in the lunar module *Eagle*. The next day, at 3.56 a.m. BST, Armstrong stepped on to the surface of the moon.

Francesco Petrarch (1304–1374), Italian poet, was born.

Sir Edmund Hillary, who with Sherpa Tenzing reached the summit of Mount Everest on 29th May 1953, was born in 1919.

In 1944 Adolf Hitler survived an assassination attempt by Claus von Stauffenberg. The 'bomb plot' had been organised by senior officers in the German army.

The March into Virginia
Ending in the First Manassas (July 1861)

Did all the lets and bars appear
    To every just or larger end,
Whence should come the trust and cheer?
    Youth must its ignorant impulse lend –
Age finds place in the rear.
    All wars are boyish, and are fought by boys,
The champions and enthusiasts of the state:
    Turbid ardours and vain joys
        Not barrenly abate –
    Stimulants to the power mature,
        Preparatives of fate.

Who here forecasteth the event?
What heart but spurns at precedent
And warnings of the wise,
Contemned foreclosures of surprise?
The banners play, the bugles call,
The air is blue and prodigal.
    No berrying party, pleasure-wooed,
No picnic party in the May,
Ever went less loth than they
    Into that leafy neighbourhood.

In Bacchic glee they file toward Fate,
Moloch's uninitiate;
Expectancy, and glad surmise
Of battle's unknown mysteries.

All they feel is this: 'tis glory,
A rapture sharp, though transitory,
Yet lasting in belaureled story.
So they gaily go to fight,
Chatting left and laughing right.

But some who this blithe mood present,
   As on in lightsome files they fare,
Shall die experienced ere three days are spent –
   Perish, enlightened by the volleyed glare;
Or shame survive, and, like to adamant,
   The throe of Second Manassas share.

Herman Melville

ON THIS DAY:

The first major battle of the American Civil War took place at Bull Run in 1861.

The Tate Gallery on Millbank in London opened in 1897.

Alan B. Shepard Jr (1923–1998), first American in space, died.

July 22

After Trinity

We have done with dogma and divinity
    Easter and Whitsun past,
The long, long Sundays after Trinity
    Are with us at last;
The passionless Sundays after Trinity,
    Neither feast-day nor fast.

Christmas comes with plenty,
    Lent spreads out its pall,
But these are five and twenty,
    The longest Sundays of all;
The placid Sundays after Trinity,
    Wheat-harvest, fruit-harvest, Fall.

Spring with its burst is over,
    Summer has had its day.
The scented grasses and clover
    Are cut, and dried into hay;
The singing-birds are silent,
    And the swallows flown away.

Post pugnam pausa fiet;
    Lord, we have made our choice;
In the stillness of autumn quiet,
    We have heard the still, small voice.
We have sung *Oh where shall Wisdom?*
    Thick paper, folio, Boyce.

Let it not all be sadness,
    Not *omnia vanitas*,
Stir up a little gladness
    To lighten the *Tibi cras*;
Send us that little summer
    That comes with Martinmas.

When still the cloudlet dapples
    The windless cobalt-blue,
And the scent of gathered apples
    Fills all the store-rooms through,
The gossamer silvers the bramble,
    The lawns are gemmed with dew.

An end of tombstone Latinity,
    Stir up sober mirth,
Twenty-fifth after Trinity,
    Kneel with the listening earth,
Behind the Advent trumpets
    They are singing Emmanuel's birth.

John Meade Falkner

ON THIS DAY:

Today is the feast day of St Mary Magdalene.

Gregor Mendel (1822–1884), Austrian botanist who developed the theory of heredity, was born.

Sir Mortimer Wheeler (1890–1976), archaeologist, died.

Meeting at Night

The grey sea and the long black land;
And the yellow half-moon large and low;
And the startled little waves that leap
In fiery ringlets from their sleep,
As I gain the cove with pushing prow,
And quench its speed i' the slushy sand.

Then a mile of warm sea-scented beach;
Three fields to cross till a farm appears;
A tap at the pane, the quick sharp scratch
And blue spurt of a lighted match,
And a voice less loud, thro' its joys and fears,
Than the two hearts beating each to each!

Robert Browning

ON THIS DAY:

Coventry Patmore (1823–1896), poet, was born.

Raymond Chandler (1888–1959), writer who created the detective Philip Marlowe, was born.

The Ford Motor Company sold its first car in 1903.

Michael Foot, leader of the Labour Party 1980–1983, was born in 1913.

July 24

The Sky Lark

The rolls and harrows lie at rest beside
The battered road and spreading far and wide
Above the russet clods the corn is seen
Sprouting its spirey points of tender green
Where squats the hare to terrors wide awake
Like some brown clod the harrows failed to break
While neath the warm hedge boys stray far from home
To crop the early blossoms as they come
Where buttercups will make them easy run
Opening their golden caskets to the sun
To see who shall be first to pluck the prize
And from their hurry up the skylark flies,
And oer her half formed nest, with happy wings
Winnows the air – till in the clouds she sings,
Then hangs a dust spot in the sunny skies,
And drops and drops, till in her nest she lies
Where boys unheeding past – neer dreaming then
That birds which flew so high – would drop agen
To nests upon the ground, where any thing
May come at to destroy had they the wing
Like such a bird themselves would be too proud,
And build on nothing but a passing cloud
As free from danger as the heavens are free
From pain and toil – there would they build and be
And sail about the world to scenes unheard
Of and unseen – O were they but a bird
So think they while they listen to its song,
And smile and fancy and so pass along;
While its low nest moist with the dews of morn
Lye safely with the leveret in the corn.

John Clare

ON THIS DAY:
Amelia Earhart (1898–1937), female aviator, was born.
Robert Graves (1895–1985), poet, was born.
The speaking clock was launched in Britain in 1936.

281

July 25

from A Ballad on the Marriage of Philip and Mary

The egles byrde hath spred his wings
And from far of, hathe taken flyght
In whiche meane way by no leurings
On bough or braunch this bird wold light
Till on the rose, both red and whight
He lighteth now, moste lovinglie
And therto moste behovinglie.

The monthe ensuing next to June
This birde, this floure for perche doth take
Rejoysinglie him selfe to prune
He rousith, rypelie to awake
Upon this perche to chose his make
Concluding strayght for rype right rest
In the lions boure, to bilde his nest

A birde, a beast to make to choose
Namelie the beaste most furious
It may seeme straunge, and so it doose
And to this birde injurious
It semthe a case right curious
To make construction in suche sens
As may stande for this birds defens

But marke, this lion so by name
Is properlie a lambe tassyne
No lion wilde, a lion tame
No rampant lion masculyne
The lamblike lion feminyne
Whose milde meeke propertie aleurth
This birde to light, and him asseurth

The egles birde, the egles eyre
All other birds far surmounting
The crounid lion, matcheth feyre
Croune unto croune, this birde dothe bring
A queenelie queene, a kinglie king
Thus, lyke to lyke here matched is
What matche may match more mete then this

John Heywood

ON THIS DAY:

Mary I and Philip (later Philip II) of Spain were married in 1554.

Today is the feast day of St James the Great (died AD 44). He was the first apostle to die for the Christian faith, and one of the most popular Christian pilgrimages is to his shrine at Santiago de Compostela in Spain.

Samuel Taylor Coleridge (1772–1834), poet, died.

July 26

from On the Death of the Late Earl of Rochester

Mourn, mourn, ye Muses, all your loss deplore,
The young, the noble *Strephon* is no more.
Yes, yes, he fled quick as departing light,
And ne'er shall rise from Death's eternal night,
So rich a prize the *Stygian* gods ne'er bore,
Such wit, such beauty, never graced their shore.
He was but lent this duller world t'improve
In all the charms of poetry, and love;
Both were his gift, which freely he bestowed,
And like a god, dealt to the wond'ring crowd.
Scorning the little vanity of fame,
Spight of himself attained a glorious name.
But oh! in vain was all his peevish pride,
The sun as soon might his vast lustre hide,
As piercing, pointed, and more lasting bright,
As suffering no vicissitudes of night.
    Mourn, mourn, ye Muses, all your loss deplore,
    The young, the noble *Strephon* is no more.

Aphra Behn

ON THIS DAY:

John Wilmot, second Earl of Rochester (1647–1680), poet, satirist and libertine, died.

George Bernard Shaw (1856–1950), playwright, was born.

Aldous Huxley (1894–1963), novelist, was born.

The Federal Bureau of Investigation (FBI) was established (as the Office of the Chief Examiner) in 1908.

July 27

To the Evening Star

Star that bringest home the bee,
And sett'st the weary labourer free!
If any star shed peace, 'tis Thou
  That send'st it from above,
Appearing when Heaven's breath and brow
  Are sweet as hers we love.

Come to the luxuriant skies,
Whilst the landscape's odours rise,
Whilst far-off lowing herds are heard
  And songs when toil is done,
From cottages whose smoke unstirr'd
  Curls yellow in the sun.

Star of love's soft interviews,
Parted lovers on thee muse;
Their remembrancer in Heaven
  Of thrilling vows thou art,
Too delicious to be riven
  By absence from the heart.

Thomas Campbell

ON THIS DAY:

The Bank of England was established by Royal Charter in 1694.

Sir Geoffrey de Havilland (1882–1965), aircraft designer, was born.

The Korean War ended with the signing of an armistice in 1953.

July 28

Melrose Abbey

If thou would'st view fair Melrose aright,
Go visit it by the pale moonlight;
For the gay beams of lightsome day
Gild, but to flout, the ruins grey.
When the broken arches are black in night,
And each shafted oriel glimmers white;
When the cold light's uncertain shower
Streams on the ruined central tower;
When buttress and buttress, alternately,
Seem framed of ebon and ivory;
When silver edges the imagery,
And the scrolls that teach thee to live and die;
When distant Tweed is heard to rave,
And the owlet to hoot o'er the dead man's grave,
Then go—but go alone the while—
Then view St. David's ruined pile;
And, home returning, soothly swear,
Was never scene so sad and fair!

Sir Walter Scott

ON THIS DAY:

Melrose Abbey was dedicated to the Blessed Virgin Mary in 1146. Founded by the Scottish king David I (c.1085–1153, reigned 1124–1153) in 1136 it took fewer than ten years to build. It was however very vulnerable to attacks from the English and suffered at their hands for many years.

Gerard Manley Hopkins (1844–1889), poet, was born.

Beatrix Potter (1866–1943), author and conservationist, was born.

Sir Garfield 'Gary' Sobers, cricketer and West Indies captain, was born in 1936.

July 29

The Other Little Boats – July 1588

A pause came in the fighting and England held her breath
For the battle was not ended and the ending might be death.
Then out they came, the little boats, from all the Channel shore
Free men were these who set the sails and laboured at the oars.
From Itchenor and Shoreham, from Deal and Winchelsea,
They put out into the Channel to keep their country free.
Not of Dunkirk this story, but of boatmen long ago,
When our Queen was Gloriana and King Philip was our foe
And galleons rode the Narrow Sea, and Effingham and Drake
Were out of shot and powder, with all England still at stake.
They got the shot and powder, they charged their guns again,
The guns that guarded England from the galleons of Spain,
And the men who helped them to do it, helped them still to hold the sea
Men from Itchenor and Shoreham, men from Deal and Winchelsea,
Looked out happily from Heaven and cheered to see the work
Of their grandsons' grandsons' grandsons on the beaches of Dunkirk.

Edward Shanks

ON THIS DAY:

The ships of the Spanish Armada were defeated by the English fleet in 1588.

George Bradshaw (1801–1853), printer whose name was given to the first printed national railway timetable, *Bradshaw's*, was born.

Benito Mussolini (1883–1945), the fascist Italian dictator, was born.

Evening

I

'Tis evening, the black snail has got on his track,
And gone to its nest is the wren;–
And the packman snail too, with his home on his back;
Clings on the bowed bents like a wen.

II

The shepherd has made a rude mark with his foot,
Where his shaddow reached when he first came;
And it just touched the tree where his secret love cut,
Two letters that stand for love's name.

III

The evening comes in with the wishes of love;–
And the shepherd he looks on the flowers;–
And thinks who would praise the soft song of the dove,
And meet joy in these dewfalling hours.

IV

For nature is love, and the wishers of love;
When nothing can hear or intrude;
It hides from the eagle, and joins with the dove:
In beautiful green solitude.

John Clare

ON THIS DAY:

Samuel Rogers (1763–1855), poet, and highly successful art collector, was born. In 1850, Rogers declined to accept the position of Poet Laureate because he believed he was too old for the post.

Thomas Gray (1716–1771) died and was buried next to his mother at Stoke Poges, Buckinghamshire (the church said to be the inspiration for his poem 'Elegy written in a Country Churchyard').

July 31

The Bibliomaniac's Prayer

Keep me, I pray, in wisdom's way
That I may truths eternal seek;
I need protecting care today, –
My purse is light, my flesh is weak.
So banish from my erring heart
All baleful appetites and hints
Of Satan's fascinating art,
Of first editions, and of prints.
Direct me in some godly walk
Which leads away from bookish strife,
That I with pious deed and talk
May extra-illustrate my life.

But if, O Lord, it pleaseth Thee
To keep me in temptation's way,
I humbly ask that I may be
Most notably beset today;
Let my temptation be a book,
Which I shall purchase, hold, and keep,
Whereon when other men shall look,
They'll wail to know I got it cheap.
Oh, let it such a volume be
As in rare copperplates abounds,
Large paper, clean, and fair to see,
Uncut, unique, unknown to Lowndes.

Eugene Field

ON THIS DAY:

William Thomas Lowndes (?–1843) died. He was the author of *The Bibliographer's Manual of English Literature* (1838) which took fourteen years to compile, and *The British Librarian* (1839).

John Ericsson (1803–1889), inventor, and designer of armoured warships for the United States navy, was born.

Hedley Verity (1905–1943), Yorkshire and England cricketer, died of wounds as a prisoner of war in Italy. Verity, a Captain in The Green Howards, was hit during the Eighth Army's first attack on German positions at Catania, in Sicily.

AUGUST

August 1

It was upon a Lammas Night

It was upon a Lammas night
　　When corn rigs are bonnie,
Beneath the moon's unclouded light
　　I held awa' to Annie,
The time flew by wi'tentless heed,
　　Till 'tween the late and early,
Wi' sma' persuasion she agreed,
　　To see me thro' the barley,

　　Corn rigs an' barley rigs,
　　An' corn rigs are bonnie:
　　I'll ne'er forget that happy night,
　　Amang the rigs wi' Annie.

The sky was blue, the wind was still
　　The moon was shining clearly;
I set her down wi'right good will
　　Amang the rigs o' barley;
I ken't her heart was a' my ain;
　　I loved her most sincerely;
I kissed her owre and owre again
　　Amang the rigs o' barley.

　　Corn rigs an' barley rigs,
　　An' corn rigs are bonnie:
　　I'll ne'er forget that happy night,
　　Amang the rigs wi' Annie.

I locked her in my fond embrace;
　　Her was beating rarely;
My blessings on that happy place,
　　Amang the rigs o' barley!
But by the moon and stars so bright,
　　That shone that hour so clearly,
She aye shall bless that happy night
　　Amang the rigs o' barley.

Corn rigs an' barley rigs,
An' corn rigs are bonnie:
I'll ne'er forget that happy night,
Amang the rigs wi' Annie.

I hae been blythe wi' comrades dear;
I hae been merry drinking;
I hae been joyfu' gatherin' gear;
I hae been happy thinkin:
But a' the pleasures e'er I saw,
Tho' three times doubled fairly
That happy night was worth them a',
Amang the rigs o' barley.

Corn rigs an' barley rigs,
An' corn rigs are bonnie:
I'll ne'er forget that happy night,
Amang the rigs wi' Annie.

Robert Burns

ON THIS DAY:

Today is Lammas Day which traditionally marked the day that hay meadows were re-opened for common grazing.

Queen Anne died without issue and was succeeded by George I (1660–1727, reigned 1714–1727).

Thomas Arne's masque *Alfred* was performed at Cliveden House in 1740 and the first rendition of 'Rule Britannia' was heard.

Herman Melville (1819–1891), writer and poet, was born.

London Bridge opened in 1831. This bridge was later sold and moved to the USA.

The Slavery Emancipation Act came into force in 1834.

August 2

Piazza di Spagna, Early Morning

I can't forget
How she stood at the top of that long marble stair
Amazed, and then with a sleepy pirouette
Went dancing slowly down to the fountain-quieted square;

Nothing upon her face
But some impersonal loneliness, – not then a girl,
But as it were a reverie of the place,
A called-for falling glide and whirl;

As when a leaf, petal, or thin chip
Is drawn to the falls of a pool and, circling a moment above it,
Rides on over the lip –
Perfectly beautiful, perfectly ignorant of it.

Richard Wilbur

ON THIS DAY:

The East India Company was dissolved in 1858, and the government of India passed to the Crown.

Alexander Graham Bell (1847–1922), inventor of the telephone, died.

Alan Whicker, broadcaster and journalist, was born in 1925.

Heaven

Fish (fly-replete, in depth of June,
Dawdling away their wat'ry noon)
Ponder deep wisdom, dark or clear,
Each secret fishy hope or fear.
Fish say, they have their Stream and Pond;
But is there anything Beyond?
This life cannot be All, they swear,
For how unpleasant, if it were!
One may not doubt that, somehow, Good
Shall come of Water and of Mud;
And, sure, the reverent eye must see
A Purpose in Liquidity.
We darkly know, by Faith we cry,
The future is not Wholly Dry.
Mud unto mud! – Death eddies near –
Not here the appointed End, not here!
But somewhere, beyond Space and Time,
Is wetter water, slimier slime!
And there (they trust) there swimmeth One
Who swam ere rivers were begun,
Immense, of fishy form and mind,
Squamous, omnipotent, and kind;
And under that Almighty Fin,
The littlest fish may enter in.
Oh! never fly conceals a hook,
Fish say, in the Eternal Brook,
But more than mundane weeds are there,
And mud, celestially fair;
Fat caterpillars drift around,
And Paradisal grubs are found;
Unfading moths, immortal flies,
And the worm that never dies.
And in that Heaven of all their wish,
There shall be no more land, say fish.

Rupert Brooke

ON THIS DAY:

Rupert Brooke (1887–1915), poet, was born.

August 4

The Send-Off

Down the close, darkening lanes they sang their way
To the siding-shed,
And lined the train with faces grimly gay.

Their breasts were stuck all white with wreath and spray
As men's are, dead.

Dull porters watched them, and a casual tramp
Stood staring hard,
Sorry to miss them from the upland camp.
Then, unmoved, signals nodded, and a lamp
Winked to the guard.

So secretly, like wrongs hushed-up, they went.
They were not ours:
We never heard to which front these were sent.

Nor there if they yet mock what women meant
Who gave them flowers.

Shall they return to beatings of great bells
In wild train-loads?
A few, a few, too few for drums and yells,
May creep back, silent, to still village wells
Up half-known roads.

Wilfred Owen

ON THIS DAY:

Britain declared war on Germany in 1914 following the German invasion of Belgium. The conflict had been precipitated by a number of factors, including the assassination of Archduke Franz Ferdinand in June 1914.

August 5

The Volunteer

Here lies a clerk who half his life had spent
Toiling at ledgers in a city grey,
Thinking that so his days would drift away
With no lance broken in life's tournament:
Yet ever 'twixt the books and his bright eyes
The gleaming eagles of the legions came,
And horsemen, charging under phantom skies,
Went thundering past beneath the oriflamme.

And now those waiting dreams are satisfied;
From twilight to the halls of dawn he went;
His lance is broken; but he lies content
With that high hour, in which he lived and died.
And falling thus, he wants no recompense,
Who found his battle in the last resort;
Nor needs he any hearse to bear him hence,
Who goes to join the men of Agincourt.

Herbert Asquith

ON THIS DAY:

John Huston (1906–1987), film director, was born. His films included *The African Queen*, shot on location with Humphrey Bogart (1899–1957) and Katharine Hepburn (1909–2003).

Jacquetta Hawkes (1910–1996), writer and archaeologist who was married to the writer J. B. Priestley (1894–1984), was born.

Neil Armstrong, astronaut and the first man to step on to the surface of the moon, was born in 1930.

August 6, 1945

Fred Braun has just leaned out on a low windowsill
that needs painting. There are cracks in it,
but so far they have let no rain through.
They can wait a little longer.
This moment is his to enjoy,
looking at his apple orchard and two small plum trees
and under them a red napkin of bee balm.
It is beautiful and peaceful. His wife
is troweling a flower bed
along the house wall. He hears
the thud of an apple falling, part
of the nice lethargy of the day. And today
across the world
behind a plane, the Enola Gay, there floats in the air,
    slowly descending,
a hardly visible thin tube
with a small fuse at one end
that will fire one of two parts at the other end
and explode this almost unnoticeable filament
with a light brighter than the sun. Below,
in the wooden city of Hiroshima
can it not be that a man
has just rolled back one of his living-room shutters
and is looking out on his garden, thinking,
The morning glories on their bamboo sticks,
the blue sky,
how beautiful everything is! Let me enjoy it.
I should be painting shutters,
but they can wait.
The rain does not yet come through.

Millen Brand

ON THIS DAY:

In 1945, towards the end of the Second World War, the United States of America dropped the first atomic bomb. The target was the Japanese city of Hiroshima. The bomb destroyed most of the city and killed many thousands of civilians. The bomb was dropped by a B29 Bomber named the *Enola Gay*.

Alfred Tennyson, first Baron Tennyson (1809–1892), poet who succeeded William Wordsworth (1770–1850) as Poet Laureate, was born.

Evening Shadows

The shadows of my chimneys stretch afar
Across the plot, and on to the privet bower,
And even the shadows of their smokings show,
And nothing says just now that where they are
They will in future stretch at this same hour,
Though in my earthen cyst I shall not know.

And at this time the neighbouring Pagan mound,
Whose myths the Gospel news now supersede,
Upon the greensward also throws its shade,
And nothing says such shade will spread around
Even as to-day when men will no more heed
The Gospel news than when the mound was made.

Thomas Hardy

ON THIS DAY:

In 1485 Henry Tudor, later Henry VII, landed at Milford Haven, from France, en route to Bosworth Field.

President George Washington (1732–1799) created the badge of military merit in 1782. The honour later became known as the Purple Heart.

The RMS *Queen Mary* made the fastest westbound transatlantic crossing in 1938, completing the journey in three days, twenty-three hours and forty-eight minutes.

August 8

Possibilities

Where are the poets, unto whom belong
   The Olympian heights; whose singing shafts were sent
   Straight to the mark, and not from bows half bent,
    But with the utmost tension of the thong?
Where are the stately argosies of song,
   Whose rushing keels made music as they went
   Sailing in search of some new continent,
    With all sail set, and steady winds and strong?
Perhaps there lives some dreamy boy, untaught
   In schools, some graduate of the field or street,
An admiral sailing the high seas of thought,
   Fearless and first, and steering with his fleet
   For lands not yet laid down in any chart.

Henry Wadsworth Longfellow

ON THIS DAY:

The British Academy received its Royal Charter from Edward VII in 1902.

In 1974 Richard Nixon (1913–1994) announced that he was to resign as President of the United States following the Watergate scandal. He held office from 1969 to 1974 and was the first President to resign.

Sir Frank Whittle (1907–1996), inventor and aeronautical engineer involved in development of the jet engine, died.

After Midsummer

Love, we curve downwards, we are set to night
After our midsummer of longest light,
After hay harvest, though the days are warmer
And fruit is rounding on the lap of summer.

Still as in youth in this time of our fruition
Thought sifts to space through the words of definition,
But strangeness darkens now to a constant mood
Like hands shone dark with use or hafts of wood;

And over our dense days of activity
Brooding like stillness and satiety
The wonder deepens as clouds mass over corn
That here we are wakened and to this world born

That with its few colours so steeps and dyes
Our hearts, and with its runic signs implies
Meaning we doubt we read, yet love and fear
The forms more for the darkened light they bear.

It was so in youth too; now youth's spaces gone
And death of parents and our time's dark tone
Shadow our days – even children too, whose birth
And care through by-ways bring our thoughts to death;

Whose force of life speaks of the distant future,
Their helplessness of helpless animal nature;
Who, like the old in their shroud of age, close bound
In childhood, impress our natural pattern and end.

The springy twigs arch over walls and beds
Of lilac buddleia, and the long flower-heads
Run down the air like valleys. Not by force
But weight, the flowers of summer bend our course;

And whether we live or die; from this time on
We must know death better; though here as we stand upon
The rounded summit we think how softly the slope
And the sky have changed, and the further dales come up.

E. J. Scovell

ON THIS DAY:

In 1945 the United States of America dropped a second atomic bomb on Japan. The target was the city of Nagasaki, much of which was destroyed and many thousands of people killed. This action forced the Japanese to surrender and the Second World War came to an end.

Star-gazer

Forty-two years ago (to me if to no one else
The number is of some interest) it was a brilliant starry night
And the westward train was empty and had no corridors
So darting from side to side I could catch the unwonted sight
Of those almost intolerably bright
Holes, punched in the sky, which excited me partly because
Of their Latin names and partly because I had read in the textbooks
How very far off they were, it seemed their light
Had left them (some at least) long years before I was.

And this remembering now I mark that what
Light was leaving some of them at least then,
Forty-two years ago, will never arrive
In time for me to catch it, which light when
It does get here may find that there is not
Anyone left alive
To run from side to side in a late night train
Admiring it and adding noughts in vain.

Louis MacNeice

ON THIS DAY:

Charles II (1630–1685, reigned 1660–1685) laid the foundation stone for the Royal Observatory at Greenwich in 1675.

The Smithsonian Institute in Washington, DC was founded in 1846 with a bequest made by the scientist James Smithson (1765–1829).

The jockey Sir Gordon Richards (1904–1986) retired from racing in 1954. He had ridden 4,870 winners during his career, including, in 1953, his first and only Derby winner, Pinza.

August 11

The Poplar-Field

The Poplars are fell'd, farewell to the shade
And the whispering sound of the cool colonnade,
The winds play no longer and sing in the leaves,
Nor Ouse on his bosom their image receives.

Twelve years have elapsed since I first took a view
Of my favourite field and the bank where they grew,
And now in the grass behold they are laid,
And the tree is my seat that once lent me a shade.

The black-bird has fled to another retreat
Where the hazels afford him a screen from the heat,
And the scene where his melody charm'd me before,
Resounds with his sweet-flowing ditty no more.

My fugitive years are all hasting away,
And I must e'er long lie as lowly as they,
With a turf on my breast and a stone at my head
E'er another such grove shall arise in its stead.

'Tis a sight to engage me, if any thing can,
To muse on the perishing pleasures of Man;
Though his life be a dream, his enjoyments, I see,
Have a Being less durable even than he.

William Cowper

ON THIS DAY:

Eugene Lauste (1857–1935) applied for a patent for his device of recording sound on film.

The SOS signal was used for the first time in 1909.

In 1999 a full solar eclipse was seen over Europe and Asia. It was the last full solar eclipse of the 20th century.

August 12

The Well of St Keyne

A well there is in the west country,
  And a clearer one never was seen;
There is not a wife in the west country
  But has heard of the Well of St Keyne.

An oak and an elm-tree stand beside,
  And behind doth an ash-tree grow,
And a willow from the bank above
  Droops to the water below.

A traveller came to the well of St Keyne;
  Joyfully he drew nigh,
For from cock-crow he had been travelling,
  And there was not a cloud in the sky.

He drank of the water so cool and clear,
  For thirsty and hot was he,
And he sat down upon the bank
  Under the willow-tree.

There came a man from the house hard by
  At the Well to fill his pail;
On the Well-side he rested it,
  And he bade the Stranger hail.

'Now art thou a bachelor, Stranger?' quoth he,
  'For an if thou hast a wife,
The happiest draught thou hast drank this day
  That ever thou didst in thy life.

'Or has thy good woman, if one thou hast,
  Ever here in Cornwall been?
For an if she have, I'll venture my life
  She has drank of the Well of St Keyne.'

'I have left a good woman who never was here,'
    The Stranger he made reply,
'But that my draught should be the better for that,
    I pray you answer me why?'

'St Keyne,' quoth the Cornish-man, 'many a time
    Drank of this crystal Well,
And before the Angel summon'd her,
    She laid on the water a spell.

'If the Husband of this gifted Well
    Shall drink before his Wife,
A happy man thenceforth is he,
    For he shall be Master for life.

'But if the Wife should drink of it first
    God help the Husband then!'
The Stranger stoopt to the Well of St Keyne,
    And drank of the water again.

'You drank of the Well I warrant betimes?'
    He to the Cornish-man said:
But the Cornish-man smiled as the Stranger spake,
    And sheepishly shook his head.

'I hasten'd as soon as the wedding was done,
    And left my Wife in the porch;
But i'faith she had been wiser than me,
    For she took a bottle to Church.'

Robert Southey

ON THIS DAY:

Robert Southey (1774–1843), poet and Poet Laureate, was born.

William Blake (1757–1827), poet and painter, died.

Wing Commander Guy Gibson, VC (1918–1944), pilot and commander of 617 Squadron, was born.

Building started on the Berlin Wall in 1961.

In 1981 IBM released its first personal computer.

After Blenheim

It was a summer evening,
　　Old Kaspar's work was done,
And he before his cottage door
　　Was sitting in the sun;
And by him sported on the green
His little grandchild Wilhelmine.

She saw her brother Peterkin
　　Roll something large and round
Which he beside the rivulet
　　In playing there had found;
He came to ask what he had found
That was so large and smooth and round.

Old Kaspar took it from the boy
　　Who stood expectant by;
And the old man shook his head,
　　And with a natural sigh
''Tis some poor fellow's skull,' said he,
'Who fell in the great victory.'

'I find them in the garden,
　　For there's many here about;
And often when I go to plough
　　The ploughshare turns them out.
For many thousand men,' said he,
'Were slain in that great victory.'

'Now tell us what 'twas all about,'
　　Young Peterkin he cries;
And little Wilhelmine looks up
　　With wonder-waiting eyes;
'Now tell us all about the war,
And what they fought each other for.'

'It was the English,' Kaspar cried,
  'Who put the French to rout;
But what they fought each other for
  I could not well make out.
But everybody said,' quoth he,
'That 'twas a famous victory.

'My father lived at Blenheim then,
  Yon little stream hard by;
They burnt his dwelling to the ground,
  And he was forced to fly:
So with his wife and child he fled,
Nor had he where to rest his head.

'With fire and sword the country round
  Was wasted far and wide,
And many a chiding mother then
  And newborn baby died:
But things like that, you know, must be
At every famous victory.

'They say it was a shocking sight
  After the field was won;
For many thousand bodies here
  Lay rotting in the sun:
But things like that, you know, must be
After a famous victory.

'Great praise the Duke of Marlbro' won
  And our good Prince Eugene;'
'Why, 'twas a very wicked thing!'
  Said little Wilhelmine;
'Nay.. nay.. my little girl,' quoth he,
'It was a famous victory.

'And everybody praised the Duke
Who this great fight did win.'
'But what good came of it at last?'
Quoth little Peterkin:–
'Why that I cannot tell,' said he,
'But 'twas a famous victory.'

Robert Southey

ON THIS DAY:

The English forces, under the Duke of Marlborough (1650–1722), defeated the French at the battle of Blenheim in 1704.

John Logie Baird (1888–1946), television pioneer, was born.

Alfred Hitchcock (1899–1980), film director who worked mostly in Hollywood, was born.

Sir Basil Spence (1907–1976), architect who designed the new Coventry Cathedral, was born.

The animated film *Bambi* was released by Walt Disney in 1942 at a premiere in New York.

I travelled among unknown Men

I travelled among unknown Men,
   In Lands beyond the Sea;
Nor England! did I know till then
   What love I bore to thee.

'Tis past, that melancholy dream!
   Nor will I quit thy shore
A second time; for still I seem
   To love thee more and more.

Among thy mountains did I feel
   The joy of my desire;
And She I cherished turned her wheel
   Beside an English fire.

Thy mornings shewed, thy nights concealed
   The bowers where Lucy played;
And thine is, too, the last green field
   Which Lucy's eyes surveyed!

William Wordsworth

ON THIS DAY:

John Galsworthy (1867–1933), playwright and novelist, was born.

In 1948 Sir Donald Bradman (1908–2001) played in his last Test match at the Oval cricket ground in London.

Bertolt Brecht (1898–1956), poet and author of plays including *Mother Courage and her Children* and *The Threepenny Opera* (with Kurt Weill, 1900–1950), died.

J. B. Priestley (1894–1984), novelist whose works included *The Good Companions* and *Bright Day*, died.

August 15

Partition

Unbiased at least he was when he arrived on his mission,
Having never set eyes on this land he was called to partition
Between two people fanatically at odds,
With their different diets and incompatible gods.
'Time,' they had briefed him in London, 'is short. It's too late
For mutual reconciliation or rational debate:
The only solution now lies in separation.
The Viceroy thinks, as you will see from his letter,
That the less you are seen in his company the better,
So we've arranged to provide you with other accommodation.
We can give you four judges, two Moslem and two Hindu,
To consult with, but the final decision must rest with you.'

Shut up in a lonely mansion, with police night and day
Patrolling the gardens to keep assassins away,
He got down to work, to the task of settling the fate
Of millions. The maps at his disposal were out of date
And the Census Returns almost certainly incorrect,
But there was no time to check them, no time to inspect
Contested areas. The weather was frightfully hot,
And a bout of dysentery kept him constantly on the trot,
But in seven weeks it was done, the frontiers decided,
A continent for better or worse divided.

The next day he sailed for England, where he quickly forgot
The case, as a good lawyer must. Return he would not,
Afraid, as he told his Club, that he might get shot.

W. H. Auden

ON THIS DAY:

In 1947, India and Pakistan were constituted as separate independent Dominions within the Common-wealth. Boundaries between the two countries were established by two Boundary Commissions, both led by Sir Cyril Radcliffe (1899–1977).

In 1938 the RMS *Queen Mary* made the fastest eastbound transatlantic crossing in three days and twenty hours.

The Japanese surrendered to the Allies on this day in 1945. Known as VJ Day, it marks the end of the Second World War.

The Vine

I dreamed this mortal part of mine
Was metamorphosed to a vine,
Which crawling one and every way
Enthralled my dainty Lucia.
Methought her long small legs and thighs
I with my tendrils did surprise;
Her belly, buttocks, and her waist
By my soft nervelets were embraced.
About her head I writhing hung,
And with rich clusters (hid among
The leaves) her temples I behung,
So that my Lucia seemed to me
Young Bacchus ravished by his tree.
My curls about her neck did crawl,
And arms and hands they did enthrall,
So that she could not freely stir
(All parts there made one prisoner).
But when I crept with leaves to hide
Those parts which maids keep unespied,
Such fleeting pleasures there I took
That with the fancy I awoke;
And found (ah me!) this flesh of mine
More like a stock than like a vine.

Robert Herrick

ON THIS DAY:

In 1952, flash floods in north Devon caused devastation in several areas, and the village of Lynmouth was badly damaged. Thirty-four people lost their lives.

Vladimir Putin (b.1952) became Prime Minister of Russia in 1999.

Idi Amin (c.1925–2003), former President of Uganda, died.

August 1914

What in our lives is burnt
In the fire of this?
The heart's dear granary?
The much we shall miss?

Three lives hath one life—
Iron, honey, gold.
The gold, the honey gone—
Left is the hard and cold.

Iron are our lives
Molten right through our youth.
A burnt space through ripe fields,
A fair mouth's broken tooth.

Isaac Rosenberg

ON THIS DAY:

Sir V. S. Naipaul, writer, was born in 1932.

Rudolf Hess (1894–1987), German war criminal, died.

In 1999 the town of Izmit, western Turkey was hit by a powerful earthquake.

August 18

Iron Age Flying

I

What's the red light? Oh Boarding Boarding.
I'm walking down a ramp into a tunnel.
Jesus, it's raining. Top of the plane
Seems a wet slick whale's back.
Jonah to England, with my sins
All upon me.
Why does it feel so like dying?
Riding the river in the speedboat with father,
I didn't feel fearful.
I wasn't so personal.
A kid's just anyone,
One drop of light into the sun's bright water.

Inside it's a cave.
Maybe find a seat by a window.
Important personalities are Cadillacs.
Black shams, limousines
Appropriate for funerals. The child soul inside.
How do you believe in this idiotic century?
I wasn't inventing the things I remembered.
Father as if mowing the evening,
The light in particles of dust
But they were shining.
Seatbelt. Good, we're moving.

Faster and faster. Like rising
Toward heaven. Is this how it will be?
Regret and desire. Memories.
The red fire jumping as if speaking in tongues.
He drove away the tanker for our lives, through
The gasoline sea of her fear.

My neck feels cramped. What time
Could it be? Must have been asleep.
Move the pillow from the window.
And *where* could we be?
With lights down below.
A city. A galaxy.
Beautiful with distance and darkness.
Perhaps my life,
If seen from that remove –
With irregular beads, it becomes a necklace
Stringing a peninsula –
Are there rocks by the lights and black-foil water?
It's a bay within the land's last arms.

II

We are going and we have been:
To climb along the Somerset headlands
Resurrected from an underground England.
We'll scramble clay holes through
Iron age forts – no stones of Camelot –
Considering the blades from Saxon barrows.

Iron age, hand
In a rusty glove handle
My throat, my thoughts,
Gently.

I began with a boy, whose sight
Was marked by a snake.
Though his brown time drains
With the Pamlico River,
Everything seen in his life
Flows in an underground stream
Where a new sun burns.

Over our horizon to the east, the constant
Night of Earth's own shadow
Cones standing still
So that children, animals, weeds, and jewels
Spin through it, where a vision
Lies buried
Like treasure: one gleaming
Bearing the world revolves on,
Earth-lidded eyeball, wink of the Cyclops.

Underground sun, give us prospect
On our landscape's mud, our poor map of paths
Which spin, recombine, in the head,
Like threads dyed red
From sheepfolds,
To stitch incorrigible imagination's pastoral.

Iron age flying, over
The planet's body where dawn still hides,
Telescope fields: the contours
Planted with a garden not realized.
Egg of earth holds the sun inside.

James Applewhite

ON THIS DAY:

Today is the feast day of St Helen (c.250–330). She was the mother of Emperor Constantine the Great (ruled 306–337).

Jim Mollison (1905–1959) successfully made the first solo westbound transatlantic flight in 1932. He flew from Ireland to New Brunswick. Mollison was briefly married to Amy Johnson (1903–1941).

In 1941 Britain's National Fire Service was established.

August 19

To the Evening Star

Thou fair-hair'd angel of the evening,
Now, while the sun rests on the mountains, light
Thy bright torch of love; thy radiant crown
Put on, and smile upon our evening bed!
Smile on our loves; and, while thou drawest the
Blue curtains of the sky, scatter thy silver dew
On every flower that shuts its sweet eyes
In timely sleep. Let thy west wind sleep on
The lake; speak silence with thy glimmering eyes,
And wash the dusk with silver. Soon, full soon,
Dost thou withdraw; then the wolf rages wide,
And the lion glares thro' the dun forest:
The fleeces of our flocks are cover'd with
Thy sacred dew: protect them with thine influence.

William Blake

ON THIS DAY:

John Dryden (1631–1700), poet and Poet Laureate, was born.

John Flamsteed (1646–1719), founder of the Greenwich Observatory and first Astronomer Royal of England, was born.

Orville Wright (1871–1948), aviation pioneer, who with his brother Wilbur Wright (1867–1912) made the first powered flight, was born.

August 20

Dawlish Fair

Over the hill and over the dale,
And over the bourne to Dawlish –
Where Gingerbread Wives have a scanty sale
And gingerbread nuts are smallish.

Rantipole Betty she ran down a hill
And kicked up her petticoats fairly
Says I I'll be Jack if you will be Gill.
So she sat on the Grass debonnairly.

Here's somebody coming, here's somebody coming!
Says I 'tis the Wind at a parley
So without any fuss any hawing and humming
She lay on the grass debonnairly,

Here's somebody here and here's somebody there!
Says I hold your tongue you young Gipsey.
So she held her tongue and lay plump and fair
And dead as a venus tipsy.

O who wouldn't hie to Dawlish fair
O who wouldn't stop in a Meadow
O who would not rumple the daisies there
And make the wild fern for a bed do.

John Keats

ON THIS DAY:
William Booth (1829–1912), founder of the Salvation Army (in 1865), died.
In 1913 stainless steel was first cast in Sheffield.
German troops occupied Brussels in 1914.

Blueberrying in August

Sprung from the hummocks
of this island, stemmed,
sea-spray-fed chromosomes
trait-coded, say, for eyes
of that surprising blue
some have, that you have:
they're everywhere, these
mimic apertures the color
of distances, of drowning –

of creekside bluebells
islanded in the lost world
of childhood; of the
illusory indigo that moats
these hillocks when
the air is windless.

Today, though, there is
wind: a slate sag occludes
the afternoon with old,
hound-throated mutterings.
Offshore, the lighthouse
fades to a sheeted,
sightless ghost. August
grows somber. Though the blue-
eyed chromosome gives way,
living even so, minute to
minute, was never better.

Amy Clampitt

ON THIS DAY:

The *Mona Lisa* was stolen from the Louvre Museum in Paris in 1911.

Ettore Bugatti (1881–1947), Italian car manufacturer, died.

The new Globe Theatre was opened in 1996 and the first play performed was Shakespeare's *Two Gentlemen of Verona*.

The Scarecrow

All winter through I bow my head
    Beneath the driving rain;
The North Wind powders me with snow
    And blows me black again;
At midnight in a maze of stars
    I flame with glittering rime,
And stand, above the stubble, stiff
    As mail at morning-prime.
But when that child, called Spring, and all
    His host of children, come,
Scattering their buds and dew upon
    These acres of my home,
Some rapture in my rags awakes;
    I lift void eyes and scan
The skies for crows, those ravening foes,
    Of my strange master, Man.
I watch him striding lank behind
    His clashing team, and know
Soon will the wheat swish body high
    Where once lay sterile snow;
Soon shall I gaze across a sea
    Of sun-begotten grain,
Which my unflinching watch hath sealed
    For harvest once again.

Walter de la Mare

ON THIS DAY:

Richard III was defeated at the battle of Bosworth Field in 1485 by Henry Tudor, who succeeded to the throne as Henry VII.

Henri Cartier-Bresson (1908–2004), photographer, was born.

August 23

Beech Tree

I planted in February
A bronze-leafed beech,
In the chill brown soil
I spread out its silken fibres.

Protected it from the goats
With wire netting,
And fixed it firm against
The worrying wind.

Now it is safe, I said,
April must stir
My precious baby
To greenful loveliness.

It is August now, I have hoped,
But I hope no more—
My beech tree will never hide sparrows
From hungry hawks.

Patrick Kavanagh

ON THIS DAY:

The Scottish patriot William Wallace (c.1274–1305) was executed in London (he was hung, drawn and quartered and the quarters were sent to Newcastle, Berwick, Stirling and Perth).

In 1617 the first one-way streets were introduced in London.

Rudolph Valentino (1895–1926), silent film star, died. His death caused hysteria among his many fans.

Sonnet to William Wilberforce, Esq.

Thy country, Wilberforce, with just disdain,
Hears thee, by cruel men and impious, call'd
Fanatic, for thy zeal to loose th'enthrall'd
From exile, public sale, and slav'ry's chain.
Friend of the poor, the wrong'd, the fetter-gall'd,
Fear not lest labour such as thine be vain!
Thou has achiev'd a part; hast gain'd the ear
Of Britain's senate to thy glorious cause;
Hope smiles, joy springs, and tho' cold caution pause
And weave delay, the better hour is near,
That shall remunerate thy toils severe
By peace for Afric, fenc'd with British laws.
Enjoy what thou hast won, esteem and love
From all the just on earth, and all the blest above!

William Cowper

ON THIS DAY:

In AD 79 Mount Vesuvius erupted and lava buried the Italian town of Pompeii.

The White House, Washington, DC was attacked and burnt by British troops in 1814.

William Wilberforce (1759–1833), English reformer, was born.

The Eve of Crecy

Gold on her head, and gold on her feet,
And gold where the hems of her kirtle meet,
And a golden girdle round my sweet;
    Ah! qu'elle est belle La Marguerite.

Margaret's maids are fair to see,
Freshly dress'd and pleasantly;
Margaret's hair falls down to her knee;
    Ah! qu'elle est belle La Marguerite.

If I were rich I would kiss her feet;
I would kiss the place where the gold hems meet,
And the golden kirtle round my sweet:
    Ah! qu'elle est belle La Marguerite.

Ah me! I have never touch'd her hand;
When the arrière-ban goes through the land,
Six basnets under my pennon stand;
    Ah! qu'elle est belle La Marguerite.

And many an one grins under his hood:
Sir Lambert du Bois, with all his men good,
Has neither food nor firewood;
    Ah! qu'elle est belle La Marguerite.

If I were rich I would kiss her feet,
And the golden girdle of my sweet,
And thereabouts where the gold hems meet;
    Ah! qu'elle est belle La Marguerite.

Yet even now it is good to think,
While my few poor varlets grumble and drink
In my desolate hall, where the fires sink,–
    Ah! qu'elle est belle La Marguerite.

Of Margaret sitting glorious there,
In glory of gold and glory of hair,
And glory of glorious face most fair;
 Ah! qu'elle est belle La Marguerite.

Likewise to-night I make good cheer,
Because this battle draweth near:
For what have I to lose or fear?
 Ah! qu'elle est belle La Marguerite.

For, look you, my horse is good to prance
A right fair measure in this war-dance,
Before the eyes of Philip of France;
 Ah! qu'elle est belle La Marguerite.

And sometime it may hap, perdie,
While my new towers stand up three and three,
And my hall gets painted fair to see–
 Ah! qu'elle est belle La Marguerite.

That folks may say: Times change, by the rood,
For Lambert, banneret of the wood,
Has heaps of food and firewood;
 Ah! qu'elle est belle La Marguerite.

William Morris

ON THIS DAY:

In 1919 the first direct international air service began with flights between London and Paris.

Frederick Forsyth, author of *The Day of the Jackal*, was born in 1938.

In 1944 the city of Paris was liberated by the Allies after four years of German occupation.

Elegy written in a Country Churchyard

The curfew tolls the knell of parting day,
　The lowing herd wind slowly o'er the lea,
The ploughman homeward plods his weary way,
　And leaves the world to darkness and to me.

Now fades the glimmering landscape on the sight,
　And all the air a solemn stillness holds,
Save where the beetle wheels his droning flight,
　And drowsy tinklings lull the distant folds;

Save that from yonder ivy-mantled tower
　The moping owl does to the moon complain
Of such, as wandering near her secret bower,
　Molest her ancient solitary reign.

Beneath those rugged elms, that yew tree's shade,
　Where heaves the turf in many a mouldering heap,
Each in his narrow cell forever laid,
　The rude forefathers of the hamlet sleep.

The breezy call of incense-breathing morn,
　The swallow twittering from the straw-built shed,
The cock's shrill clarion, or the echoing horn,
　No more shall rouse them from their lowly bed.

For them no more the blazing hearth shall burn,
　Or busy housewife ply her evening care;
No children run to lisp their sire's return,
　Or climb his knees the envied kiss to share.

Oft did the harvest to their sickle yield,
　Their furrow oft the stubborn glebe has broke;
How jocund did they drive their team afield!
　How bowed the woods beneath their sturdy stroke!

Let not Ambition mock their useful toil,
   Their homely joys, and destiny obscure;
Nor Grandeur hear with a disdainful smile
   The short and simple annals of the poor.

The boast of heraldry, the pomp of power,
   And all that beauty, all that wealth e'er gave,
Awaits alike the inevitable hour.
   The paths of glory lead but to the grave.

Nor you, ye proud, impute to these the fault,
   If Memory o'er their tomb no trophies raise,
Where through the long-drawn aisle and fretted vault
   The pealing anthem swells the note of praise.

Can storied urn or animated bust
   Back to its mansion call the fleeting breath?
Can Honour's voice provoke the silent dust,
   Or Flattery soothe the dull cold ear of Death?

Perhaps in this neglected spot is laid
   Some heart once pregnant with celestial fire;
Hands that the rod of empire might have swayed,
   Or waked to ecstasy the living lyre.

But Knowledge to their eyes her ample page
   Rich with the spoils of time did ne'er unroll;
Chill Penury repressed their noble rage,
   And froze the genial current of the soul.

Full many a gem of purest ray serene,
   The dark unfathomed caves of ocean bear:
Full many a flower is born to blush unseen,
   And waste its sweetness on the desert air.

Some village Hampden, that with dauntless breast
   The little tyrant of his fields withstood;
Some mute inglorious Milton here may rest,
   Some Cromwell guiltless of his country's blood.

The applause of listening senates to command,
   The threats of pain and ruin to despise,
To scatter plenty o'er a smiling land,
   And read their history in a nation's eyes,

Their lot forbade: nor circumscribed alone
   Their growing virtues, but their crimes confined;
Forbade to wade through slaughter to a throne,
   And shut the gates of mercy on mankind,

The struggling pangs of conscious truth to hide,
   To quench the blushes of ingenuous shame,
Or heap the shrine of Luxury and Pride
   With incense kindled at the Muse's flame.

Far from the madding crowd's ignoble strife,
   Their sober wishes never learned to stray;
Along the cool sequestered vale of life
   They kept the noiseless tenor of their way.

Yet even these bones from insult to protect
   Some frail memorial still erected nigh,
With uncouth rhymes and shapeless sculpture decked,
   Implores the passing tribute of a sigh.

Their name, their years, spelt by the unlettered Muse,
   The place of fame and elegy supply:
And many a holy text around she strews,
   That teach a rustic moralist to die.

For who to dumb Forgetfulness a prey,
    This pleasing anxious being e'er resigned,
Left the warm precincts of the cheerful day,
    Nor cast one longing lingering look behind?

On some fond breast the parting soul relies,
    Some pious drops the closing eye requires;
Even from the tomb the voice of Nature cries,
    Even in our ashes live their wonted fires.

For thee, who mindful of the unhonoured dead
    Dost in these lines their artless tale relate;
If chance, by lonely contemplation led,
    Some kindred spirit shall inquire thy fate,

Haply some hoary-headed swain may say,
    'Oft have we seen him at the peep of dawn
Brushing with hasty steps the dews away
    To meet the sun upon the upland lawn.

'There at the foot of yonder nodding beech
    That wreathes its old fantastic roots so high,
His listless length at noontide would he stretch,
    And pore upon the brook that babbles by.

'Hard by yon wood, now smiling as in scorn,
    Muttering his wayward fancies he would rove,
Now drooping, woeful wan, like one forlorn,
    Or crazed with care, or crossed in hopeless love.

'One morn I missed him on the customed hill,
    Along the heath and near his favourite tree;
Another came; nor yet beside the rill,
    Nor up the lawn, nor at the wood was he;

'The next with dirges due in sad array
    Slow through the churchway path we saw him borne.
Approach and read (for thou canst read) the lay,
    Graved on the stone beneath yon aged thorn.'

The Epitaph

Here rests his head upon the lap of Earth
    A youth to Fortune and to Fame unknown.
Fair science frowned not on his humble birth,
    And Melancholy marked him for her own.

Large was his bounty, and his soul sincere,
    Heaven did a recompense as largely send:
He gave to Misery all he had, a tear,
    He gained from Heaven ('twas all he wished) a friend.
No farther seek his merits to disclose,
    Or draw his frailties from their dread abode
(There they alike in trembling hope repose),
    The bosom of his Father and his God.

Thomas Gray

ON THIS DAY:

In 1346 the English defeated the French at the battle of Crécy (one of the battles of the Hundred Years War).

The XXth Olympiad opened in Munich, Germany in 1972. The games are now infamous for the kidnap and murder of eleven members of the Israeli team by an Arab group called Black September. The terrorists had called for the release of hundreds of Palestinians from prison in Israel.

The yachtsman Sir Francis Chichester (1901–1972) died.

August 27

Musings

Before the falling summer sun
   The boughs are shining all as gold,
And down below them waters run,
   As there in former years they rolled;
The poolside wall is glowing hot,
   The pool is in a dazzling glare,
And makes it seem as, ah! 'tis not,
   A summer when my life was fair.

The evening, gliding slowly by,
   Seems one of those that long have fled;
The night comes on to star the sky
   As then it darkened round my head.
A girl is standing by yon door,
   As one in happy times was there,
And this day seems, but is no more,
   A day when all my life was fair.

We hear from yonder feast the hum
   Of voices, as in summers past;
And hear the beatings of the drum
   Again come throbbing on the blast.
There neighs a horse in yonder plot,
   As once there neighed our petted mare,
And summer seems, but ah! is not
   The summer when our life was fair.

William Barnes

ON THIS DAY:

Sir Donald Bradman (1908–2001), record-breaking Australian cricketer, was born.

In 1979 Earl Mountbatten of Burma (1900–1979) was murdered by the IRA whilst on a sailing holiday in Ireland. Several other members of his family died and many were injured.

August 28

The Stone Beach

A walk, not more than a mile
along the barricade of land
between the ocean and the grey lagoon.
Six of us, hand in hand,

connected by blood. Underfoot
a billion stones and pebbles –
new potatoes, mint imperials,
the eggs of birds –

each rock more infinitely formed
than anything we own.
Spoilt for choice – which one to throw,
which to pocket and take home.

The present tense, although
some angle of the sun, some slant of light
back-dates us thirty years.
Home-movie. Super 8.

Seaweed in ropes and rags.
The weightless, empty armour
of a crab. A jawbone, bleached
and blasted, manages a smile.

Long-shore-drift,
the ocean sorts and sifts,
giving with this, getting back
with the next.

A sailboat thinks itself
across the bay.
Susan, nursing a thought of her own
unthreads and threads

the middle button of her coat.
Disturbed,
a colony of nesting terns
makes one full circle of the world

then drops.
But the beach, full of itself,
each round of rock
no smaller than a bottle top,

no bigger than a nephew's fist.
One minute more, as Jonathan, three, autistic,
hypnotised by flight and fall,
picks one more shape

and under-arms the last wish of the day –
look, like a stone – into the next wave.

Simon Armitage

ON THIS DAY:

Sir John Betjeman (1906–1984), poet with a passion for churches and church architecture, was born.

A telegraph cable running under the English Channel and linking Dover and Cap Gris Nez, Calais was completed in 1850.

A Wet August

Nine drops of water bead the jessamine,
And nine-and-ninety smear the stones and tiles:
– 'Twas not so in that August – full-rayed, fine –
When we lived out-of-doors, sang songs, strode miles.

Or was there then no noted radiancy
Of summer? Were dun clouds, a dribbling bough,
Gilt over by the light I bore in me,
And was the waste world just the same as now?

It can have been so: yea, that threatenings
Of coming down-drip on the sunless gray,
By the then golden chances seen in things
Were wrought more bright than brightest skies to-day.

Thomas Hardy

ON THIS DAY:

In 1842 the Treaty of Nanking was signed, in which China ceded Hong Kong to Great Britain.

Ingrid Bergman (1915–1982), Swedish actress who starred with Humphrey Bogart in *Casablanca*, was born. She also died on this day.

The Soviet Parliament suspended the Communist Party in 1991.

Today

So here hath been dawning
Another blue Day:
Think wilt thou let it
Slip useless away.

Out of Eternity
This new Day is born;
Into Eternity,
At night, will return.

Behold it aforetime
No eye ever did:
So soon it forever
From all eyes is hid.

Here hath been dawning
Another blue Day:
Think wilt thou let it
Slip useless away.

Thomas Carlyle

ON THIS DAY:

Mary Shelley (1797–1851), wife of Percy Bysshe Shelley (1792–1822) and author of *Frankenstein*, was born.

Ernest Rutherford (1871–1937), the New Zealand scientist who was the first man to split the atom, was born.

In 1901 Hubert Cecil Booth (1871–1955) patented the vacuum cleaner.

The river Nile flooded in 1938 and the city of Cairo was surrounded by flood-water.

An August Midnight

I

A shaded lamp and a waving blind,
And the beat of a clock from a distant floor:
On this scene enter – winged, horned, and spined –
A longlegs, a moth, and a dumbledore;
While 'mid my page there idly stands
A sleepy fly, that rubs its hands...

II

Thus meet we five, in this still place,
At this point of time, at this point in space.
– My guests besmear my new-penned line,
Or bang at the lamp and fall supine.
'God's humblest, they!' I muse. Yet why?
They know Earth-secrets that know not I.

Thomas Hardy

ON THIS DAY:

John Bunyan (1628–1688), author of *The Pilgrim's Progress*, died.

President Dwight D. Eisenhower (1890–1969) and Prime Minister Harold Macmillan (1894–1986) made a historic live television transmission from 10 Downing Street in 1959.

Chris Bonington (b.1934) and Ian Clough (1937–1970) succeeded in becoming the first Britons to scale the north face of the Eiger in 1962.

Henry Moore (1898–1986), sculptor, died.

SEPTEMBER

September 1, 1939

I sit in one of the dives
On Fifty-Second Street
Uncertain and afraid
As the clever hopes expire
Of a low dishonest decade:
Waves of anger and fear
Circulate over the bright
And darkened lands of the earth,
Obsessing our private lives;
The unmentionable odour of death
Offends the September night.

Accurate scholarship can
Unearth the whole offence
From Luther until now
That has driven a culture mad,
Find what occurred at Linz,
What huge imago made
A psychopathic god:
I and the public know
What all schoolchildren learn,
Those to whom evil is done
Do evil in return.

Exiled Thucydides knew
All that a speech can say
About Democracy,
And what dictators do,
The elderly rubbish they talk
To an apathetic grave;
Analysed all in his book,
The enlightenment driven away,
The habit-forming pain,
Mismanagement and grief:
We must suffer them all again.

Into this neutral air
Where blind skyscrapers use
Their full height to proclaim
The strength of Collective Man,
Each language pours its vain
Competitive excuse:
But who can live for long
In an euphoric dream;
Out of the mirror they stare,
Imperialism's face
And the international wrong.

Faces along the bar
Cling to their average day:
The lights must never go out,
The music must always play,
All the conventions conspire
To make this fort assume
The furniture of home;
Lest we should see where we are,
Lost in a haunted wood,
Children afraid of the night
Who have never been happy or good.

The windiest militant trash
Important Persons shout
Is not so crude as our wish:
What mad Nijinsky wrote
About Diaghilev
Is true of the normal heart;
For the error bred in the bone
Of each woman and each man
Craves what it cannot have,
Not universal love
But to be loved alone.

From the conservative dark
Into the ethical life
The dense commuters come,
Repeating their morning vow,

'I *will* be true to the wife,
I'll concentrate more on my work',
And helpless governors wake
To resume their compulsory game:
Who can release them now,
Who can reach the deaf,
Who can speak for the dumb?

All I have is a voice
To undo the folded lie,
The romantic lie in the brain
Of the sensual man-in-the-street
And the lie of Authority
Whose buildings grope the sky:
There is no such thing as the State
And no one exists alone;
Hunger allows no choice
To the citizen or the police;
We must love one another or die.

Defenceless under the night
Our world in stupor lies;
Yet, dotted everywhere,
Ironic points of light
Flash out wherever the Just
Exchange their messages:
May I, composed like them
Of Eros and of dust,
Beleaguered by the same
Negation and despair,
Show an affirming flame.

W. H. Auden

ON THIS DAY:

In 1939 Germany invaded Poland, precipitating the Second World War.

Adrian IV (Nicholas Breakspear, c.1100–1159, Pope 1154–1159), the first and only Englishman to become pope, died. He was interred in the Castel Sant'Angelo on the banks of the river Tiber, not far from the Vatican City.

In 1972 Bobby Fischer (b.1943) beat Boris Spassky (b.1937) to become the United States' first world chess champion.

September 2

The War Films

O living pictures of the dead,
    O songs without a sound,
O fellowship whose phantom tread
    Hallows a phantom ground –
How in a gleam have these revealed
    The faith we had not found.

We have sought God in a cloudy Heaven,
    We have passed by God on earth:
His seven sins and his sorrows seven,
    His wayworn mood and mirth,
Like a ragged cloak have hid from us
    The secret of his birth.

Brother of men, when now I see
    The lads go forth in line,
Thou knowest my heart is hungry in me
    As for thy bread and wine:
Thou knowest my heart is bowed in me
    To take their death for mine.

Sir Henry Newbolt

ON THIS DAY:

In 1666 the Great Fire of London started in the bakery of Thomas Farryner, Pudding Lane and lasted three days and three nights.

The poet William Somerville (1675–1742) was born.

Thomas Telford (1757–1834), engineer, died.

In 1906 Roald Amundsen (1872–1928) succeeded in negotiating the Northwest Passage in Canada.

J. R. R. Tolkien (1892–1973), author of *The Hobbit*, *The Lord of the Rings* and *The Silmarillion*, died.

In 1985 the wreckage of the RMS *Titanic* was located on the ocean floor off the coast of Newfoundland.

In Carrowdore Churchyard

(at the grave of Louis MacNeice)

Your ashes will not stir, even on this high ground,
However the wind tugs, the headstones shake.
This plot is consecrated, for your sake,
To what lies in the future tense. You lie
Past tension now, and spring is coming round
Igniting flowers on the peninsula.

Your ashes will not fly, however the rough winds burst
Through the wild brambles and the reticent trees.
All we may ask of you we have; the rest
Is not for publication, will not be heard.
Maguire, I believe, suggested a blackbird
And over your grave a phrase from Euripides.

Which suits you down to the ground, like this churchyard
With its play of shadow, its humane perspective.
Locked in the winter's fist, these hills are hard
As nails, yet soft and feminine in their turn
When fingers open and the hedges burn.
This, you implied, is how we ought to live –

The ironical, loving crush of roses against snow,
Each fragile, solving ambiguity. So
From the pneumonia of the ditch, from the ague
Of the blind poet and the bombed-out town you bring
The all-clear to the empty holes of spring,
Rinsing the choked mud, keeping the colours new.

Derek Mahon

ON THIS DAY:

The poet Louis MacNeice (1907–1963) died suddenly from pneumonia, which he had contracted whilst working on an assignment. He is buried next to his mother.

Oliver Cromwell (1599–1658) died.

The Treaty of Paris, in which England recognised America's independence, was signed and the War of Independence was brought to an end in 1783.

In 1939 Britain and France declared war on Germany.

The Mermaid Tavern

Souls of Poets dead and gone,
What Elysium have ye known,
Happy field or mossy cavern,
Choicer than the Mermaid Tavern?
Have ye tippled drink more fine
Than mine host's Canary wine?
Or are fruits of Paradise
Sweeter than those dainty pies
Of Venison? O generous food!
Drest as though bold Robin Hood
Would, with his Maid Marian,
Sup and bowse from horn and can.

I have heard that on a day
Mine host's signboard flew away
Nobody knew whither, till
An astrologer's old quill
To a sheepskin gave the story –
Said he saw you in your glory
Underneath a new-old Sign
Sipping beverage divine,
And pledging with contented smack
The Mermaid in the Zodiac!

Souls of Poets dead and gone
What Elysium have ye known –
Happy field or mossy cavern –
Choicer than the Mermaid Tavern?

John Keats

ON THIS DAY:

In 1666 the Mermaid Tavern was destroyed during the Great Fire of London. It had been the meeting place for the 'Friday Night Club' of poets and writers.

In 1888 George Eastman (1854–1932) patented his roll-film camera, and registered the name 'Kodak'.

In 1964 the Forth Road Bridge opened to traffic.

Peace

My soul, there is a country
    Far beyond the stars,
Where stands a wingèd sentry
    All skilful in the wars:
There above noise and danger
    Sweet Peace sits crowned with smiles,
And One born in a manger
    Commands the beauteous files.
He is thy gracious friend
    And—O my soul, awake!—
Did in pure love descend
    To die here for thy sake.
If thou canst get but thither,
    There grows the flower of Peace,
The Rose that cannot wither,
    Thy fortress, and thy ease.
Leave then thy foolish ranges
    For none can thee secure,
But one who never changes,
    Thy God, thy life, thy cure.

Henry Vaughan

ON THIS DAY:

John Wisden (1826–1884), the founder (in 1864) of the *Wisden Cricketers' Almanack*, was born.

In 1922 James Doolittle completed the first coast-to-coast flight across the United States of America in under twenty-four hours. The journey took twenty-one hours and nineteen minutes.

London after the Great Fire, 1666

Methinks already from this chymic flame
I see a city of more precious mould,
Rich as the town which gives the Indies name,
With silver paved and all divine with gold.

Already, labouring with a mighty fate,
She shakes the rubbish from her mounting brow,
And seems to have renewed her charter's date,
Which Heaven will to the death of time allow.

More great than human now and more August,
New deified she from her fires does rise:
Her widening streets on new foundations trust,
And, opening, into larger parts she flies.

Before, she like some shepherdess did show
Who sat to bathe her by a river's side,
Not answering to her fame, but rude and low,
Nor taught the beauteous arts of modern pride.

Now like a maiden queen she will behold
From her high turrets hourly suitors come;
The East with incense and the West with gold
Will stand like suppliants to receive her doom.

The silver Thames, her own domestic flood,
Shall bear her vessels like a sweeping train,
And often wind, as of his mistress proud,
With longing eyes to meet her face again.

The wealthy Tagus and the wealthier Rhine
The glory of their towns no more shall boast,
And Seine, that would with Belgian rivers join,
Shall find her lustre stained and traffic lost.

The venturous merchant who designed more far
And touches on our hospitable shore,
Charmed with the splendour of this northern star,
Shall here unlade him and depart no more.

John Dryden

ON THIS DAY:

In 1666 the Great Fire of London was finally extinguished.

The first free lending library was opened in Manchester in 1852.

The first public telephone exchange in Britain was opened in Lombard Street, London in 1879.

Kay Kendall (1926–1959), actress and star of *Genevieve*, died. She was married to Sir Rex Harrison (1908–1990).

London under Bombardment

I, who am known as London, have faced stern times before,
Having fought and ruled and traded for a thousand years and more;
I knew the Roman legions and the harsh-voiced Danish hordes;
I heard the Saxon revels, saw blood on the Norman swords.
But, though I am scarred by battle, my grim defenders vow
Never was I so stately nor so well-beloved as now.
The lights that burn and glitter in the exile's lonely dream,
The lights of Piccadilly, and those that used to gleam
Down Regent-street and Kingsway may now no longer shine,
But other lights keep burning, and their splendour, too, is mine,
Seen in the work-worn faces and glimpsed in the steadfast eyes
When little homes lie broken and death descends from the skies.
The bombs have shattered my churches, have torn my streets apart,
But they have not bent my spirit and they shall not break my heart.
For my people's faith and courage are lights of London town
Which still would shine in legends though my last broad bridge were down.

Greta Briggs

ON THIS DAY:

The first attack on the city of London by German Luftwaffe bombers took place on the night of 7th September 1940 and what became known as the Battle of Britain continued for fifty-seven nights.

Dame Edith Sitwell (1887–1965), poet, was born.

In 1929 Flying Officer H. R. D. Waghorn won the Schneider Trophy race in a Supermarine S6 Seaplane, powered by a 1800hp Rolls-Royce engine. The seaplane was conceived by Sir Henry Royce (1863–1933).

September 8

Summer Dawn

Pray but one prayer for me 'twixt thy closed lips;
　Think but one thought of me up in the stars.
The summer night waneth, the morning light slips,
　Faint and grey 'twixt the leaves of the aspen,
　　betwixt the cloud-bars,
That are patiently waiting there for the dawn:
　Patient and colourless, though Heaven's gold
Waits to float through them along with the sun.
Far out in the meadows, above the young corn,
　The heavy elms wait, and restless and cold
The uneasy wind rises; the roses are dun;
Through the long twilight they pray for the dawn,
Round the lone house in the midst of the corn.
　Speak but one word to me over the corn,
　Over the tender, bowed locks of the corn.

William Morris

ON THIS DAY:

Siegfried Sassoon (1886–1967), poet and soldier, was born.

Michael Frayn, author and dramatist, was born in 1933.

Rod Laver (b.1938) won the US Open tennis championship in 1969 and achieved his second tennis grand slam.

Leni Riefenstahl (1902–2003), actress, photographer, film-maker and director who amongst other subjects chronicled the rise of Nazi Germany, died.

Lament for Flodden

I've heard them lilting at our ewe-milking,
    Lasses a' lilting before dawn o' day;
But now they are moaning on ilka green loaning–
    The Flowers of the Forest are a' wede away.

At bughts, in the morning, nae blythe lads are scorning,
    Lasses are lonely and dowie and wae;
Nae daffin', nae gabbin', but sighing and sabbing,
    Ilk ane lifts her leglin and hies her away.

In har'st, at the shearing, nae youths now are jeering,
    Bandsters are lyart, and runkled, and grey;
At fair or at preaching, nae wooing, nae fleeching–
    The Flowers of the Forest are a' wede away.

At e'en, in the gloaming, nae younkers are roaming
    'Bout stacks wi' the lasses at bogle to play;
But ilk ane sits drearie, lamenting her dearie–
    The Flowers of the Forest are weded away.

Dool and wae for the order, sent our lads to the Border!
    The English, for ance, by guile wan the day;
The Flowers of the Forest, that fought ay the foremost,
    The prime of our land, are cauld in the clay.

We'll hear nae mair lilting at the ewe-milking;
    Women and bairns are heartless and wae;
Sighing and moaning on ilka green loaning–
    The Flowers of the Forest are a' wede away.

Jean Elliott

ON THIS DAY:

In 1513 the battle of Flodden Field took place in Northumberland between the English and Scottish forces. Although Scotland was newly allied to England following James IV's (1473–1513) marriage to Princess Margaret, Henry VIII's aspirations in France caused anger at the Scottish court and conflict ensued. The English forces' strength and tactics defeated the Scottish, and James IV was killed.

William I of England (reigned 1066–1087) died after a fall from a horse.

Cardinal Richelieu (1585–1642), chief minister of France, was born.

Breakfast

We ate our breakfast lying on our backs
Because the shells were screeching overhead.
I bet a rasher to a loaf of bread
That Hull United would beat Halifax
When Jimmy Stainthorpe played full-back instead
Of Billy Bradford. Ginger raised his head
And cursed, and took the bet, and dropt back dead.
We ate our breakfast lying on our backs
Because the shells were screeching overhead.

Wilfrid Gibson

ON THIS DAY:

Thomas Wolsey (c.1475–1530) became Archbishop of York in 1514.

In 1967 Gibraltar voted to remain British (12,138 voted 'for' and 44 voted 'against').

In 2002 Switzerland joined the United Nations.

September 11

Aspens

All day and night, save winter, every weather,
Above the inn, the smithy, and the shop,
The aspens at the cross-roads talk together
Of rain, until their last leaves fall from the top.

Out of the blacksmith's cavern comes the ringing
Of hammer, shoe, and anvil; out of the inn
The clink, the hum, the roar, the random singing –
The sounds that for these fifty years have been.

The whisper of the aspens is not drowned,
And over lightless pane and footless road,
Empty as sky, with every other sound
Not ceasing, calls their ghosts from their abode,

A silent smithy, a silent inn, nor fails
In the bare moonlight or the thick-furred gloom,
In tempest or the night of nightingales,
To turn the cross-roads to a ghostly room.

And it would be the same were no house near.
Over all sorts of weather, men, and times,
Aspens must shake their leaves and men may hear
But need not listen, more than to my rhymes.

Whatever wind blows, while they and I have leaves
We cannot other than an aspen be
That ceaselessly, unreasonably grieves,
Or so men think who like a different tree.

Edward Thomas

ON THIS DAY:

The Scotsman William Wallace (c.1274–1305) and his forces defeated the English at the battle of Stirling Bridge in 1297.

James Thomson (1700–1748), poet, was born. His poem *Rule Britannia* was set to music by Thomas Arne in 1740.

D. H. Lawrence (1885–1930), poet and novelist, was born.

Ode on a Distant Prospect
of Eton College

Ye distant spires, ye antique towers,
That crown the watery glade,
Where grateful Science still adores
Her Henry's holy shade;
And ye, that from the stately brow
Of Windsor's heights the expanse below
Of grove, of lawn, of mead survey,
Whose turf, whose shade, whose flowers among
Wanders the hoary Thames along
His silver-winding way.

Ah happy hills, ah pleasing shade,
Ah fields beloved in vain,
Where once my careless childhood strayed,
A stranger yet to pain!
I feel the gales, that from ye blow,
A momentary bliss bestow,
As waving fresh their gladsome wing,
My weary soul they seem to soothe,
And, redolent of joy and youth,
To breathe a second spring.

Say, Father Thames, for thou hast seen
Full many a sprightly race
Disporting on thy margent green
The paths of pleasure trace,
Who foremost now delight to cleave
With pliant arm thy glassy wave?
The captive linnet which enthrall?
What idle progeny succeed
To chase the rolling circle's speed,
Or urge the flying ball?

While some on earnest business bent
Their murmuring labours ply
'Gainst graver hours, that bring constraint
To sweeten liberty:
Some bold adventurers disdain
The limits of their little reign,
And unknown regions dare descry:
Still as they run they look behind,
They hear a voice in every wind,
And snatch a fearful joy.

Gay hope is theirs by fancy fed,
Less pleasing when possessed;
The tear forgot as soon as shed,
The sunshine of the breast:
Theirs buxom health of rosy hue,
Wild wit, invention ever new,
And lively cheer of vigour born;
The thoughtless day, the easy night,
The spirits pure, the slumbers light,
That fly the approach of morn.

Alas, regardless of their doom,
The little victims play!
No sense have they of ills to come,
Nor care beyond today.
Yet see how all around 'em wait
The ministers of human fate,
And black Misfortune's baleful train!
Ah, show them where in ambush stand
To seize their prey the murderous band!
Ah, tell them they are men!

These shall the fury Passions tear,
The vultures of the mind,
Disdainful Anger, pallid Fear,
And Shame that skulks behind;
Or pining Love shall waste their youth,
Or Jealousy with rankling tooth,
That inly gnaws the secret heart,
And Envy wan, and faded Care,
Grim-visaged comfortless Despair,
And Sorrow's piercing dart.

Ambition this shall tempt to rise,
Then whirl the wretch from high,
To bitter Scorn a sacrifice,
And grinning Infamy.
The stings of Falsehood those shall try,
And hard Unkindness' altered eye,
That mocks the tear it forced to flow;
And keen Remorse with blood defiled,
And moody Madness laughing wild
Amid severest woe.

Lo, in the vale of years beneath
A grisly troop are seen,
The painful family of Death,
More hideous than their Queen:
This racks the joints, this fires the veins,
That every labouring sinew strains,
Those in the deeper vitals rage:
Lo, Poverty, to fill the band,
That numbs the soul with icy hand,
And slow-consuming Age.

To each his sufferings: all are men,
Condemned alike to groan;
The tender for another's pain,
The unfeeling for his own.
Yet ah! why should they know their fate?
Since sorrow never comes too late,
And happiness too swiftly flies.
Thought would destroy their paradise.
No more; where ignorance is bliss,
'Tis folly to be wise.

Thomas Gray

ON THIS DAY:

In 1440 Eton College was founded by Henry VI followed a year later by the foundation of King's College, Cambridge.

In 1609 the English navigator Henry Hudson (c.1550–1611) first sailed into the river in North America which would later carry his name.

In 2005 the England cricket team, captained by Michael Vaughan, regained the Ashes by winning the Test series against Australia by two matches to one. It was England's first Ashes series victory since 1987.

from In Memoriam A.H.H.

Old Yew, which graspest at the stones
    That name the under-lying dead,
    Thy fibres net the dreamless head,
Thy roots are wrapt about the bones.

The seasons bring the flower again,
    And bring the firstling to the flock;
    And in the dusk of thee, the clock
Beats out the little lives of men.

O not for thee the glow, the bloom,
    Who changest not in any gale,
    Nor branding summer suns avail
To touch thy thousand years of gloom:

And gazing on thee, sullen tree,
    Sick for thy stubborn hardihood,
    I seem to fail from out my blood
And grow incorporate into thee.

Alfred, Lord Tennyson

ON THIS DAY:

Michel de Montaigne (1533–1592), lawyer and author, died.

J. B. Priestley (1894–1984), author and playwright, was born in Bradford, Yorkshire.

Roald Dahl (1916–1990), author of children's novels such as *James and the Giant Peach* and *Charlie and the Chocolate Factory*, was born.

William Heath Robinson (1872–1944), illustrator and cartoonist, died.

Drawing Details in an Old Church

I hear the bell-rope sawing,
And the oil-less axle grind,
As I sit alone here drawing
What some Gothic brain designed;
And I catch the toll that follows
    From the lagging bell,
Ere it spreads to hills and hollows
    Where people dwell.

I ask not whom it tolls for,
Incurious who he be;
So, some morrow, when those knolls for
One unguessed, sound out for me,
A stranger, loitering under
    In nave or choir,
May think, too, 'Whose, I wonder?'
    But not inquire.

Thomas Hardy

ON THIS DAY:

Sir Peter Scott (1909–1989), ornithologist, artist and son of Robert Falcon Scott, was born.

Sam Neill, winemaker and actor who has appeared in films such as *Jurassic Park*, was born in 1947.

Princess Grace of Monaco (1929–1982), who as film actress Grace Kelly appeared in several films directed by Alfred Hitchcock including *To Catch a Thief* and later married Prince Rainier of Monaco (1923–2005), died as a result of a car accident.

Fleet Fighter

'Good show!' he said, leaned back his head and laughed.
'They're wizard types!' he said, and held his beer
Steadily, looked at it and gulped it down
Out of its jam-jar, took a cigarette
And blew a neat smoke ring into the air.
'After this morning's prang I've got the twitch;
I thought I'd had it in that teased-out kite.'
His eyes were blue, and older than his face,
His single stripe had known a lonely war
But all his talk and movements showed his age.
His whole life was the air and his machine,
He had no thought but of the latest 'mod',
His jargon was of aircraft or of beer.
'And what will you do afterwards?' I said,
Then saw his puzzled face and held my breath.
There was no afterwards for him, but death.

Olivia Fitzroy

ON THIS DAY:

The Battle of Britain Day is now celebrated annually on 15th September. It was the first major battle of the Second World War and was unique in that it was fought entirely in the air. From 10th July to 31st October 1940, the fighter pilots of the Royal Air Force resisted all efforts of the German Luftwaffe to gain aerial supremacy. The RAF's victory turned the course of the war.

In 1830 the Liverpool and Manchester railway was opened and among other locomotives present was George Stephenson's *Rocket*. The day was marred by tragedy when the *Rocket* injured William Huskisson, MP for Liverpool. He died later the same day from his injuries.

Sir Donald Bailey (1901–1985), engineer who designed pre-fabricated bridges used extensively during the Second World War, was born.

On the University Carrier who sickn'd in the time of his vacancy, being forbid to go to London, by reason of the Plague

Here lies old *Hobson*, Death hath broke his girt,
And here alas, hath laid him in the dirt,
Or els the ways being foul, twenty to one,
He's here stuck in a slough, and overthrown.
'Twas such a shifter, that if truth were known,
Death was half glad when he had got him down;
For he had any time this ten yeers full,
Dodg'd with him, betwixt *Cambridge* and the Bull.
And surely, Death could never have prevail'd,
Had not his weekly course of carriage fail'd;
But lately finding him so long at home,
And thinking now his journeys end was come,
And that he had tane up his latest Inne,
In the kind office of a Chamberlin
Shew'd him his room where he must lodge that night,
Pull'd off his Books, and took away the light:
If any ask for him, it shall be sed,
Hobson has supt, and's newly gone to bed.

John Milton

ON THIS DAY:

Alexander Korda (1893–1956), film producer, was born.

The two tiers of postage – first and second class – were introduced in the UK in 1968.

Maria Callas (1923–1977), opera singer, died.

To Wordsworth

Those who have laid the harp aside
   And turn'd to idler things,
From very restlessness have tried
   The loose and dusty strings;
And, catching back some favourite strain,
Run with it o'er the chords again.

But Memory is not a Muse,
   O Wordsworth! – though 'tis said
They all descend from her, and use
   To haunt her fountain-head:
That other men should work for me
In the rich mines of Poesie,

Pleases me better than the toil,
   Of smoothing under hardened hand,
With attic emery and oil,
   The shining point for Wisdom's wand;
Like those thou temperest 'mid the rills
Descending from thy native hills.

Without his governance, in vain
   Manhood is strong, and youth is bold.
If oftentimes the o'er-piled strain
   Clogs in the furnace, and grows cold,
Beneath his pinions deep and frore,
And swells, and melts, and flows no more,

That is because the heat beneath,
   Pants in its cavern poorly fed.
Life springs not from the couch of Death,
   Nor Muse nor Grace can raise the dead;
Unturn'd then let the mass remain,
Intractable to sun or rain.

A marsh, where only flat leaves lie,
And showing but the broken sky,
Too surely is the sweetest lay
That wins the ear and wastes the day;
Where youthful Fancy pouts alone,
And lets not Wisdom touch her zone.
He who would build his fame up high,
The rule and plummet must apply,
Nor say – I'll do what I have plann'd,
Before he try if loam or sand
Be still remaining in the place
Delved for each polish'd pillar's base.
With skilful eye and fit device,
Thou raisest every edifice:
Whether in sheltered vale it stand
Or overlook the Dardan strand,
Amid those cypresses that mourn
Laodamia's love forlorn.

We both have run o'er half the space
Bounded for mortal's earthly race;
We both have crossed life's fervid line,
And other stars before us shine.
May they be bright and prosperous
As those that have been stars for us!
Our course by Milton's light was sped,
And Shakespeare shining overhead:
Chatting on deck was Dryden too,
The Bacon of the rhyming crew;
None ever crost our mystic sea,
More richly stored with thought than he;
Tho' never tender nor sublime,
He struggles with and conquers Time.
To learn my lore on Chaucer's knee,
I've left much prouder company.
Thee, gentle Spenser fondly led;
But me he mostly sent to bed.

I wish them every joy above
That highly blessed spirits prove,
Save one – and that too shall be theirs,
But after many rolling years,
When 'mid their light, thy light appears.

Walter Savage Landor

ON THIS DAY:

Walter Savage Landor (1775–1864), poet, died.

William Fox Talbot (1800–1877), mathematician and photography pioneer, died.

William Carlos Williams (1883–1963), poet, was born.

Sir Francis Chichester (1901–1972), yachtsman, was born. In his yacht *Gypsy Moth IV*, Chichester circumnavigated the world, arriving back in Plymouth on 28th May 1967, nine months and one day after he left.

September 18

The Next Poem

How much better it seems now
than when it is finally done–
the unforgettable first line,
the cunning way the stanzas run.

The rhymes soft-spoken and suggestive
are barely audible at first,
an appetite not yet acknowledged
like the inkling of a thirst.

While gradually the form appears
as each line is coaxed aloud–
the architecture of a room
seen from the middle of a crowd.

The music that of common speech
but slanted so that each detail
sounds unexpected as a sharp
inserted in a simple scale.

No jumble box of imagery
dumped glumly in the reader's lap
or elegantly packaged junk
the unsuspecting must unwrap.

But words that could direct a friend
precisely to an unknown place,
those few unshakeable details
that no confusion can erase.

And the real subject left unspoken
but unmistakable to those
who don't expect a jungle parrot
in the black and white of prose.

How much better it seems now
than when it is finally written.
How hungrily one waits to feel
the bright lure seized, the old hook bitten.

Dana Gioia

ON THIS DAY:

Dr Samuel Johnson (1709–1784), author of, among other works, *A Dictionary of the English Language* and *The Lives of the English Poets*, was born.

The *New York Times* was first published in 1851.

Sir Owen Searman (1861–1936), poet and editor of *Punch* (1906–1932), was born.

When Oats Were Reaped

That day when oats were reaped, and wheat was ripe, and barley ripening,
　　The road-dust hot, and the bleaching grasses dry,
　　　　I walked along and said,
While looking just ahead to where some silent people lie:

'I wounded one who's there, and now know well I wounded her;
　　But, ah, she does not know that she wounded me!'
　　　　And not an air stirred,
Nor a bill of any bird; and no response accorded she.

Thomas Hardy

ON THIS DAY:

George Cadbury (1839–1922), manufacturer of chocolate, Quaker, and reformer who believed that a worker's environment was crucial to his well-being, was born. He created a new factory and housing in the area still known as Bournville.

William Hesketh Lever, first Viscount Leverhulme (1851–1925), maker of soap whose factory and model town (built specially for his workforce) is known as Port Sunlight, was born.

Sir William Golding (1911–1993), author and winner of the Nobel Prize for literature in 1983, was born.

In 1945 William Joyce ('Lord Haw-Haw', 1906–1946) was found guilty of treason at the Old Bailey and sentenced to death. He was executed on 3rd January 1946.

Tichborne's Elegy

(written with his own hand in the Tower before his execution)

My prime of youth is but a froste of cares:
My feaste of joy, is but a dishe of payne:
My cropp of corne, is but a field of tares:
And all my good is but vaine hope of gain:
The daye is gone, and yet I sawe no sonn:
And nowe I live, and nowe my life is donn.

My springe is paste, and yet it hath not sprong,
My frute is deade, and yet the leaves are greene
My youth is gone, and yet I am but yonge
I sawe the woorld, and yet I was not seene
My threed is cutt and yet it was not sponn
And nowe I lyve, and nowe my life is donn.

I saught my death, and founde it in my wombe,
I lookte for life and sawe it was a shade.
I trode the earth and knewe it was my Tombe
And nowe I die, and nowe I am but made
The glasse is full, and nowe the glass is rune,
And nowe I live, and nowe my life is donn

Chidiock Tichborne

ON THIS DAY:

In 1586 Chidiock Tichborne (?–1586) was hanged for treasonous acts against Elizabeth I.

Sir Titus Salt (1803–1876), textiles manufacturer and designer of the Yorkshire town Saltaire which was completed shortly before his death, was born.

Stevie Smith (1902–1971), poet, was born.

Joan Littlewood (1914–2002), theatre director, died.

For the Fallen – September 1914

With proud thanksgiving, a mother for her children,
England mourns for her dead across the sea.
Flesh of her flesh they were, spirit of her spirit,
Fallen in the cause of the free.

Solemn the drums thrill: Death august and royal
Sings sorrow up into immortal spheres.
There is music in the midst of desolation
And a glory that shines upon our tears.

They went with songs to the battle, they were young,
Straight of limb, true of eye, steady and aglow.
They were staunch to the end against odds uncounted,
They fell with their faces to the foe.

They shall not grow old, as we that are left grow old:
Age shall not weary them, nor the years condemn.
At the going down of the sun and in the morning
We will remember them.

They mingle not with their laughing comrades again;
They sit no more at familiar tables of home;
They have no lot in our labour of the day-time;
They sleep beyond England's foam.

But where our desires are and our hopes profound,
Felt as a well-spring that is hidden from sight,
To the innermost heart of their own land they are known
As the stars are known to the Night;

As the stars that shall be bright when we are dust,
Moving in marches upon the heavenly plain,
As the stars that are starry in the time of our darkness,
To the end, to the end, they remain.

Laurence Binyon

ON THIS DAY:

Laurence Binyon's poem was first published in *The Times* on 21st September 1914.

In 1915 a Mr C. H. Chubb bought Stonehenge and thirty acres of land which surrounded it at auction (for £6,600) and presented it to the nation.

To Autumn

Season of mists and mellow fruitfulness!
   Close bosom-friend of the maturing sun;
Conspiring with him how to load and bless
   With fruit the vines that round the thatch-eaves run;
To bend with apples the mossed cottage-trees,
   And fill all fruit with ripeness to the core;
     To swell the gourd, and plump the hazel shells
With a sweet kernel; to set budding more,
   And still more, later flowers for the bees,
   Until they think warm days will never cease,
     For Summer has o'erbrimmed their clammy cells.

Who hath not seen thee oft amid thy store?
   Sometimes whoever seeks abroad may find
Thee sitting careless on a granary floor,
   Thy hair soft-lifted by the winnowing wind,
Or on a half-reaped furrow sound asleep,
   Drowsed with the fume of poppies, while thy hook
     Spares the next swath and all its twinèd flowers;
And sometimes like a gleaner thou dost keep
   Steady thy laden head across a brook;
   Or by a cider-press, with patient look,
     Thou watchest the last oozings hours by hours.

Where are the songs of Spring? Ay, where are they?
   Think not of them, thou hast thy music too,–
While barred clouds bloom the soft-dying day,
   And touch the stubble-plains with rosy hue;
Then in a wailful choir the small gnats mourn
   Among the river sallows, borne aloft
     Or sinking as the light wind lives or dies;
And full-grown lambs loud bleat from hilly bourn;
   Hedge-crickets sing; and now with treble soft
   The redbreast whistles from a garden-croft;
     And gathering swallows twitter in the skies.

John Keats

ON THIS DAY:

Michael Faraday (1791–1867), English scientist, was born.

September 23

Song at the Beginning of Autumn

Now watch this autumn that arrives
In smells. All looks like summer still;
Colours are quite unchanged, the air
On green and white serenely thrives.
Heavy the trees with growth and full
The fields. Flowers flourish everywhere.

Proust who collected time within
A child's cake would understand
The ambiguity of this –
Summer still raging while a thin
Column of smoke stirs from the land
Proving that autumn gropes for us.

But every season is a kind
Of rich nostalgia. We give names –
Autumn and summer, winter, spring –
As though to unfasten from the mind
Our moods and give them outward forms.
We want the certain, solid thing.

But I am carried back against
My will into a childhood where
Autumn is bonfires, marbles, smoke;
I lean against my window fenced
From evocations in the air.
When I said autumn, autumn broke.

Elizabeth Jennings

ON THIS DAY:

The autumnal equinox occurs around this date.

Sigmund Freud (1856–1939), who developed psychoanalysis for treatment of mental disorders, was born.

The BBC launched its Ceefax text service in 1974.

Lambeth Lyric

Some seven score Bishops late at Lambeth sat,
Gray-whiskered and respectable debaters:
Each had on head a well-strung curly hat;
       And each wore gaiters.

And when these prelates at their talk had been
Long time, they made yet longer proclamation,
Saying: 'These creeds are childish! both Nicene,
       And Athanasian.

True, they were written by the Holy Ghost;
So, to re-write them were perhaps a pity.
Refer we their revision to a most
       Select Committee!

In ten years' time we wise Pan Anglicans
Once more around this Anglo Catholic table
Will meet, to prove God's word more weak than man's,
       His truth, less stable.'

So saying homeward the good Fathers go;
Up Mississippi some and some up Niger.
For thine old mantle they have clearly no
       More use, Elijah!

Instead, an apostolic apron girds
Their loins, which ministerial fingers tie on:
And Babylon's songs they sing, new tune and words,
       All over Zion.

The Creeds, the Scriptures, all the Faith of old,
They hack and hew to please each bumptious German,
Windy and vague as mists and clouds that fold
       Tabour and Hermon.

Happy Establishment in this thine hour!
Behold thy bishops to their sees retreating!
'Have at the Faith!' each cries: 'good bye till our
Next merry meeting!'

Lionel Johnson

ON THIS DAY:

The first Lambeth Conference of the Church of England was held on this day in 1867. Seventy-six bishops attended.

In 1940 the George Cross was instituted by George VI as an award primarily for civilians for acts of great heroism or conspicuous courage in circumstances of extreme danger. Military personnel are eligible for this award for acts of heroism away from the field of battle.

The Pipes at Lucknow

Pipes of the misty moorlands,
　　Voice of the glens and hills;
The droning of the torrents,
　　The treble of the rills!
Not the braes of broom and heather,
　　Nor the mountains dark with rain,
Nor maiden bower, nor border tower,
　　Have heard your sweetest strain!

Dear to the Lowland reaper,
　　And plaided mountaineer, –
To the cottage and the castle
　　The Scottish pipes are dear –
Sweet sounds the ancient pibroch
　　O'er mountain, loch, and glade;
But the sweetest of all music
　　The pipes at Lucknow played.

Day by day the Indian tiger
　　Louder yelled, and nearer crept;
Round and round the jungle-serpent
　　Near and nearer circles swept.
'Pray for rescue, wives and mothers, –
Pray to-day!' the soldier said;
　　'To-morrow, death's between us
And the wrong and shame we dread.'

Oh, they listened, looked, and waited,
　　Till their hope became despair;
And the sobs of low bewailing
　　Filled the pauses of their prayer.
Then up spake a Scottish maiden,
　　With her ear unto the ground:
'Dinna ye hear it? – dinna ye hear it?
　　The pipes o' Havelock sound!'

373

Hushed the wounded man his groaning;
　　Hushed the wife her little ones;
Alone they heard the drum-roll
　　And the roar of Sepoy guns.
But to sounds of home and childhood
　　The Highland ear was true; –
As her mother's cradle-crooning
　　The mountain pipes she knew.

Like the march of soundless music
　　Through the vision of the seer,
More of feeling than of hearing,
　　Of the heart than of the ear
She knew the droning pibroch,
　　She knew the Campbell's call
'Hark! hear ye no' MacGregor's,
　　The grandest o' them all!'

Oh, they listened, dumb and breathless,
　　And they caught the sound at last;
Faint and far beyond the Goomtee
　　Rose and fell the piper's blast!
Then a burst of wild thanksgiving
　　Mingled woman's voice and man's;
'God be praised! – the march of Havelock!
　　The piping of the clans!'

Louder, nearer, fierce as vengeance,
　　Sharp and shrill as swords at strife,
Came the wild MacGregor's clan-call,
　　Stinging all the air to life.
But when the far-off dust-cloud
　　To plaided legions grew,
Full tenderly and blithesomely
　　The pipes of rescue blew!

Round the silver domes of Lucknow,
    Moslem mosque and Pagan shrine,
Breathed the air to Britons dearest,
    The air of Auld Lang Syne.
O'er the cruel roll of war-drums
    Rose that sweet and homelike strain;
And the tartan clove the turban,
    As the Goomtee cleaves the plain.

Dear to the corn-land reaper
    And plaided mountaineer, –
To the cottage and the castle
    The piper's song is dear.
Sweet sounds the Gaelic pibroch
    O'er mountain, glen, and glade;
But the sweetest of all music
    The Pipes at Lucknow played!

John Greenleaf Whittier

ON THIS DAY:

The first relief of Lucknow occurred on this day in 1857. However, the relieving forces themselves were then besieged until the second relief of the city on 17th November 1857.

The first transfusion using human blood was performed at Guy's Hospital in 1818.

The transatlantic telephone service began in 1956.

September 26

Number 534

For ages you were rock, far below light,
Crushed, without shape, earth's unregarded bone.
Then Man in all the marvel of his might
Quarried you out and burned you from the stone.

Then, being pured to essence, you were nought
But weight and hardness, body without nerve;
Then Man in all the marvel of his thought,
Smithied you into form of leap and curve;

And took you, so, and bent you to his vast,
Intense great world of passionate design,
Curve after changing curving, braced and masst
To stand all tumult that can tumble brine,

And left you, this, a rampart of a ship,
Long as a street and lofty as a tower,
Ready to glide in thunder from the slip
And shear the sea with majesty of power.

I long to see you leaping to the urge
Of the great engines, rolling as you go,
Parting the seas in sunder in a surge,
Shredding a trackway like a mile of snow

With all the wester streaming from your hull
And all gear twanging shrilly as you race,
And effortless above your stern a gull
Leaning upon the blast and keeping place.

May shipwreck and collision, fog and fire,
Rock, shoal and other evils of the sea,
Be kept from you; and may the heart's desire
Of those who speed your launching come to be.

John Masefield

ON THIS DAY:

Queen Mary (1867–1953) launched the Cunard liner RMS *Queen Mary* at Clydebank in 1934. Prior to being named the ship had been known only by its work number '534'.

September, 1819

Departing summer hath assumed
An aspect tenderly illumed,
The gentlest look of spring;
That calls from yonder leafy shade
Unfaded, yet prepared to fade,
A timely carolling.

No faint and hesitating trill,
Such tribute as to winter chill
The lonely redbreast pays!
Clear, loud, and lively is the din,
From social warblers gathering in
Their harvest of sweet lays.

Nor doth the example fail to cheer
Me, conscious that my leaf is sere,
And yellow on the bough: —
Fall, rosy garlands, from my head!
Ye myrtle wreaths, your fragrance shed
Around a younger brow!

Yet will I temperately rejoice;
Wide is the range, and free the choice
Of undiscordant themes;
Which, haply, kindred souls may prize
Not less than vernal ecstasies,
And passion's feverish dreams.

For deathless powers to verse belong,
And they like Demi-gods are strong
On whom the Muses smile;
But some their function have disclaimed,
Best pleased with what is aptliest framed
To enervate and defile.

Not such the initiatory strains
Committed to the silent plains
In Britain's earliest dawn:

Trembled the groves, the stars grew pale,
While all-too-daringly the veil
Of nature was withdrawn!

Nor such the spirit-stirring note
When the live chords Alcæus smote,
Inflamed by sense of wrong;
Woe! woe to Tyrants! from the lyre
Broke threateningly, in sparkles dire
Of fierce vindictive song.

And not unhallowed was the page
By wingèd Love inscribed, to assuage
The pangs of vain pursuit;
Love listening while the Lesbian Maid
With finest touch of passion swayed
Her own Æolian lute.

O ye, who patiently explore
The wreck of Herculanean lore,
What rapture! could ye seize
Some Theban fragment, or unroll
One precious, tender-hearted scroll
Of pure Simonides.

That were, indeed, a genuine birth
Of poesy; a bursting forth
Of genius from the dust:
What Horace gloried to behold,
What Maro loved, shall we enfold?
Can haughty Time be just!

William Wordsworth

ON THIS DAY:

In 1825 the Stockton to Darlington Railway, the first public railway in England, was opened by George Stephenson (1781–1848), who drove the engine *Locomotion*.

The *Queen Elizabeth* was launched at Clydebank, by Queen Elizabeth (1900–2002), consort of George VI in 1938.

The RMS *Queen Mary* completed her final transatlantic voyage in 1967.

Sir William Empson (1906–1984), poet, was born.

At Melville's Tomb

Often beneath the wave, wide from this ledge
The dice of drowned men's bones he saw bequeath
An embassy. Their numbers as he watched,
Beat on the dusty shore and were obscured.

And wrecks passed without sound of bells,
The calyx of death's bounty giving back
A scattered chapter, livid hieroglyph,
The portent wound in corridors of shells.

Then in the circuit calm of one vast coil,
Its lashings charmed and malice reconciled,
Frosted eyes there were that lifted altars;
And silent answers crept across the stars.

Compass, quadrant and sextant contrive
No farther tides… High in the azure steeps
Monody shall not wake the mariner.
This fabulous shadow only the sea keeps.

Hart Crane

ON THIS DAY:

Herman Melville (1819–1891), author of *Moby Dick*, died.

William of Normandy (1027–1087) invaded England in 1066.

Bavarian Gentians

Not every man has gentians in his house
in Soft September, at slow, Sad Michaelmas.

Bavarian gentians, big and dark, only dark
darkening the day-time torch-like with the smoking blueness of Pluto's gloom,
ribbed and torch-like, with their blaze of darkness spread blue
down flattening into points, flattened under the sweep of white day
torch-flower of the blue-smoking darkness, Pluto's dark-blue daze,
black lamps from the halls of Dis, burning dark blue,
giving off darkness, blue darkness, as Demeter's pale lamps give off light,
lead me then, lead me the way.

Reach me a gentian, give me a torch
let me guide myself with the blue, forked torch of this flower
down the darker and darker stairs, where blue is darkened on blueness,
even where Persephone goes, just now, from the frosted September
to the sightless realm where darkness is awake upon the dark
and Persephone herself is but a voice
or a darkness invisible enfolded in the deeper dark
of the arms Plutonic, and pierced with the passion of dense gloom,
among the splendour of torches of darkness, shedding darkness on the lost
   bride and her groom.

D. H. Lawrence

ON THIS DAY:

The feast day of St Michael and all Angels, which is known as Michaelmas, falls on 29th September.

Horatio Nelson (1758–1805) was born.

The Metropolitan Police service was founded in 1829.

W. H. Auden (1907–1973), poet, died.

September 30

Oxford Canal

When you have wearied of the valiant spires of this County Town,
Of its wide white streets and glistening museums, and black monastic walls,
Of its red motors and lumbering trams, and self-sufficient people,
I will take you walking with me to a place you have not seen –
Half town and half country – the land of the Canal.

It is dearer to me than the antique town: I love it more than the rounded hills:
Straightest, sublimest of rivers is the long Canal.
I have observed great storms and trembled: I have wept for fear of the dark.
But nothing makes me so afraid as the clear water of this idle canal on a
  summer's noon.
Do you see the great telephone poles down in the water, how every wire is
  distinct?
If a body fell into the canal it would rest entangled in those wires for ever,
  between earth and air.
For the water is as deep as the stars are high.
One day I was thinking how if a man fell from that lofty pole
He would rush through the water toward me till his image was scattered by
  his splash,
When suddenly a train rushed by: the brazen dome of the engine flashed: the
  long white carriages roared;
The sun veiled himself for a moment, and the signals loomed in fog;
A savage woman screamed at me from a barge: little children began to cry;
The untidy landscape rose to life; a sawmill started;
A cart rattled down to the wharf, and workmen clanged over the iron
  footbridge;
A beautiful old man nodded from the first storey window of a square red house,
And a pretty girl came out to hang up clothes in a small delightful garden.
O strange motion in the suburb of a county town: slow regular movement of
  the dance of death!
Men and not phantoms are these that move in light.
Forgotten they live, and forgotten die.

James Elroy Flecker

ON THIS DAY:

James Brindley (1716–1772), canal engineer, died. Work on the Oxford Canal began in 1769 and the
canal opened on 1st January 1790.

OCTOBER

October

O leafy yellowness you create for me
A world that was and now is poised above time,
I do not need to puzzle out Eternity
As I walk this arboreal street on the edge of a town.
The breeze, too, even the temperature
And pattern of movement, is precisely the same
As broke my heart for youth passing. Now I am sure
Of something. Something will be mine wherever I am.
I want to throw myself on the public street without caring
For anything but the prayering that the earth offers.
It is October over all my life and the light is staring
As it caught me once in a plantation by the fox coverts.
A man is ploughing ground for winter wheat
And my nineteen years weigh heavily on my feet.

Patrick Kavanagh

ON THIS DAY:

In 1868 the Midland Railway Company opened St Pancras Station.

William Boeing (1881–1956), timber merchant, and founder of the aeroplane manufacturing company that bears his name, was born.

Stanley Holloway (1890–1982), actor and raconteur, was born.

Written in October

The blasts of Autumn as they scatter round
   The faded foliage of another year,
And muttering many a sad and solemn sound,
   Drive the pale fragments o'er the stubble sere,
Are well attuned to my dejected mood;
   (Ah! better far than airs that breathe of Spring!)
   While the high rooks, that hoarsely clamouring
Seek in black phalanx the half-leafless wood,
   I rather hear, than that enraptured lay
Harmonious, and of Love and Pleasure born,
Which from the golden furze, or flowering thorn
   Awakes the Shepherd in the ides of May;
Nature delights *me* most when most she mourns,
For never more to me the Spring of Hope returns!

Charlotte Smith

ON THIS DAY:

Roy Campbell (1901–1957), poet, was born.

Graham Greene (1904–1991), author, was born.

Lord Robert Runcie (1921–2000), Archbishop of Canterbury, was born.

The Polish government, which had been exiled to Paris following the invasion of Poland by German forces and the outbreak of the Second World War, was recognised by the United States of America in 1939.

In 1959 a new film company, Beaver Films, was set up by Richard Attenborough and Bryan Forbes.

Grown and Flown

I loved my love from green of Spring
    Until sere Autumn's fall;
But now that leaves are withering
    How should one love at all?
    One heart's too small
For hunger, cold, love, everything.

I loved my love on sunny days
    Until late Summer's wane;
But now that frost begins to glaze
    How should one love again?
    Nay, love and pain
Walk wide apart in diverse ways.

I loved my love–alas to see
    That this should be, alas!
I thought that this could scarcely be,
    Yet has it come to pass:
    Sweet sweet love was,
Now bitter bitter grown to me.

Christina Rossetti

ON THIS DAY:

St Francis of Assisi (c.1181/2–1226), founder of the Franciscan Order, died.

Ben Jonson (1572–1637), poet and playwright, died.

Pierre Bonnard (1867–1947), painter, was born.

The rationing of tea ended in Britain in 1952.

October 4

Cathedral

Songbirds live
in the old cathedral,
caged birds bought at the street market
and freed as a kind of offering.
Now doves and finches and parakeets
nest in the crooks of the nave's highest arches,
roosting on the impossibly high
sills of stained glass windows,
looking down into the valley of the altar
as if from cliffs.

Twice a day, you'll hear them singing:
at dawn
when the blue light
of angels' wings
and the yellow light of halos
flood into their nests to wake them;
and during mass
when the organ fills
the valley below with thunder.
These birds love thunder,
never having seen a drop of rain.
They love it when the people below stand up
and sing. They fly
in mad little loops
from window to window,
from the tops of arches
down toward the candles and tombs,
making the sign of the cross.

If you look up during mass
to the world's light falling
through the arms of saints,
you can see birds flying

through blue columns of incense
as if it were simple wood smoke
rising from a cabin's chimney
in a remote and hushed forest.

Richard Jones

ON THIS DAY:

Today is the feast day of St Francis of Assisi.

In 1535 Miles Coverdale (1488–1568) published the first English translation of the entire Bible.

Buster Keaton (1896–1966), American film comedian, was born.

The USSR launched *Sputnik I*, the first man-made satellite, in 1957.

Jarrow

Nothing is left to dig, little to make.
Night has engulfed both firelit hall and sparrow.
Wind and car-noise pour across the Slake.
Nothing is left to dig, little to make
A stream of rust where a great ship might grow.
And where a union-man was hung for show
Nothing is left to dig, little to make.
Night has engulfed both firelit hall and sparrow.

Carol Rumens

ON THIS DAY:

In 1936, 200 unemployed men set off from Jarrow to march to London to deliver a petition to the government in protest at the exceptionally high level of unemployment in the town. Local people raised money to support them on their march, paying for the leather and nails to mend their boots en route.

Václav Havel, playwright, poet and first non-Communist President of Czechoslovakia, was born in 1936.

The charity Oxfam was founded in 1942.

October 6

Talkies

Already there is gossip in Hollywood
About something new. Even the stars will need tests.

In the beginning was the caption,
Ringlets, a balletic flow of knees;

Crowds opened their mouths, then closed them.
Now some will never be heard of again

If between camera-loving, soundless lips
Is a foreign accent, or that timbre of voice which means

The microphone doesn't like you.
Friends swell into enormous heart-throbs:

Their voices are good. 'Retraining?
Let me get you another drink.'

At the neat wrought-iron table,
Legs crossed, she stares at the studio,

A hangar, a camp, a silo. Work
Means something else now, something other

Than what she set her heart on, black and white silk, panache.
With a longer lifespan she might become

A nostalgia executive, a Last of the, a rediscovery.
But the dates are wrong; leaving her speechless

At this technology crackling over California
Eagerly, far out of sight.

Robert Crawford

ON THIS DAY:

In 1927 the feature-length 'talkie', *The Jazz Singer*, starring Al Jolson, was shown publicly for the first time in New York.

Helen Wills Moody (1905–1998), tennis player and eight times winner of the Ladies' Championship at Wimbledon, was born.

Autumn Ploughing

After the ranks of stubble have lain bare,
And field mice and the finches' beaks have found
The last spilled seed corn left upon the ground;
And no more swallows miracle in air;

When the green tuft no longer hides the hare,
And dropping starling flights at evening come;
When birds, except the robin, have gone dumb,
And leaves are rustling downwards everywhere;

Then out, with the great horses, come the ploughs,
And all day long the slow procession goes,
Darkening the stubble fields with broadening strips.

Gray sea-gulls settle after to carouse:
Harvest prepares upon the harvest's close,
Before the blackbird pecks the scarlet hips.

John Masefield

ON THIS DAY:

Archbishop William Laud (1573–1645), Archbishop of Canterbury who was executed for treason, was born.

Edgar Allen Poe (1809–1849), novelist, died.

In 1938 Germany ordered all Jews to hand over their passports to the authorities.

October 8

In Autumn...

In Autumn when the woods are red
And skies are grey and clear,
The sportsmen seek the wild fowls' bed
Or follow down the deer;
And Cupid hunts by haugh and head,
By riverside and mere,
I walk, not seeing where I tread
And keep my heart with fear,
Sir, have an eye, on where you tread,
And keep your heart with fear,
For something lingers here;
A touch of April not yet dead,
In Autumn when the woods are red
And skies are grey and clear.

Robert Louis Stevenson

ON THIS DAY:

St Mark's Cathedral, Venice was consecrated in 1085.

Dame Betty Boothroyd, the first woman to be Speaker of the House of Commons, was born in 1929.

In 1962 Judge Elizabeth Lane (1905–1988) became the first woman to sit in the High Court.

The Post Office Tower opened in 1965.

Shortening Days at the Homestead

The first fire since the summer is lit, and is smoking into the room:
    The sun-rays thread it through, like woof-lines in a loom.
    Sparrows spurt from the hedge, whom misgivings appal
That winter did not leave last year for ever, after all.
    Like shock-headed urchins, spiny-haired,
    Stand pollard willows, their twigs just bared.

Who is this coming with pondering pace,
Black and ruddy, with white embossed,
His eyes being black, and ruddy his face,
And the marge of his hair like morning frost?
    It's the cider-maker,
    And appletree-shaker,
And behind him on wheels, in readiness,
His mill, and tubs, and vat, and press.

Thomas Hardy

ON THIS DAY:

Today is the feast day of St Denis, the patron saint of France.

Quintin Hogg, Lord Hailsham (1907–2001, Lord Chancellor from 1970 to 1974 and 1979 to 1987), was born. His father, Douglas Hogg, Viscount Hailsham (1872–1950), was Lord Chancellor from 1928 to 1929 and again from 1935 to 1938.

Jacques Tati (1908–1982), film director and actor who played the character Monsieur Hulot in numerous films, was born.

Ars Poetica

A poem should be palpable and mute
As a globed fruit,

Dumb
As old medallions to the thumb,

Silent as the sleeve-worn stone
Of casement ledges where the moss has grown –

A poem should be wordless
As the flight of birds.

*

A poem should be motionless in time
As the moon climbs,

Leaving, as the moon releases
Twig by twig the night-entangled trees,

Leaving, as the moon behind the winter leaves,
Memory by memory the mind –

A poem should be motionless in time
As the moon climbs.

*

A poem should be equal to:
Not true.

For all the history of grief
An empty doorway and a maple leaf.

For love
The leaning grasses and two lights above the sea –

A poem should not mean
But be.

Archibald MacLeish

ON THIS DAY:

Sir John Betjeman appointed Poet Laureate in 1972.

Wyatt Resteth Here

Wyatt resteth here, that quick could never rest;
Whose heavenly gifts increasèd by disdain,
And virtue sank the deeper in his breast;
Such profit he of envy could obtain.
A head where wisdom mysteries did frame,
Whose hammers beat still in that lively brain
As on a stithy, where some work of fame
Was daily wrought, to turn to Britain's gain.
A visage stern and mild, where both did grow,
Vice to contemn, in virtues to rejoice,
Amid great storms, whom grace assurèd so,
To live upright, and smile at fortune's choice.
A hand that taught what might be said in rhyme;
That reft Chaucer the glory of his wit;
A mark, the which – unperfited, for time –
Some may approach, but never none shall hit.
A tongue that served in foreign realms his king;
Whose courteous talk to virtue did enflame
Each noble heart; a worthy guide to bring
Our English youth, by travail, unto fame.
An eye whose judgement no affect could blind,
Friends to allure, and foes to reconcile;
Whose piercing look did represent a mind
With virtue fraught, reposèd, void of guile.
A heart where dread yet never so impressed
To hide the thought that might the truth advance;
In neither fortune lost, nor so repressed,
To swell in wealth, nor yield unto mischance.
A valiant corps, where force and beauty met,
Happy, alas! too happy, but for foes,
Livèd, and ran the race that nature set;
Of manhood's shape, where she the mould did lose.
But to the heavens that simple soul is fled,

Which left with such as covet Christ to know
Witness of faith that never shall be dead,
Sent for our health, but not receivèd so.
Thus, for our guilt, this jewel have we lost;
The earth his bones, the heavens possess his ghost.

Henry Howard, Earl of Surrey

ON THIS DAY:

Ulrich Zwingli (1484–1531), theologian and reformer, died at the battle of Keppel

The Second Anglo-Boer War began in 1899.

In 1982 the wreck of the *Mary Rose*, Henry VIII's flagship, was raised from the seabed.

October 12

The Discovery of America

All the mill-horses of Europe
   Were plodding round and round;
All the mills were droning
   The same old sound.

The drivers were dozing, the millers
   Were deaf – as millers will be;
When, startling them all, without warning
   Came a great shout from the sea!

It startled them all. The horses,
   Lazily plodding round,
Started and stopp'd; and the mills dropp'd
   Like a mantle their sound.

The millers look'd over their shoulders,
   The drivers open'd their eyes:
A silence, deeper than deafness,
   Had fallen out of the skies.

'Halloa there!' – this time distinctly
   It rose from the barren sea;
And Europe, turning in wonder,
   Whisper'd, 'What can it be?'

'Come down, come down to the shore here!'
   And Europe was soon on the sand; –
It was the great Columbus
   Dragging his prize to land.

James Logie Robertson

ON THIS DAY:

In 1492 Christopher Columbus reached the Bahamas and ended a voyage that had begun ten weeks earlier in Palos, Spain. In the USA it is celebrated as Columbus Day, a tradition that began in 1792.

In 1915 Nurse Edith Cavell (1865–1915) was executed by the Germans for treasonous acts. She ran a school for nurses in Brussels but was prosecuted for harbouring Belgians of military age and for assisting English and French soldiers to escape across the Dutch border.

Crossing the Bar

Sunset and evening star,
    And one clear call for me!
And may there be no moaning of the bar,
    When I put out to sea,

But such a tide as moving seems asleep,
    Too full for sound and foam,
When that which drew from out the boundless deep
    Turns again home.

Twilight and evening bell,
    And after that the dark!
And may there be no sadness of farewell,
    When I embark;

For though from out our bourne of Time and Place
    The flood may bear me far,
I hope to see my Pilot face to face
    When I have crost the bar.

Alfred, Lord Tennyson

ON THIS DAY:

Sir Henry Irving (John Henry Brodribb, 1838–1905), the first actor to receive a knighthood, died.

In 1988 the British government failed to stop the book *Spycatcher* by Peter Wright (1916–1995), a former member of MI5, from being published.

A Sheep Fair

The day arrives of the autumn fair,
    And torrents fall,
Though sheep in throngs are gathered there,
    Ten thousand all,
Sodden, with hurdles round them reared:
And, lot by lot, the pens are cleared,
And the auctioneer wrings out his beard,
And wipes his book, bedrenched and smeared,
And rakes the rain from his face with the edge of his hand,
    As torrents fall.

The wool of the ewes is like a sponge
    With the daylong rain:
Jammed tight, to turn, or lie, or lunge,
    They strive in vain.
Their horns are soft as finger-nails,
Their shepherds reek against the rails,
The tied dogs soak with tucked-in tails,
The buyers' hat-brims fill like pails,
Which spill small cascades when they shift their stand
    In the daylong rain.

Postscript

Time has trailed lengthily since met
    At Pummery Fair
Those panting thousands in their wet
    And woolly wear:
And every flock long since has bled,
And all the dripping buyers have sped,
And the hoarse auctioneer is dead,
Who 'Going – going!' so often said,
As he consigned to doom each meek, mewed band
    At Pummery Fair.

Thomas Hardy

ON THIS DAY:

King Harold (c.1022–1066) was killed while fighting William of Normandy's invading forces at the battle of Hastings (Senlac Hill).

To Daffodils

Fair daffodils, we weep to see
    You haste away so soon:
As yet the early-rising sun
    Has not attained his noon.
        Stay, stay,
    Until the hasting day
        Has run
    But to the evensong;
And, having prayed together, we
    Will go with you along.

We have short time to stay as you;
    We have as short a spring;
As quick a growth to meet decay,
    As you or anything.
        We die,
    As your hours do, and dry
        Away
    Like to the summer's rain;
Or as the pearls of morning's dew,
    Ne'er to be found again.

Robert Herrick

ON THIS DAY:

The poet Robert Herrick (1591–1674) was buried in 1674.

Virgil (70BC–19BC), poet, was born.

In 1928 the German airship the *Graf Zeppelin* completed its first transatlantic flight.

Mikhail Gorbachev (b.1931) received the Nobel Peace Prize in 1990.

The Charge of the Light Brigade

Half a league, half a league,
　Half a league onward,
All in the valley of Death
　Rode the six hundred.
'Forward, the Light Brigade!
Charge for the guns!' he said:
Into the valley of Death
　Rode the six hundred.

'Forward, the Light Brigade!'
Was there a man dismay'd?
Not tho' the soldier knew
　Some one had blunder'd:
Their's not to make reply,
Their's not to reason why,
Their's but to do and die:
Into the valley of Death
　Rode the six hundred.

Cannon to right of them,
Cannon to left of them,
Cannon in front of them
　Volley'd and thunder'd;
Storm'd at with shot and shell,
Boldly they rode and well,
Into the jaws of Death,
Into the mouth of Hell
　Rode the six hundred.

Flash'd all their sabres bare,
Flash'd as they turn'd in air
Sabring the gunners there,
Charging an army, while
　All the world wonder'd:

Plunged in the battery-smoke
Right thro' the line they broke;
Cossack and Russian
Reel'd from the sabre-stroke
   Shatter'd and sunder'd.
Then they rode back, but not
   Not the six hundred.

Cannon to right of them,
Cannon to left of them,
Cannon behind them
   Volley'd and thunder'd;
Storm'd at with shot and shell,
While horse and hero fell,
They that had fought so well
Came thro' the jaws of Death,
Back from the mouth of Hell,
All that was left of them,
   Left of six hundred.

When can their glory fade?
O the wild charge they made!
   All the world wonder'd.
Honour the charge they made!
Honour the Light Brigade,
   Noble six hundred!

Alfred, Lord Tennyson

ON THIS DAY:

Lord Cardigan (1797–1868), soldier who led the charge at the battle of Balaclava, was born.

In 1834 the Houses of Parliament were destroyed by fire.

In 1987 a severe storm swept across southern England during the night, causing great devastation and disruption to essential services. Six of the seven oak trees at Sevenoaks were lost.

Elegy 9: The Autumnal

No spring, nor summer beauty hath such grace,
　　As I have seen in one autumnal face.
Young beauties force your love, and that's a rape,
　　This doth but counsel, yet you cannot scape.
It 'twere a shame to love, here 'twere no shame,
　　Affection here takes reverence's name.
Were her first years the Golden Age; that's true,
　　But now she's gold oft tried, and ever new.
That was her torrid and inflaming time,
　　This is her tolerable tropic clime.
Fair eyes, who asks more heat than comes from hence,
　　He in a fever wishes pestilence.
Call not these wrinkles, graves; if graves they were,
　　They were Love's graves; for else he is no where.
Yet lies not Love dead here, but here doth sit
　　Vowed to this trench, like an anachorit.
And here, till hers, which must be his death, come,
　　He doth not dig a grave, but build a tomb.
Here dwells he, though he sojourn everywhere,
　　In Progress, yet his standing house is here.
Here, where still evening is; not noon, nor night;
　　Where no voluptuousness, yet all delight.
In all her words, unto all hearers fit,
　　You may at revels, you at council, sit.
This is Love's timber, youth his underwood;
　　There he, as wine in June, enrages blood,
Which then comes seasonabliest, when our taste
　　And appetite to other things is past.
Xerxes' strange Lydian love, the platan tree,
　　Was loved for age, none being so large as she,
Or else because, being young, nature did bless
　　Her youth with age's glory, barrenness.

If we love things long sought, age is a thing
    Which we are fifty years in compassing.
If transitory things, which soon decay,
    Age must be loveliest at the latest day.
But name not winter-faces, whose skin's slack;
    Lank, as an unthrift's purse; but a soul's sack;
Whose eyes seek light within, for all here's shade;
    Whose mouths are holes, rather worn out, than made;
Whose every tooth to a several place is gone,
    To vex their souls at Resurrection;
Name not these living death's-heads unto me,
    For these, not ancient, but antiques be.
I hate extremes; yet I had rather stay
    With tombs, than cradles, to wear out a day.
Since such love's natural lation is, may still
    My love descend, and journey down the hill,
Not panting after growing beauties, so,
    I shall ebb out with them, who homeward go.

John Donne

ON THIS DAY:

Sir Philip Sidney (1554–1586), soldier and poet, died.

Georg Büchner (1813–1837), poet, playwright and author of *Woyzeck*, was born.

Arthur Miller (1915–2005), writer and author of the plays *Death of a Salesman* and *The Crucible*, was born.

Calder Hall in Cumbria, the first full-scale nuclear power station, was opened in 1956.

October 18

Autumn Violets

Keep love for youth, and violets for the spring:
   Or if these bloom when worn-out autumn grieves,
   Let them lie hid in double shade of leaves,
Their own, and others dropped down withering;
For violets suit when home birds build and sing,
   Not when the outbound bird a passage cleaves;
   Not with dry stubble of mown harvest sheaves,
But when the green world buds to blossoming.
Keep violets for the spring, and love for youth,
   Love that should dwell with beauty, mirth, and hope:
   Or if a later sadder love be born,
Let this not look for grace beyond its scope,
But give itself, nor plead for answering truth –
   A grateful Ruth tho' gleaning scanty corn.

Christina Rossetti

ON THIS DAY:

Antonio Canaletto (1697–1768), painter whose favourite subjects included Venice and London, was born.

Thomas Love Peacock (1785–1866), poet, was born.

Martina Navratilova, tennis player, and nine times winner of the Ladies' Singles at Wimbledon over a period of three decades, was born in 1956.

Lord Emmanuel ('Manny') Shinwell (1884–1985), Labour politician, was born.

The Solitary Reaper

Behold her, single in the field,
   Yon solitary Highland Lass!
Reaping and singing by herself;
   Stop here, or gently pass!
Alone she cuts and binds the grain,
And sings a melancholy strain;
O listen! for the vale profound
Is overflowing with the sound.

No nightingale did ever chaunt
   More welcome notes to weary bands
Of travellers in some shady haunt,
   Among Arabian sands:
A voice so thrilling ne'er was heard
In spring-time from the cuckoo-bird,
Breaking the silence of the seas
Among the farthest Hebrides.

Will no one tell me what she sings? –
   Perhaps the plaintive numbers flow
For old, unhappy, far-off things,
   And battles long ago:
Or is it some more humble lay,
Familiar matter of to-day?
Some natural sorrow, loss, or pain,
That has been, and may be again?

Whate'er the theme, the maiden sang
   As if her song could have no ending;
I saw her singing at her work,
   And o'er the sickle bending; –
I listened, motionless and still;
And, as I mounted up the hill,
The music in my heart I bore,
Long after it was heard no more.

William Wordsworth

ON THIS DAY:

Auguste Lumière (1862–1954), who with his brother Louis Jean Lumière (1864–1948) invented the motion picture camera and developed a colour photography process, was born.

I am

I am – yet what I am, none cares or knows;
   My friends forsake me like a memory lost:
I am the self-consumer of my woes –
   They rise and vanish in oblivion's host
Like shadows in love – frenzied stifled throes
And yet I am, and live – like vapours tossed

Into the nothingness of scorn and noise,
   Into the living sea of waking dreams,
Where there is neither sense of life or joys,
   But the vast shipwreck of my life's esteems;
Even the dearest that I love the best
Are strange – nay, rather, stranger than the rest.

I long for scenes, where man hath never trod
   A place where woman never smiled or wept
There to abide with my Creator, God,
   And sleep as I in childhood sweetly slept,
Untroubling and untroubled where I lie
The grass below – above, the vaulted sky.

John Clare

ON THIS DAY:

Thomas Linacre (c.1460–1524), founder of the Royal College of Surgeons, died.

Sir Christopher Wren (1632–1723), the architect of St Paul's Cathedral and many other London churches, following the destruction caused by the Great Fire of London, was born.

HM Queen Elizabeth II opened the Sydney Opera House in Australia in 1973.

Ye Mariners of England

Ye Mariners of England
   That guard our native seas!
Whose flag has braved a thousand years
   The battle and the breeze!
Your glorious standard launch again
   To match another foe;
And sweep through the deep,
   While the stormy winds do blow!
While the battle rages loud and long
   And the stormy winds do blow.

The spirits of your fathers
   Shall start from every wave –
For the deck it was their field of fame,
   And Ocean was their grave:
Where Blake and mighty Nelson fell
   Your manly hearts shall glow,
As ye sweep through the deep,
   While the stormy winds do blow!
While the battle rages loud and long
   And the stormy winds do blow.

Britannia needs no bulwarks,
   No towers along the steep;
Her march is o'er the mountain-waves,
   Her home is on the deep.
With thunders from her native oak
   She quells the floods below,
As they roar on the shore,
   When the stormy winds do blow!
When the battle rages loud and long,
   And the stormy winds do blow.

The meteor flag of England
   Shall yet terrific burn;
Till danger's troubled night depart
   And the star of peace return.
Then, then, ye ocean-warriors!
   Our song and feast shall flow
To the fame of your name,
   When the storm has ceased to blow!
When the fiery fight is heard no more,
   And the storm has ceased to blow.

Thomas Campbell

ON THIS DAY:

The Royal Navy fleet commanded by Nelson defeated the combined fleets of France and Spain off Cape Trafalgar in 1805.

Alfred Nobel (1833–1896), Swedish inventor who discovered and manufactured dynamite and endowed the Nobel prizes, was born.

The Guggenheim Museum in New York opened in 1959. The architect was Frank Lloyd Wright (1869–1959).

The Soldier Addresses his Body

I shall be mad if you get smashed about,
we've had good times together, you and I;
although you groused a bit when luck was out,
say a girl turned us down, or we went dry.

But there's a world of things we haven't done,
countries not seen, where people do strange things;
eat fish alive, and mimic in the sun
the solemn gestures of their stone-grey kings.

I've heard of forests that are dim at noon
where snakes and creepers wrestle all day long;
where vivid beasts grow pale with the full moon,
gibber and cry, and wail a mad old song;

because at the full moon the Hippogriff
with crinkled ivory snout and agate feet,
with his green eye will glare them cold and stiff
for the coward Wyvern to come down and eat.

Vodka and kvass, and bitter mountain wines
we've never drunk; nor snatched the bursting grapes
to pelt slim girls among Sicilian vines,
who'd flicker through the leaves, faint frolic shapes.

Yes, there's a world of things we've never done,
but it's a sweat to knock them into rhyme,
let's have a drink, and give the cards a run
and leave dull verse to the dull peaceful time.

Edgell Rickword

ON THIS DAY:

Edgell Rickword (1898–1982), critic and poet, was born.

In 1797 André-Jacques Garnerin (1769–1823) made the first parachute descent, from a balloon.

Seasons and Times

Awhile in the dead of the winter,
The wind hurries keen through the sunshine,
But finds no more leaves that may linger
On tree-boughs to strew on the ground.

Long streaks of bright snow-drift, bank-shaded,
Yet lie on the slopes, under hedges;
But still all the road out to Thorndon
Would not wet a shoe on the ground.

The days, though the cold seems to strengthen,
Outlengthen their span, and the evening
Seeks later and later its westing,
To cast its dim hue on the ground,

Till tree-heads shall thicken their shadow
With leaves of a glittering greenness,
And daisies shall fold up their blossoms
At evening, in dew on the ground;

And then, in the plum-warding garden,
Or shadowy orchard, the house-man
Shall smile at his fruit, really blushing,
Where sunheat shoots through on the ground.

What season do you feel the fairest –
The season of sowing or growing,
Or season of mowing and ripeness,
When hay may lie new on the ground?

And like you the glittering morning,
Or short-shaded noon, or the coming
Of slant-lighted evening, or moonlight,
When footsteps are few on the ground?

William Barnes

ON THIS DAY:
Douglas Jardine (1900–1958), captain of the England cricket team, was born.

October 24

Walking in Autumn

for Diana Lodge

We have overshot the wood.
The track has led us beyond trees
to the tarmac edge. Too late now
at dusk to return a different way,
hazarding barbed wire or an unknown bull.
We turn back onto the darkening path.
Pale under-leaves of whitebeam, alder
gleam at our feet like stranded fish
or Hansel's stones.
A wren, unseen, churrs alarm:
each tree drains to blackness.
Halfway now, we know
by the leaning crab-apple:
feet crunching into mud
the hard slippery yellow moons.
We hurry without reason
stumbling over roots and stones.
A night creature lurches, cries out,
crashes through brambles.
Skin shrinks inside our clothes;
almost we run
falling through darkness to the wood's end,
the gate into the sloping field.
Home is lights and woodsmoke, voices –
and, our breath caught, not trembling now,
a strange reluctance to enter within doors.

Frances Horovitz

ON THIS DAY:

Francis Palgrave (1824–1897), poet and editor of the *Golden Treasury*, died.

The United Nations became reality on this day in 1945 following the signing of the charter by 50 (of 51) original member states on 26th June 1945.

Concorde made its final flight in 2003.

413

A Carol of Agincourt

Deo gracias, Anglia,
Redde pro victoria.

Oure kinge went forth to Normandy
With grace and might of chivalry.
Ther God for him wrought mervelusly:
Wherefore Englonde may calle and cry.

He sette a sege, the sothe for to say,
To Harflu towne with ryal array:
That towne he wan and made affray
That Fraunce shall riwe till Domesday.

Than went oure kinge with alle his hoste
Thorwe Fraunce, for alle the Frenshe boste:
He spared, no drede, of lest ne moste,
Till he come to Agincourt coste.

Than, forsoth, that knight comely
In Agincourt feld he faught manly.
Thorw grace of God most mighty
He had bothe the felde and the victory.

There dukis and erlis, lorde and barone,
Where take and slaine, and that well sone,
And summe were ladde into Lundone
With joye and merthe and grete renone.

Now gracious God he save oure kinge,
His peple and alle his well-willinge:
Yef him gode life and gode ending,
That we with merthe mowe safely singe,

Anonymous

ON THIS DAY:

Henry V defeated the French at the battle of Agincourt in 1415, the most decisive victory of the Hundred Years War.

Aberdeen Train

Rubbing a glistening circle
on the steamed-up window I framed
a pheasant in a field of mist.
The sun was a great red thing somewhere low,
struggling with the milky scene. In the furrows
a piece of glass winked into life,
hypnotised the silly dandy; we
hooted past him with his head cocked,
contemplating a bottle-end.
And this was the last of October,
a Chinese moment in the Mearns.

Edwin Morgan

ON THIS DAY:

François Mitterrand (1916–1996) was born.

John Arden, writer and playwright, was born in 1930.

Andrew Motion, poet and Poet Laureate since 1999, was born in 1952.

Poem in October

It was my thirtieth year to heaven
Woke to my hearing from harbour and neighbour wood
   And the mussel pooled and the heron
         Priested shore
       The morning beckon
With water praying and call of seagull and rook
And the knock of sailing boats on the net webbed wall
      Myself to set foot
        That second
In the still sleeping town and set forth.

   My birthday began with the water-
Birds and the birds of the winged trees flying my name
   Above the farms and the white horses
        And I rose
      In the rainy autumn
And walked abroad in a shower of all my days.
High tide and the heron dived when I took the road
      Over the border
        And the gates
Of the town closed as the town awoke.

   A springful of larks in a rolling
Cloud and the roadside bushes brimming with whistling
    Blackbirds and the sun of October
        Summery
      On the hill's shoulder,
Here were fond climates and sweet singers suddenly
Come in the morning where I wandered and listened
      To the rain wringing
        Wind blow cold
In the wood faraway under me.

Pale rain over the dwindling harbour
And over the sea wet church the size of a snail
   With its horns through mist and the castle
    Brown as owls
   But all the gardens
Of spring and summer were blooming in the tall tales
Beyond the border and under the lark full cloud.
   There could I marvel
    My birthday
 Away but the weather turned around.

 It turned away from the blithe country
And down the other air and the blue altered sky
  Streamed again a wonder of summer
    With apples
   Pears and red currants
And I saw in the turning so clearly a child's
Forgotten mornings when he walked with his mother
   Through the parables
    Of sunlight
And the legends of the green chapels

 And the twice told fields of infancy
That his tears burned my cheeks and his heart moved in mine.
  These were the woods the river and sea
    Where a boy
   In the listening
Summertime of the dead whispered the truth of his joy
To the trees and the stones and the fish in the tide.
   And the mystery
    Sang alive
 Still in the water and singingbirds.

And there could I marvel my birthday
Away but the weather turned around. And the true
Joy of the long dead child sang burning
In the sun.
It was my thirtieth
Year to heaven stood there then in the summer noon
Though the town below lay leaved with October blood.
O may my heart's truth
Still be sung
On this high hill in a year's turning.

Dylan Thomas

ON THIS DAY:

Dylan Thomas (1914–1953), poet, was born.

James Cook (1728–1779), explorer who discovered Botany Bay, was born.

Sylvia Plath (1932–1963), poet and wife of Ted Hughes (1930–1998), was born.

October 28

The New Colossus

Not like the brazen giant of Greek fame,
With conquering limbs astride from land to land;
Here at our sea-washed, sunset gates shall stand
A mighty woman with a torch, whose flame
Is the imprisoned lightning, and her name
Mother of Exiles. From her beacon-hand
Glows world-wide welcome; her mild eyes command
The air-bridged harbor that twin cities frame.
'Keep, ancient lands, your storied pomp!' cries she
With silent lips. 'Give me your tired, your poor,
Your huddled masses yearning to breathe free,
The wretched refuse of your teeming shore.
Send these, the homeless, tempest-tost to me,
I lift my lamp beside the golden door!'

Emma Lazarus

ON THIS DAY:

The Statue of Liberty was dedicated by President Grover Cleveland (1837–1908) in 1886. The statue was a gift from France to the United States of America. *The New Colossus* was recited at the dedication.

The oldest American university, Harvard, was founded in 1636.

Ted Hughes (1930–1998), Poet Laureate, died.

October 29

Late Lamented Fame of the
Giant City of New York

I

Who is there still remembers
The fame of the giant city of New York
In the decade after the Great War?

II

What a melting pot was America in those days – celebrated by poets!
God's own country!
Invoked just by the initials of its names:
U.S.A.
Like an unmistakable childhood friend whom everyone knows.

III

This inexhaustible melting pot, so it was said
Received everything that fell into it and converted it
Within twice two weeks into something identifiable.
All races which landed on this zestful continent
Eagerly abandoned themselves and forgot their profoundest characteristics
Like bad habits
In order to become
As quickly as possible like those who were so much at home there.
And they received them with careless generosity as if they were utterly different
(Differing only through the difference of their miserable existences).
Like a good leaven they feared no
Mass of dough, however enormous: they knew
They would penetrate everything.
What fame! What a century!

IV

Ah, those voices of their women coming from the sound-boxes!
Thus they sang (take good care of those records!) in the golden age.
Harmony of the evening waters at Miami!
Uncontainable gaiety of the generations driving fast over unending roads!

420

Mighty lamentations of women singing, faithfully mourning
Broad-chested men, but ever surrounded by
Broad-chested men!

V

They collected whole parks of rare human specimens
Fed them scientifically, bathed them and weighed them
So that their incomparable gestures might be perpetuated in photographs
For all who came after.

VI

They raised up their gigantic buildings with incomparable waste
Of the best human material. Quite openly, before the whole world
They squeezed from their workers all that was in them
Fired rifles into the coal mines and threw their used-up bones and
Exhausted muscles on the streets with
Good-natured laughter.
But in sporting acknowledgement they reported
The same rough obstinacy in workers on strike
With homeric exaggeration.

VII

Poverty was considered despicable there.
In the films of this blessed nation
Men down on their luck, on seeing the homes of the poor (which included
   pianos and leather couches)
Killed themselves out of hand.

VIII

What fame! What a century!
Oh we too demanded such broad-gauge overcoats of rough material
With the padded shoulders which make men so broad
That three of them fill the entire sidewalk.
We too sought to brake our gestures
Thrust our hands slowly into our pockets and work ourselves slowly
Out of the armchairs in which we had reclined (as for all eternity)
Like a whole State turning over

421

And we too stuffed our mouths full of chewing gum (Beechnut)
Which was supposed eventually to push forward the jawbone
And sat with jaws ruminating as in endless greed.
To our faces too we wished to lend that feared impenetrability
Of the *poker-faced man* who propounded himself to his fellow-citizens
As an insoluble riddle.
We too perpetually smiled, as if before or after a good piece of business
Which is the proof of a well-ordered digestion.
We too liked to slap our companions (all of them future customers)
On arm and thigh and between the shoulder-blades
Testing how to get such fellows into our hands
By the same caressing or grabbing motions as for dogs.
So we imitated this renowned race of men who seemed destined
To rule the world by helping it to progress.

IX

What confidence! What an inspiration!
Those machine rooms: the biggest in the world!
The car factories campaigned for an increase in the birthrate: they had
    started making cars (on hire purchase)
For the unborn. Whoever threw away
Practically unused clothing (but so
That it rotted at once, preferably in quicklime)
Was paid a bonus. Those bridges
Which linked flourishing land with flourishing land! Endless!
The longest in the world! Those skyscrapers –
The men who piled their stones so high
That they towered over all, anxiously watched from their summits the
    new buildings
Springing up from the ground, soon to overtower
Their own mammoth size.
(Some were beginning to fear that the growth of such cities
Could no longer be stopped, that they would have to finish their days
With twenty storeys of other cities above them
And would be stacked in coffins which would be buried
One on top of the other.)

X

But apart from that: what confidence! Even the dead
Were made up and given a cosy smile
(These are characteristics I am setting down from memory; others
I have forgotten) for not even those who had got away
Were allowed to be without hope.

XI

What people they were! Their boxers the strongest!
Their inventors the most practical! Their trains the fastest!
And also the most crowded!
And it all looked like lasting a thousand years
For the people of the city of New York put it about themselves:
That their city was built on the rock and hence
Indestructible.

XII

Truly their whole system of communal life was beyond compare.
What fame! What a century!

XIII

Admittedly that century lasted
A bare eight years.

XIV

For one day there ran through the world the rumour of strange collapses
On a famous continent, and its banknotes, hoarded only yesterday
Were rejected in disgust like rotten stinking fish.

XV

Today, when the word has gone round
That these people are bankrupt
We on the other continents (which are indeed bankrupt as well)
See many things differently and, so we think, more clearly.

XVI

What of the skyscrapers?
We observe them more coolly.
What contemptible hovels skyscrapers are when they no longer yield rents!
Rising so high, so full of poverty? Touching the clouds, full of debt?
What of the railroad trains?
In the railroad trains, which resemble hotels on wheels, they say
Often nobody lives.
He travels nowhere
With incomparable rapidity.
What of the bridges? The longest in the world, they now link
Scrapheap with scrapheap.
And what of the people?

XVII

They still make up, we hear, but now
It's to grab a job. Twenty-two year old girls
Sniff cocaine now before setting out
To capture a place at a typewriter.
Desperate parents inject poison into their daughters' thighs
To make them look red hot.

XVIII

Gramophone records are still sold, not many of course
But what do they tell us, these cows who have not learned
To sing? What
Is the sense of these songs? What have they really
Been singing to us all these years long?
Why do we now dislike these once celebrated voices?
Why
Do these photos of cities no longer make the slightest impression on us?
Because word has gone round
That these people are bankrupt.

XIX

For their machines, it is said, lie in huge heaps (the biggest in the world)
And rust
Like the machines of the Old World (in smaller heaps).

XX

World championships are still contested before a few spectators who have
    absent-mindedly stayed in their places:
Each time the strongest competitor
Stands no chance against the mysterious law
That drives people away from shops stocked to bursting.

XXI

Clutching their smile (but nothing else now) the retired world champions
Stand in the way of the last few streetcars left running.
Three of these broad-gauge fellows fill the sidewalk, but
What will fill *them* before nightfall?
The padding warms only the shoulders of those who in interminable columns
Hurry day and night through the empty canyons of lifeless stonepiles.
Their gestures are slow, like those of hungry and enfeebled beasts.
Like a whole State turning over
They work themselves slowly out of the gutters in which they seem to be
    lying as for all eternity.
Their confidence, it is said
Is still there; it is based on the hope that
Tomorrow the rain will fall upwards.

XXII

But some, we hear, can still find jobs: in those places
Where whole waggon-loads of wheat are being shovelled into the ocean
Called pacific.
And those who spend their nights on benches are, we hear, apt to
Think quite impermissible thoughts as they see
Those empty skyscrapers before dropping off to sleep.

XXIII

What a bankruptcy! How
Great a fame has departed! What a discovery:
That their system of communal life displays
The same miserable flaw as that of
More modest people.

Bertolt Brecht

ON THIS DAY:

Panic selling on the New York Stock Exchange precipitated the Wall Street Crash in 1929. Between 29th October and 13th November, $30 billion disappeared from the US economy. The greatest financial crisis in US history ushered in the Great Depression and a world economic crisis.

Luke Hansard (1752–1828), printer to the House of Commons, died. *Hansard* is produced daily when Parliament is in session.

Muhammad Ali at the Ringside, 1985

The arena is darkened. A feast of blood
Will follow duly; the spotlights have been borrowed
For a while. These ringside prances
Merely serve to whet the appetite. Gladiators,
Clad tonight in formal mufti, customized,
Milk recognition, savor the night-off, show-off
Rites. Ill fitted in this voyeur company,
The desperate arm wrap of the tiring heart
Gives place to social hugs, the slow count
One to ten to a snappy 'Give me five!'
Toothpaste grins replace the death-mask
Rubber gumshield grimaces. Promiscuous
Peck-a-cheek supplants the maestro's peek-a-boo.
The roped arena waits; an umpire tests the floor,
Tests whiplash boundaries of the rope.
The gallant's exhibition rounds possess
These foreplay moments. Gloves in silk-white sheen
Rout lint and leather. Paco Rabanne rules the air.
A tight-arsed soubriette checks her placard smile
To sign the rounds for blood and gore.

Eased from the navel of Bitch-Mother Fame
A microphone, neck-ruffed silver filigree – as one
Who would usurp the victor's garland – stabs the air
For instant prophecies. In cosy insulation, bathed
In teleglow, distant homes have built
Their own vicarious rings – the forecast claimed
Four million viewers on the cable deal alone;
Much 'bread' was loaded on the scales
At weighing hour – till scores are settled. One
Will leave the fickle womb tonight
Smeared in combat fluids, a broken fetus.
The other, toned in fire, a dogged phoenix
Oblivious of the slow countdown of inner hurts
Will thrust his leaden fists in air
Night prince of the world of dreams.

One sits still. His silence is a dying count.
At last the lens acknowledges the tested
Hulk that dominates, even in repose
The giddy rounds of furs and diamond pins.
A brief salute – the camera is kind,
Discreetly pans, and masks the doubletalk
Of medicine men – 'Has the syndrome
But not the consequence.' Promoters, handlers
It's time to throw in the towel – Parkinson's
Polysyllables have failed to tease a rhyme
From the once nimble Louisville Lips.

The camera flees, distressed. But not before
The fire of battle flashes in those eyes
Rekindled by the moment's urge to center stage.
He rules the night space even now, bestrides
The treacherous domain with thighs of bronze,
A dancing mural of delights. Oh Ali! Ale-e-e…

What music hurts the massive head tonight, Ali!
The drums, the tins cans, the guitars and *mbira* of Zaire?
Aa-lee! Aa-lee! Aa-lee *Bomaye! Bomaye!*
The Rumble in the Jungle? Beauty and the Beast?
Roll call of Bum-a-Month? The rope-a-dope?
The Thrilla in Manila? – Ah-lee! Ah-lee!
'The closest thing to death,' you said. Was that
The greatest, saddest prophesy of all? Oh, Ali!

Black tarantula whose antics hypnotize the foe!
Butterfly sideslipping death from rocket probes.
Bee whose sting, unsheathed, picks the teeth
Of the raging hippopotamus, then fans
The jaw's convergence with its flighty wings.
Needle that threads the snapping fangs
Of crocodiles, knots the tusks of elephants
On rampage. Cricket that claps and chirrups
Round the flailing horn of the rhinoceros,

Then shuffles, does a bugalloo, tap-dances on its tip.
Space that yields, then drowns the intruder
In showers of sparks – oh Ali! Ali!
Esu with faces turned to all four compass points
Astride a weather vane; they sought to trap him,
Slapped the wind each time. He brings a message –
All know the messenger, the neighbourhood is roused –

Yet no one sees his face, he waits for no reply,
Only that combination three-four calling card,
The wasp-tail legend: I've been here and gone.
Mortar that goads the pestle: Do you call that
Pounding? The yam is not yet smooth –
Pound, dope, pound! When I have eaten the yam,
I'll chew the fibre that once called itself
A pestle! Warrior who said, 'I will not fight,'
And proved a prophet's call to arms against a war.
Cassius Marcellus, Warrior, Muhammad Prophet,
Flesh is clay, all, all too brittle mould.
The bout is over. Frayed and split and autographed,
The gloves are hung up in the Hall of Fame –
Still loaded, even from that first blaze of gold
And glory. Awed multitudes will gaze,
New questers feast on these mementos
And from their shell-shocked remnants
Reinvoke the spell. But the sorcerer is gone,
The lion withdrawn to a lair of time and space
Inaccessible as the sacred lining of a crown
When kings were kings, and lords of rhyme and pace.
The enchantment is over but the spell remains.

Wole Soyinka

ON THIS DAY:

Muhammad Ali beat George Foreman to regain the world heavyweight boxing title in 1974 in Kinshasa, Zaire.

Jean Henri Dunant (1828–1910), founder of the International Red Cross, died.

Autumn Fruits

Obedient to the breeze and beating ray,
From the deep-loaded bough a mellow shower
Incessant melts away. The juicy pear
Lies in a soft profusion scattered round.
A various sweetness swells the gentle race,
By Nature's all-refining hand prepared,
Of tempered sun, and water, earth, and air,
In ever-changing composition mixed.
Such, falling frequent through the chiller night,
The fragrant stores, the wide-projected heaps
Of apples, which the lusty-handed year
Innumerous o'er the blushing orchard shakes.
A various spirit, fresh, delicious, keen,
Dwells in their gelid pores, and active points
The piercing cider for the thirsty tongue –
Thy native theme, and boon inspirer too,
Phillips, Pomona's bard! the second thou
Who nobly durst in rhyme-unfettered verse
With British freedom sing the British song –
How from Silurian vats high-sparkling wines
Foam in transparent floods, some strong to cheer
The wintry revels of the labouring hind,
And tasteful some to cool the summer hours.

James Thomson

ON THIS DAY:

Martin Luther (1483–1546) published his 95 Theses on indulgences by nailing them to the door of the Castle Church, Wittenberg in 1517.

John Keats (1795–1821), poet, was born.

NOVEMBER

November 1

Blunden's Beech

I named it Blunden's Beech; and no one knew
That this – of local beeches – was the best.
Remembering lines by Clare, I'd sometimes rest
Contentful on the cushioned moss that grew
Between its roots. Finches, a flitting crew,
Chirped their concerns. Wiltshire, from east to west
Contained my tree. And Edmund never guessed
How he was there with me till dusk and dew.

Thus, fancy-free from ownership and claim,
The mind can make its legends live and sing
And grow to be the genius of some place.
And thus, where sylvan shadows held a name,
The thought of Poetry will dwell, and bring
To summer's idyll an unheeded grace.

Siegfried Sassoon

ON THIS DAY:

Edmund Blunden (1896–1974), poet, was born. Blunden and Siegfried Sassoon (1886–1967) were lifelong friends and shared a passion for the game of cricket. They first met when Blunden sent Sassoon a collection of his verse whilst Sassoon was Literary Editor at the *Daily Herald.*

Today is All Saints' Day, the festival on which there is a general celebration of the saints, instituted early in the 7th century by Pope Boniface IV (Pope 608–615).

In 1512 the public were admitted into the Sistine Chapel and saw for the first time Michelangelo's (1475–1564) frescoes on the ceiling.

President John Adams (1735–1826), President of the United States 1797–1801, became the first occupant of the White House when he moved there in 1800. The White House was commissioned by George Washington, who oversaw construction but died before it was completed, and the architect was James Hoban.

W. H. Smith opened its first bookstall at Euston station in 1848.

Going, Going

I thought it would last my time –
The sense that, beyond the town,
There would always be fields and farms,
Where the village louts could climb
Such trees as were not cut down;
I knew there'd be false alarms

In the papers about old streets
And split-level shopping, but some
Have always been left so far;
And when the old parts retreat
As the bleak high-risers come
We can always escape in the car.

Things are tougher than we are, just
As earth will always respond
However we mess it about;
Chuck filth in the sea, if you must:
The tides will be clean beyond.
–But what do I feel now? Doubt?

Or age, simply? The crowd
Is young in the M1 café;
Their kids are screaming for more –
More houses, more parking allowed,
More caravan sites, more pay:
On the Business Page, a score

Of spectacled grins approve
Some takeover bid that entails
Five per cent profit (and ten
Per cent more in the estuaries): move
Your works to the unspoilt dales
(Grey area grants)! And when

You try to get near the sea
In summer...
                    It seems, just now,
To be happening so very fast;
Despite all the land left free
For the first time I feel somehow
That it isn't going to last,

That before I snuff it, the whole
Boiling will be bricked in
Except for the tourist parts –
First slum of Europe: a role
It won't be so hard to win,
With a cast of crooks and tarts.

And that will be England gone,
The shadows, the meadows, the lanes,
The guildhalls, the carved choirs.
There'll be books; it will linger on
In galleries; but all that remains
For us will be concrete and tyres.

Most things are never meant.
This won't be, most likely: but greeds
And garbage are too thick-strewn
To be swept up now, or invent
Excuses that make them all needs.
I just think it will happen, soon.

Philip Larkin

ON THIS DAY:

The M1 motorway, linking London and the north of England, was officially opened in 1959.

Today is All Souls' Day, the festival on which prayers are offered for the souls of the 'faithful departed'. It is said to have been instituted at Cluny at the end of the 10th century.

The *Daily Mirror* was launched in 1903.

In 1936 the BBC transmitted its first regular television service from Alexandra Palace.

Channel 4 Television was launched in 1982.

November

He has hanged himself – the Sun.
    He dangles
A scarecrow in thin air.

He is dead for love – the Sun,
    He who in forest tangles
Wooed all things fair

That great lover – the Sun,
    Now spangles
The wood with blood-stains.

He has hanged himself – the Sun.
    How thin he dangles
In these gray rains!

F. W. Harvey

ON THIS DAY:

Karl Baedeker (1801–1859), founder of the Baedeker publishing company specialising in guidebooks for tourists, was born.

In 1977 industrial action by the trade unions caused a blackout at the State Opening of Parliament. Prime Minister James Callaghan (1912–2005) warned that there would be further disruption over the winter months as a result of action by the unions.

November 4

Futility

Move him into the sun –
Gently its touch awoke him once,
At home, whispering of fields unsown.
Always it woke him, even in France,
Until this morning and this snow.
If anything might rouse him now
The kind old sun will know.

Think how it wakes the seeds, –
Woke, once, the clays of a cold star.
Are limbs, so dear-achieved, are sides,
Full-nerved – still warm – too hard to stir?
Was it for this the clay grew tall?
– O what made fatuous sunbeams toil
To break earth's sleep at all?

Wilfred Owen

ON THIS DAY:

Wilfred Owen (1893–1918), poet and soldier, died at Sambre Canal, France. A week later the Armistice was concluded and the First World War came to an end.

Howard Carter's (1874–1939) archaeological endeavours were rewarded when the steps to Tutan-khamun's tomb were discovered in 1922.

Charles Causley (1917–2003), poet, died.

The Burning of the Leaves

Now is the time for the burning of the leaves.
They go to the fire; the nostril pricks with smoke
Wandering slowly into the weeping mist.
Brittle and blotched, ragged and rotten sheaves!
A flame seizes the smouldering ruin, and bites
On stubborn stalks that crackle as they resist.

The last hollyhock's fallen tower is dust:
All the spices of June are a bitter reek,
All the extravagant riches spent and mean.
All burns! the reddest rose is a ghost.
Sparks whirl up, to expire in the mist: the wild
Fingers of fire are making corruption clean.

Now is the time for stripping the spirit bare,
Time for the burning of days ended and done,
Idle solace of things that have gone before,
Rootless hope and fruitless desire are there:
Let them go to the fire with never a look behind.
That world that was ours is a world that is ours no more.

They will come again, the leaf and the flower, to arise
From squalor of rottenness into the old splendour,
And magical scents to a wondering memory bring;
The same glory, to shine upon different eyes.
Earth cares for her own ruins, naught for ours.
Nothing is certain, only the certain spring.

Laurence Binyon

ON THIS DAY:

In 1605 Guy Fawkes and his co-conspirators were arrested following an attempt to blow up the Houses of Parliament. Their plans were discovered after one of the group warned a relative to stay away from the opening of Parliament. The conspirators were arrested on their return to Parliament to set the fuses alight. The Gunpowder Plot was motivated by the treatment of Catholics under the Protestant regime of James I.

The Russians were defeated by British and French troops at the battle of Inkerman in 1854.

Vivien Leigh (1913–1967), actress, and second wife of Lord Laurence Olivier (1907–1989), was born.

Lester Piggott, jockey and nine times winner of the Derby, was born in 1935.

The Cries of London

Here's fine rosemary, sage, and thyme
Come buy my ground ivy.
Here's fetherfew, gilliflowers and rue.
Come buy my knotted marjorum, ho!
Come buy my mint, my fine green mint.
Here's fine lavender for your cloaths.
Here's parsley and winter-savory,
And hearts-ease, which all do choose.
Here's balm and hissop, and cinquefoil,
All fine herbs, it is well known.
    Let none despise the merry, merry cries
    Of famous London-town!

Here's fine herrings, eight a groat.
Hot codlins, pies and tarts.
New mackerel! have to sell.
Come buy my Wellfleet oysters, ho!
Come buy my whitings fine and new.
Wives, shall I mend your husbands horns?
I'll grind your knives to please your wives,
And very nicely cut your corns.
Maids, have you any hair to sell,
Either flaxen, black, or brown?
    Let none despise the merry, merry cries
    Of famous London-town!

Anonymous

ON THIS DAY:
Charles Henry Dow (1857–1902), financial journalist, was born.
In 1869 Queen Victoria opened Blackfriars Bridge in London.
In 1999 Australia rejected a proposal to become a republic.

The Going

Why did you give no hint that night
That quickly after the morrow's dawn,
And calmly, as if indifferent quite,
You would close your term here, up and be gone
      Where I could not follow
      With wing of swallow
To gain one glimpse of you ever anon!

      Never to bid good-bye,
      Or lip me the softest call,
Or utter a wish for a word, while I
Saw morning harden upon the wall,
      Unmoved, unknowing
      That your great going
Had place that moment, and altered all.

Why do you make me leave the house
And think for a breath it is you I see
At the end of the alley of bending boughs
Where so often at dusk you used to be;
      Till in darkening dankness
      The yawning blankness
Of the perspective sickens me!

      You were she who abode
      By those red-veined rocks far West,
You were the swan-necked one who rode
Along the beetling Beeny Crest,
      And, reining nigh me,
      Would muse and eye me,
While Life unrolled us its very best.

Why, then, latterly did we not speak,
Did we not think of those days long dead,
And ere your vanishing strive to seek
That time's renewal? We might have said,
    'In this bright spring weather
    We'll visit together
Those places that once we visited.'

    Well, well! All's past amend,
    Unchangeable. It must go.
I seem but a dead man held on end
To sink down soon... O you could not know
    That such swift fleeing
    No soul foreseeing –
Not even I – would undo me so!

Thomas Hardy

ON THIS DAY:

Thomas Hardy's (1840–1928) first wife, Emma Gifford, died on this day in 1912. It has been widely recorded that Hardy was deeply shocked at her sudden death (although she had suffered with poor health for some time) and he wrote numerous poems after her death, including 'The Going' and 'The Voice'.

November 8

'I am Like a Slip of Comet…'

– I am like a slip of comet,
Scarce worth discovery, in some corner seen
Bridging the slender difference of two stars,
Come out of space, or suddenly engender'd
By heady elements, for no man knows;
But when she sights the sun she grows and sizes
And spins her skirts out, while her central star
Shakes its cocooning mists; and so she comes
To fields of light; millions of travelling rays
Pierce her; she hangs upon the flame-cased sun,
And sucks the light as full as Gideon's fleece:
But then her tether calls her; she falls off,
And as she dwindles shreds her smock of gold
Between the sistering planets, till she comes
To single Saturn, last and solitary;
And then she goes out into the cavernous dark.
So I go out: my little sweet is done:
I have drawn heat from this contagious sun:
To not ungentle death now forth I run.

Gerard Manley Hopkins

A New Song on the Birth of the Prince of Wales

There's a pretty fuss and bother both in country and in town,
Since we have got a present, and an heir unto the Crown,
A little Prince of Wales so charming and so sly,
And the ladies shout with wonder, What a pretty little boy!

He must have a little musket, a trumpet and a kite,
A little penny rattle, and silver sword so bright,
A little cap and feather with scarlet coat so smart,
And a pretty little hobby horse to ride about the park.

Prince Albert he will often take the young Prince on his lap,
And fondle him so lovingly, while he stirs about the pap,
He will pin on his flannel before he takes his nap,
Then dress him out so stylish with his little clouts and cap.

He must have a dandy suit to strut about the town,
John Bull must rake together six or seven thousand pound,
You'd laugh to see his daddy, at night he homeward runs,
With some peppermint or lollipops, sweet cakes and sugar plums.

He will want a little fiddle, and a little German flute,
A little pair of stockings and a pretty pair of boots,
With a handsome pair of spurs, and a golden headed cane,
And a stick of barley sugar, as long as Drury Lane.

An old maid ran through the palace, which did the nobs surprize,
Bawling out, he's got his daddy's mouth, his mammy's nose and eyes,
He will be as like his daddy as a frigate to a ship,
If he'd only got mustachios upon his upper lip.

Now to get these little niceties the taxes must be rose,
For the little Prince of Wales wants so many suits of clothes,
So they must tax the frying pan, the windows and the doors,
The bedsteads and the tables, kitchen pokers, and the floors.

Anonymous

ON THIS DAY:

Prince Albert Edward (later King Edward VII), first son and second child of Queen Victoria and Prince Albert, was born in 1841.

November 10

Autumn Idleness

This sunlight shames November where he grieves
   In dead red leaves, and will not let him shun
    The day, though bough with bough be over-run.
But with a blessing every glade receives
High salutation; while from hillock-eaves
    The deer gaze calling, dappled white and dun,
     As if, being foresters of old, the sun
Had marked them with the shade of forest-leaves.

Here dawn to-day unveiled her magic glass;
    Here noon now gives the thirst and takes the dew;
Till eve bring rest when other good things pass.
    And here the lost hours the lost hours renew
While I still lead my shadow o'er the grass,
    Nor know, for longing, that which I should do.

Dante Gabriel Rossetti

ON THIS DAY:

Martin Luther (1483–1546), Protestant theologian and reformer, was born.

George II was born in 1683.

In 1960, after conclusion of the obscenity trial at the Old Bailey, of *Lady Chatterley's Lover* by D. H. Lawrence, the book's first print run, 200,000 copies, sold out in the day. Publication of the book had been banned for 30 years.

November 11

Armistice Day

I stood with three comrades in Parliament Square
November her freights of grey fire unloading,
No sound from the city upon the pale air,
Above us the sea-bell eleven exploding.

Down by the bands and the burning memorial
Beats all the brass in a royal array,
But at our end we are not so sartorial:
Out of (as usual) the rig of the day.

Starry is wearing a split pusser's flannel
Rubbed, as he is, by the regular tide;
Oxo the ducks that he ditched in the Channel
In June, 1940 (when he was inside).

Kitty recalls his abandon-ship station,
Running below at the Old Man's salute
And (with a deck-watch) going down for duration
Wearing his oppo's pneumonia-suit.

Comrades, for you the black captain of carracks
Writes in Whitehall his appalling decisions,
But as was often the case in the Barracks
Several ratings are not at Divisions.

Into my eyes the stiff sea-horses stare,
Over my head sweeps the sun like a swan.
As I stand alone in Parliament Square
A cold bugle calls, and the city moves on.

Charles Causley

ON THIS DAY:

In 1918, the First World War came to an end when the German Armies surrendered to Marshall Foch in a railway carriage in the Forest of Compiègne.

Today is the feast day of St Martin of Tours, the patron saint of soldiers.

In 1920, the Cenotaph memorial in Whitehall was unveiled by George V.

Sir Vivian Fuchs (1908–1999), explorer and geologist who completed the first overland crossing of Antarctica in March 1958, died.

The Cold Earth Slept Below

The cold earth slept below,
  Above the cold sky shone;
And all around, with a chilling sound,
  From caves of ice and fields of snow,
  The breath of night like death did flow
  Beneath the sinking moon.

The wintry hedge was black,
  The green grass was not seen,
The birds did rest on the bare thorn's breast,
  Whose roots, beside the pathway track,
  Had bound their folds o'er many a crack
  Which the frost had made between.

Thine eyes glowed in the glare
  Of the moon's dying light;
As a fen-fire's beam on a sluggish stream
  Gleams dimly, so the moon shone there,
  And it yellowed the strings of thy raven hair,
  That shook in the wind of night.

The moon made thy lips pale, beloved –
  The wind made thy bosom chill –
The night did shed on thy dear head
  Its frozen dew, and thou didst lie
  Where the bitter breath of the naked sky
  Might visit thee at will.

Percy Bysshe Shelley

ON THIS DAY:

Auguste Rodin (1840–1917), sculptor, was born.

The *Tirpitz*, the last of Germany's major battleships, was sunk by three RAF Lancaster bombers in 1944 in the fjord waters of Norway.

Winston Churchill (1874–1965) received the freedom of the city of Paris in 1944.

Armistice

It is finished. The enormous dust-cloud over Europe
Lifts like a million swallows; and a light,
Drifting in craters, touches the quiet dead.

Now, at the bugle's hour, before the blood
Cakes in a clean wind on their marble faces,
Making them monuments; before the sun,

Hung like a medal on the smoky noon,
Whitens the bone that feeds the earth; before
Wheat-ear springs green, again, in the green spring

And they are bread in the bodies of the young:
Be strong to remember how the bread died, screaming;
Gangrene was corn, and monuments went mad.

Paul Dehn

ON THIS DAY:
St Augustine (354–430), author of *Confessions* and *City of God*, was born.
Edward III was born in 1312.
John Moore (1761–1809), victor of Corunna, was born.
Robert Louis Stevenson (1850–1894), novelist, was born.

From Harvest to January

The hay has long been built into the stack
And now the grain; anon the hunter's moon
Shall wax and wane in cooler skies, and soon
Again re-orb'd, speed on her wonted track,
To spend her snowy light upon the rack
Of dark November, while her brother Sun
Shall get up later for his eight-hours' run
In that cold section of the Zodiac:
Far from the Lion, from the Virgin far!
Then onward through the last dim month shall go
The two great lights, to where the kalendar
Splits the mid-winter; and the feathery snow
Ushering another spring, with falling flakes
Shall nurse the soil for next year's scythes and rakes.

Charles Turner

ON THIS DAY:

Claude Monet (1840–1926), French impressionist painter, was born.

In 1940 German bombers destroyed most of the city of Coventry, and many hundreds of people lost their lives.

Harold Larwood (1904–1995), English cricketer who participated in the 'bodyline' cricket tour of Australia in 1932–1933 under the captaincy of Douglas Jardine (1900–1958), was born.

The Thunder Mutters

The thunder mutters louder and more loud
With quicker motion hay folks ply the rake
Ready to burst slow sails the pitch black cloud
And all the gang a bigger haycock make
To sit beneath – the woodland winds awake
The drops so large wet all thro' in an hour
A tiney flood runs down the leaning rake
In the sweet hay yet dry the hay folks cower
And some beneath the wagon shun the shower.

John Clare

ON THIS DAY:

William Pitt the Elder (1708–1778) was born.

Sir William Herschel (1738–1822), astronomer, was born.

In 1899 Winston Churchill (1874–1965) was captured whilst working as a journalist during the Boer War. He later escaped.

Aneurin Bevan (1897–1960), Minister of Health in Clement Attlee's post-war Labour government who introduced the National Health Service in 1948, was born.

A Night in November

I marked when the weather changed,
And the panes began to quake,
And the winds rose up and ranged,
That night, lying half-awake.

Dead leaves blew into my room,
And alighted upon my bed,
And a tree declared to the gloom
Its sorrow that they were shed.

One leaf of them touched my hand,
And I thought that it was you
There stood as you used to stand,
And saying at last you knew!

Thomas Hardy

ON THIS DAY:

Tiberius (42BC–AD 37), second Roman emperor, was born.

John Walter (?–1812), printer and publisher of *The Times* newspaper, died.

The musical *The Sound of Music* opened on Broadway, New York in 1959.

The Wild Swans at Coole

The trees are in their autumn beauty,
The woodland paths are dry,
Under the October twilight the water
Mirrors a still sky;
Upon the brimming water among the stones
Are nine-and-fifty swans.

The nineteenth autumn has come upon me
Since I first made my count;
I saw, before I had well finished,
All suddenly mount
And scatter wheeling in great broken rings
Upon their clamorous wings.

I have looked upon those brilliant creatures,
And now my heart is sore.
All's changed since I, hearing at twilight,
The first time on this shore,
The bell-beat of their wings above my head,
Trod with a lighter tread.

Unwearied still, lover by lover,
They paddle in the cold
Companionable streams or climb the air;
Their hearts have not grown old;
Passion or conquest, wander where they will,
Attend upon them still.

But now they drift on the still water,
Mysterious, beautiful;
Among what rushes will they build,
By what lake's edge or pool
Delight men's eyes when I awake some day
To find they have flown away?

W. B. Yeats

ON THIS DAY:

In 1558 Elizabeth I acceded to the throne.

In 1603 Sir Walter Raleigh (1552–1618) stood trial for treason against Elizabeth I.

November 18

Autumn

The thistledown's flying Though the winds are all still
On the green grass now lying Now mounting the hill
The spring from the fountain Now boils like a pot
Through stones past the counting It bubbles red-hot

The ground parched and cracked is Like overbaked bread
The greensward all wrecked is Bents dried up and dead
The fallow fields glitter Like water indeed
And gossamers twitter Flung from weed unto weed

Hill-tops like hot iron Glitter hot i' the sun,
And the Rivers we're eying Burn to gold as they run
Burning hot is the ground Liquid gold is the air
Whoever looks round Sees Eternity there.

John Clare

ON THIS DAY:

St Peter's Basilica, Rome was consecrated by Pope Urban VIII (1568–1644) in 1626.

The State Funeral of the Duke of Wellington (1769–1852) took place.

W. S. Gilbert (1836–1911), librettist and playwright, was born.

When you see millions of the mouthless dead

When you see millions of the mouthless dead
Across your dreams in pale battalions go,
Say not soft things as other men have said,
That you'll remember. For you need not so.
Give them not praise. For, deaf, how should they know
It is not curses heaped on each gashed head?
Nor tears. Their blind eyes see not your tears flow.
Nor honour. It is easy to be dead.
Say only this, 'They are dead.' Then add thereto,
'Yet many a better one has died before.'
Then, scanning all the o'ercrowded mass, should you
Perceive one face that you loved heretofore,
It is a spook. None wears the face you knew.
Great death has made all his for evermore.

Charles Hamilton Sorley

ON THIS DAY:

In 1918 the British Government issued estimated casualty figures for the First World War. The estimates showed that one million service personnel were killed and two million suffered injuries.

Lines written in Kensington Gardens

In this lone, open glade I lie,
Screen'd by deep boughs on either hand;
And at its end, to stay the eye,
Those black-crown'd, red-boled pine trees stand!

Birds here make song, each bird has his,
Across the girdling city's hum.
How green under the boughs it is!
How thick the tremulous sheep-cries come!

Sometimes a child will cross the glade
To take his nurse his broken toy;
Sometimes a thrush flit overhead
Deep in her unknown day's employ.

Here at my feet what wonders pass,
What endless, active life is here!
What blowing daisies, fragrant grass!
An air-stirr'd forest, fresh and clear.

Scarce fresher is the mountain-sod
Where the tired angler lies, stretch'd out,
And, eased of basket and of rod,
Counts his day's spoil, the spotted trout.

In the huge world, which roars hard by,
Be others happy if they can!
But in my helpless cradle I
Was breathed on by the rural Pan.

I, on men's impious uproar hurl'd,
Think often, as I hear them rave,
That peace has left the upper world
And now keeps only in the grave.

Yet here is peace for ever new!
When I who watch them am away,
Still all things in this glade go through
The changes of their quiet day.

Then to their happy rest they pass!
The flowers upclose, the birds are fed,
The night comes down upon the grass,
The child sleeps warmly in his bed.

Calm soul of all things! make it mine
To feel, amid the city's jar,
That there abides a peace of thine,
Man did not make, and cannot mar.

The will to neither strive nor cry,
The power to feel with others give!
Calm, calm me more! nor let me die
Before I have begun to live.

Matthew Arnold

November 21

Extempore Effusion upon the Death of James Hogg

When first, descending from the moorlands,
I saw the Stream of Yarrow glide
Along a bare and open valley,
The Ettrick Shepherd was my guide.

When last along its banks I wandered,
Through groves that had begun to shed
Their golden leaves upon the pathways,
My steps the Border-minstrel led.

The mighty Minstrel breathes no longer,
'Mid mouldering ruins low he lies;
And death upon the braes of Yarrow,
Has closed the Shepherd-poet's eyes:

Nor has the rolling year twice measured,
From sign to sign, its steadfast course,
Since every mortal power of Coleridge
Was frozen at its marvellous source;

The rapt One, of the godlike forehead,
The heaven-eyed creature sleeps in earth:
And Lamb, the frolic and the gentle,
Has vanished from his lonely hearth.

Like clouds that rake the mountain summits,
Or waves that own no curbing hand,
How fast has brother followed brother,
From sunshine to the sunless land!

Yet I, whose lids from infant slumber
Were earlier raised, remain to hear
A timid voice, that asks in whispers,
'Who next will drop and disappear?'

Our haughty life is crowned with darkness,
Like London with its own black wreath,
On which with thee, O Crabbe! forth-looking,
I gazed from Hampstead's breezy heath.

As if but yesterday departed,
Thou too art gone before; but why,
O'er ripe fruit, seasonably gathered,
Should frail survivors heave a sigh?

Mourn rather for that holy Spirit,
Sweet as the spring, as ocean deep;
For her who, ere her summer faded,
Has sunk into a breathless sleep.

No more of old romantic sorrows,
For slaughtered Youth or lovelorn Maid!
With sharper grief is Yarrow smitten,
And Ettrick mourns with her their Poet dead.

William Wordsworth

ON THIS DAY:

James Hogg (1770–1835), Scottish writer, died.

Sir Samuel Cunard (1787–1865), civil engineer and shipping line owner, was born.

René Magritte (1898–1967), artist, was born.

The daily proceedings in the House of Commons were shown on television for the first time in 1989.

A Song for St Cecilia's Day

From harmony, from heavenly harmony
    This universal frame began;
   When Nature underneath a heap
    Of jarring atoms lay,
  And could not heave her head,
The tuneful voice was heard from high,
    Arise, ye more than dead.
Then cold and hot and moist and dry
  In order to their stations leap,
    And Music's power obey.
From harmony, from heavenly harmony
    This universal frame began:
    From harmony to harmony
Through all the compass of the notes it ran,
The diapason closing full in Man.
What passion cannot Music raise and quell?
    When Jubal struck the corded shell,
  His listening brethren stood around,
    And, wondering, on their faces fell
To worship that celestial sound:
Less than a god they thought there could not dwell
    Within the hollow of that shell,
    That spoke so sweetly, and so well.
What passion cannot Music raise and quell?
  The trumpet's loud clangour
    Excites us to arms
  With shrill notes of anger
    And mortal alarms.
  The double double double beat
    Of the thundering drum
    Cries, Hark! the foes come;
Charge, charge, 'tis too late to retreat.
  The soft complaining flute
  In dying notes discovers
  The woes of hopeless lovers,
Whose dirge is whispered by the warbling lute.

Sharp violins proclaim
Their jealous pangs and desperation,
Fury, frantic indignation,
Depth of pains and height of passion,
    For the fair, disdainful dame.

But oh! what art can teach
What human voice can reach
    The sacred organ's praise?
Notes inspiring holy love,
Notes that wing their heavenly ways
    To mend the choirs above.

Orpheus could lead the savage race,
And trees unrooted left their place,
    Sequacious of the lyre;
But bright Cecilia raised the wonder higher:
When to her organ vocal breath was given,
An angel heard, and straight appeared
    Mistaking earth for heaven.

Grand Chorus

As from the power of sacred lays
    The spheres began to move,
And sung the great Creator's praise
    To all the Blest above;
So, when the last and dreadful hour
This crumbling pageant shall devour,
The trumpet shall be heard on high,
The dead shall live, the living die,
And Music shall untune the sky.

John Dryden

ON THIS DAY:

Today is St Cecilia's Day.

Thomas Cook (1808–1892), tourism pioneer and organiser of railway tours, was born.

Mary Ann Evans (1819–1880), who wrote as George Eliot, was born.

President John F. Kennedy (1917–1963) was assassinated while visiting Dallas, Texas.

In 1990 Margaret Thatcher (b.1925) resigned the office of Prime Minister.

London Bells

Two sticks and an apple,
Ring the bells at Whitechapel.

Old Father Bald Pate,
Ring the bells Aldgate.

Maids in white aprons,
Ring the bells at St. Catherine's.

Oranges and lemons,
Ring the bells at St Clement's.

When will you pay me?
Ring the bells at the Old Bailey.

When I am rich,
Ring the bells at Fleetditch.

When will that be?
Ring the bells at Stepney.

When I am old,
Ring the great bell at Paul's.

Anonymous

ON THIS DAY:

Today is the feast day of St Clement.

In 1852 the first pillar-box was erected. Now painted red, they were originally painted green.

Sonnet XVI: November

The mellow year is hasting to its close;
The little birds have almost sung their last,
Their small notes twitter in the dreary blast –
That shrill-piped harbinger of early snows;
The patient beauty of the scentless rose,
Oft with the Morn's hoar crystal quaintly glass'd,
Hangs, a pale mourner for the summer past,
And makes a little summer where it grows:
In the chill sunbeam of the faint brief day
The dusky waters shudder as they shine,
The russet leaves obstruct the struggling way
Of oozy brooks, which no deep banks define,
And the gaunt woods, in ragged, scant array,
Wrap their old limbs with sombre ivy twine.

Hartley Coleridge

ON THIS DAY:

The river Thames has been frozen twice on this day, firstly in 1434 and again in 1715.

Laurence Sterne (1713–1768), author of *Tristram Shandy*, was born.

On the Origin of Species by Charles Darwin (1809–1882) was published in 1859.

Break of Day in the Trenches

The darkness crumbles away.
It is the same old druid Time as ever,
Only a live thing leaps my hand,
A queer sardonic rat,
As I pull the parapet's poppy
To stick behind my ear.
Droll rat, they would shoot you if they knew
Your cosmopolitan sympathies.
Now you have touched this English hand
You will do the same to a German
Soon, no doubt, if it be your pleasure
To cross the sleeping green between.
It seems you inwardly grin as you pass
Strong eyes, fine limbs, haughty athletes,
Less chanced than you for life,
Bonds to the whims of murder,
Sprawled in the bowels of the earth,
The torn fields of France.
What do you see in our eyes
At the shrieking iron and flame
Hurled through still heavens?
What quaver – what heart aghast?
Poppies whose roots are in man's veins
Drop, and are ever dropping;
But mine in my ear is safe –
Just a little white with the dust.

Isaac Rosenberg

ON THIS DAY:

The Mousetrap by Agatha Christie (1890–1976) opened at the Ambassadors Theatre in London's West End in 1952. The play transferred to St Martin's Theatre in March 1974, where it remains in production.

President John F. Kennedy (1917–1963) was buried at Arlington Cemetery.

November 26

Kelmscott Crab Apples

Fair is the world, now autumn's wearing,
And the sluggard sun lies long abed;
Sweet are the days, now winter's nearing,
And all winds feign that the wind is dead.

Dumb is the hedge where the crabs hang yellow,
Bright as the blossoms of the spring;
Dumb is the close where the pears grow mellow,
And none but the dauntless redbreasts sing.

Fair was the spring, but amidst his greening
Grey were the days of the hidden sun;
Fair was the summer, but overweening,
So soon his o'er-sweet days were done.

Come then, love, for peace is upon us.
Far off is failing, and far is fear,
Here where the rest in the end hath won us,
In the garnering tide of the happy year.

Come from the grey old house by the water,
Where, far from the lips of the hungry sea,
Green groweth the grass o'er the field of the slaughter,
And all is a tale for thee and me.

William Morris

ON THIS DAY:
A fierce storm swept through the south of England in 1703, leaving eight thousand people dead.
In 1921 Howard Carter (1874–1939) had his first glimpse of the inside of Tutankhamun's tomb.

The Pilgrims

An uphill path, sun-gleams between the showers,
Where every beam that broke the leaden sky
Lit other hills with fairer ways than ours;
Some clustered graves where half our memories lie;
And one grim Shadow creeping ever nigh:
And this was Life.

Wherein we did another's burden seek,
The tired feet we helped upon the road,
The hand we gave the weary and the weak,
The miles we lightened one another's load,
When, faint to falling, onward yet we strode:
This too was Life.

Till, at the upland, as we turned to go
Amid fair meadows, dusky in the night,
The mists fell back upon the road below;
Broke on our tired eyes the western light;
The very graves were for a moment bright:
And this was Death.

John McCrae

ON THIS DAY:

Anders Celsius (1701–1744), professor of astronomy, was born.

Sir William Orpen (1878–1931), painter and one of the first official artists of the First World War, was born.

John Major (b.1943) became the leader of the Conservative party and Prime Minister of Britain in 1990, a position he held until 1997.

Moonlit Apples

At the top of the house the apples are laid in rows,
And the skylight lets the moonlight in, and those
Apples are deep-sea apples of green. There goes
    A cloud on the moon in the autumn night.

A mouse in the wainscot scratches, and scratches, and then
There is no sound at the top of the house of men
Or mice; and the cloud is blown, and the moon again
    Dapples the apples with deep-sea light.

They are lying in rows there, under the gloomy beams;
On the sagging floor; they gather the silver streams
Out of the moon, those moonlit apples of dreams,
    And quiet is the steep stair under.

In the corridors under there is nothing but sleep.
And stiller than ever on orchard boughs they keep
Tryst with the moon, and deep is the silence, deep
    On moon-washed apples of wonder.

John Drinkwater

ON THIS DAY:

William Blake (1757–1827), poet and artist, was born.

Nancy Mitford (1904–1973), novelist and one of the five Mitford sisters, was born.

Lady Astor (1879–1964) elected MP for Plymouth in 1919 and became the first woman to sit in the House of Commons (she took her seat on 1st December 1919).

The Five Students

The sparrow dips in his wheel-rut bath,
    The sun grows passionate-eyed,
And boils the dew to smoke by the paddock-path;
    As strenuously we stride, –
Five of us; dark He, fair He, dark She, fair She, I,
    All beating by.

The air is shaken, the high-road hot,
    Shadowless swoons the day,
The greens are sobered and cattle at rest; but not
    We on our urgent way, –
Four of us; fair She, dark She, fair He, I, are there,
    But one – elsewhere.

Autumn moulds the hard fruit mellow,
    And forward still we press
Through moors, briar-meshed plantations, clay-pits yellow,
    As in the spring hours – yes,
Three of us; fair He, fair She, I, as heretofore,
    But – fallen one more.

The leaf drops: earthworms draw it in
    At night-time noiselessly,
The fingers of birch and beech are skeleton-thin,
    And yet on the beat are we, –
Two of us; fair She, I. But no more left to go
    The track we know.

Icicles tag the church-aisle leads,
    The flag-rope gibbers hoarse,
The home-bound foot-folk wrap their snow-flaked heads,
    Yet I still stalk the course –
One of us…Dark and fair He, dark and fair She, gone:
    The rest – anon.

Thomas Hardy

ON THIS DAY:

Gertrude Jekyll (1843–1932), horticulturalist, was born.
C. S. Lewis (1898–1963), novelist and author of the *Narnia* chronicles, was born.

November

November's days are thirty:
November's earth is dirty,
Those thirty days, from first to last;
And the prettiest things on ground are the paths
With morning and evening hobnails dinted,
With foot and wing-tip overprinted
Or separately charactered,
Of little beast and little bird.
The fields are mashed by sheep, the roads
Make the worst going, the best the woods
Where dead leaves upward and downward scatter.
Few care for the mixture of earth and water,
Twig, leaf, flint, thorn,
Straw, feather, all that men scorn,
Pounded up and sodden by flood,
Condemned as mud.

But of all the months when earth is greener
Not one has clean skies that are cleaner.
Clean and clear and sweet and cold,
They shine above the earth so old,
While the after-tempest cloud
Sails over in silence though winds are loud,
Till the full moon in the east
Looks at the planet in the west
And earth is silent as it is black,
Yet not unhappy for its lack.
Up from the dirty earth men stare:
One imagines a refuge there
Above the mud, in the pure bright
Of the cloudless heavenly light:
Another loves earth and November more dearly
Because without them, he sees clearly,
The sky would be nothing more to his eye
Than he, in any case, is to the sky;
He loves even the mud whose dyes
Renounce all brightness to the skies.

Edward Thomas

ON THIS DAY:
Today is the feast day of St Andrew, the patron saint of Scotland.

DECEMBER

December 1

These verses weare made By Michaell Drayton Esquier Poett Lawreatt the night before hee dyed

Soe well I love thee, as without thee I
Love Nothing, yf I might Chuse, I'de rather dye
Then bee on day debarde thy companye

Since Beasts, and plantes doe growe, and live and move
Beastes are those men, that such a life approve
Hee onlye Lives, that Deadly is In Love

The Corne that in the grownd is sowen first dies
And of on seed doe manye Eares aRise
Love this worldes Corne, by dying Multiples

The seeds of Love first by thy eyes weare throwne
Into A grownd untild, a harte unknowne
To beare such fruitt, tyll by thy handes t'was sowen

Looke as your Looking glass by Chance may fall
Devyde and breake in manye peyces smale
And yett shewes forth, the selfe same face In all

Proportions, Features Graces Just the same
And In the smalest peyce as well the name
Of Fayrest one deserves, as In the richest frame

Soe all my Thoughts are peyces but of you
Whiche put together makes a Glass soe true
As I therin noe others face but yours can Veiwe

Michael Drayton

ON THIS DAY:

Queen Alexandra (1844–1925), consort of Edward VII and mother of George V, was born.

In 1919 Lady Astor (1879–1964) became the first woman to take her seat in the House of Commons. She was not the first woman to be elected as an MP however. Countess Markievicz was elected as a Sinn Fein candidate the previous year but was prohibited from taking her seat because she refused to swear the oath of allegiance to the King.

Woody Allen, film director and musician, was born in 1935.

December 2

The Brilliancies of Winter

Last of flowers, in tufts around
Shines the gorse's golden bloom:
Milk-white lichens clothe the ground
'Mid the flowerless heath and broom:
Bright are holly-berries, seen
Red, through leaves of glossy green.

Brightly, as on rocks they leap,
Shine the sea-waves, white with spray:
Brightly, in the dingles deep,
Gleams the river's foaming way;
Brightly through the distance show
Mountain-summits clothed in snow.

Brightly, where the torrents bound,
Shines the frozen colonnade,
Which the black rocks, dripping round,
And the flying spray have made:
Bright the ice-drops on the ash
Leaning o'er the cataract's dash.

Bright the hearth, where feast and song
Crown the warrior's hour of peace,
While the snow-storm drives along,
Bidding war's worse tempest cease;
Bright the hearth-flame, flashing clear
On the up-hung shield and spear.

Bright the torchlight of the hall
When the wintry night-winds blow;
Brightest when its splendours fall
On the mead-cup's sparkling flow:
While the maiden's smile of light
Makes the brightness trebly bright.

Close the portals; pile the hearth;
Strike the harp; the feast pursue;
Brim the horns: fire, music, mirth,
Mead and love, are winter's due.
Spring to purple conflict calls
Swords that shine on winter's walls.

Thomas Love Peacock

ON THIS DAY:

Michael Drayton (1563–1631), poet, died. Although Drayton died in poverty he was buried in West-minster Abbey and Lady Anne Clifford, the Countess of Dorset, paid for the memorial monument.

Napoleon I (1769–1821) led the French army at the battle of Austerlitz in 1805, defeating the com-bined armies of Russia and Austria.

Georges Seurat (1859–1891), artist, was born.

Philip Larkin (1922–1985), poet and novelist, died.

The Stately Homes of England

Lord Elderley, Lord Borrowmere,
Lord Sickert and Lord Camp,
With every virtue, every grace,
Ah what avails the sceptred race,
Here you see – the four of us,
And there are so many more of us
Eldest sons that must succeed.
We know how Caesar conquered Gaul
And how to whack a cricket ball;
Apart from this, our education lacks co-ordination.
Though we're young and tentative
And rather rip-representative,
Scions of a noble breed,
We are the products of those homes serene and stately
Which only lately
Seem to have run to seed!

The Stately Homes of England,
How beautiful they stand,
To prove the upper classes
Have still the upper hand;
Though the fact that they have to be rebuilt
And frequently mortgaged to the hilt
Is inclined to take the gilt
Off the gingerbread,
And certainly damps the fun
Of the eldest son –
But still we won't be beaten,
We'll scrimp and scrape and save,
The playing fields of Eton
Have made us frightfully brave –
And though if the Van Dycks have to go
And we pawn the Bechstein Grand,
We'll stand
By the Stately Homes of England.

Here you see
The pick of us,
You may be heartily sick of us,
Still with sense
We're all imbued.
Our homes command extensive views
And with assistance from the Jews
We have been able to dispose of
Rows and rows and rows of
Gainsboroughs and Lawrences,
Some sporting prints of Aunt Florence's,
Some of which were rather rude.
Although we sometimes flaunt our family conventions,
Our good intentions
Mustn't be misconstrued.

The Stately Homes of England
We proudly represent,
We only keep them up for
Americans to rent,
Though the pipes that supply the bathroom burst
And the lavatory makes you fear the worst,
It was used by Charles the First
Quite informally,
And later by George the Fourth
On a journey north.
The State Apartments keep their
Historical renown,
It's wiser not to sleep there
In case they tumble down;
But still if they ever catch on fire
Which, with any luck, they might
We'll fight
For the Stately Homes of England

The Stately Homes of England,
Though rather in the lurch,
Provide a lot of chances
For Psychical Research –

There's the ghost of a crazy younger son
Who murdered, in thirteen fifty-one,
An extremely rowdy Nun
Who resented it,
And people who come to call
Meet her in the hall.
The baby in the guest wing,
Who crouches by the grate,
Was walled up in the west wing
In fourteen twenty-eight.
If anyone spots
The Queen of Scots
In a hand-embroidered shroud
We're proud
Of the Stately Homes of England.

Lord Elderley, Lord Borrowmere,
Lord Sickert and Lord Camp,
Behold us in our hours of ease,
Uncertain, coy and hard to please.
Reading in *Debrett* of us,
This fine Patrician quartette of us,
We can feel extremely proud,
Our ancient lineage we trace
Back to the cradle of the Race
Before those beastly Roman bowmen
Bitched our local Yeomen.
Though the new democracy
May pain the old Aristocracy
We've not winced nor cried aloud,
Under the bludgeonings of chance what will be –
    will be.
Our heads will still be
Bloody but quite unbowed!

The Stately Homes of England
In valley, dale and glen
Produce a race of charming,
Innocuous young men.

Though our mental equipment may be slight
And we barely distinguish left from right,
We are quite prepared to fight
For our principles,
Though none of us know so far
What they really are.
Our duty to the nation,
It's only fair to state,
Lies not in pro-creation
But what we pro-create;
And so we can cry
With kindling eye
As to married life we go,
What ho!
For the Stately Homes of England!

The Stately Homes of England,
Although a trifle bleak,
Historically speaking,
Are more or less unique.
We've a cousin who won the Golden Fleece
And a very peculiar fowling-piece
Which was sent to Cromwell's niece,
Who detested it,
And rapidly sent it back
With a dirty crack.
A note we have from Chaucer
Contains a bawdy joke.
We also have a saucer
That Bloody Mary broke.
We've two pairs of tights
King Arthur's Knights
Had completely worn away.
Sing Hey!
For the Stately Homes of England.

Sir Noël Coward

ON THIS DAY:

Octavia Hill (1838–1912), a co-founder in 1895 of the National Trust, was born.
Joseph Conrad (1857–1924), author of *Nostromo* and *Heart of Darkness*, was born.

December

No gardener need go far to find
   The Christmas rose,
The fairest of the flowers that mark
   The sweet Year's close:
Nor be in quest of places where
   The hollies grow,
Nor seek for sacred trees that hold
   The mistletoe.
All kindly tended gardens love
   December days,
And spread their latest riches out
   In winter's praise.
But every gardener's work this month
   Must surely be
To choose a very beautiful
   Big Christmas tree,
And see it through the open door
   In triumph ride,
To reign a glorious reign within
   At Christmas-tide.

Dollie Radford

ON THIS DAY:

Thomas Carlyle (1795–1881), author and historian, was born.

Edith Cavell (1865–1915), nurse who was executed by the Germans for treason, was born.

Rainer Maria Rilke (1875–1926), poet, was born.

December 5

Autumn

It is the football season once more
And the back pages of the Sunday papers
Again show the blurred anguish of goalkeepers.

In Maida Vale, Golders Green and Hampstead
Lamps ripen early in the surprising dusk;
They are furred like stale rinds with a fuzz of mist.

The pavements of Kensington are greasy;
The wind smells of burnt porridge in Bayswater,
And the leaves are mushed to silence in the gutter.

The big hotel like an anchored liner
Rides near the park; lit windows hammer the sky.
Like the slow swish of surf the tyres of taxis sigh.

On Ealing Broadway the cinema glows
Warm behind glass while mellow the church clock chimes
As the waiting girls stir in their delicate chains.

Their eyes are polished by the wind,
But the gleam is dumb, empty of joy or anger.
Though the lovers are long in coming the girls still linger.

We are nearing the end of the year.
Under the sombre sleeve the blood ticks faster
And in the dark ear of Autumn quick voices whisper.

It is a time of year that's to my taste,
Full of spiced rumours, sharp and velutinous flavours,
Dim with the mist that softens the cruel surfaces,
Makes mirrors vague. It is the mist that I most favour.

Vernon Scannell

ON THIS DAY:

Wolfgang Amadeus Mozart (1756–1791), composer, died.

Christina Rossetti (1830–1894), poet, was born.

479

December 6

The Question

I dreamed that, as I wandered by the way,
    Bare Winter suddenly was changed to Spring,
And gentle odours led my steps astray,
    Mixed with a sound of waters murmuring
Along a shelving bank of turf, which lay
    Under a copse, and hardly dared to fling
Its green arms round the bosom of the stream,
But kissed it and then fled, as thou mightest in dream.

    There grew pied wind-flowers and violets,
        Daisies, those pearled Arcturi of the earth,
The constellated flower that never sets;
        Faint oxlips; tender bluebells, at whose birth
The sod scarce heaved; and that tall flower that wets–
        Like a child, half in tenderness and mirth–
Its mother's face with Heaven's collected tears,
When the low wind, its playmate's voice, it hears.

    And in the warm hedge grew lush eglantine,
        Green cowbind and the moonlight-coloured may,
And cherry-blossoms, and white cups, whose wine
        Was the bright dew, yet drained not by the day;
And wild roses, and ivy serpentine,
        With its dark buds and leaves, wandering astray;
And flowers azure, black, and streaked with gold,
Fairer than any wakened eyes behold.

    And nearer to the river's trembling edge
        There grew broad flag-flowers, purple pranked with white,
And starry river buds among the sedge,
        And floating water-lilies, broad and bright,
Which lit the oak that overhung the hedge
        With moonlight beams of their own watery light;
And bulrushes, and reeds of such deep green
As soothed the dazzled eye with sober sheen.

Methought that of these visionary flowers
I made a nosegay, bound in such a way
That the same hues, which in their natural bowers
Were mingled or opposed, the like array
Kept these imprisoned children of the Hours
Within my hand, – and then, elate and gay,
I hastened to the spot whence I had come,
That I might there present it! – Oh! to whom?

Percy Bysshe Shelley

ON THIS DAY:
Anthony Trollope (1815–1882), novelist, died.
Osbert Sitwell (1892–1969), writer, was born.

December 7

News of Pearl Harbor

From the arched Philco with its speaker like a Gothic window
    came news from the sky. Later, newsreels showed the *Arizona*
hulled over, burning. The P-40's and slender-tailed B-17's in
    their peacetime markings lay crumpled in piles. The sky
became accelerator of change – no longer the river with
    its slow hieroglyphic, its evolution from sailing craft
and log raft to steam-huffed packet. Not the railroad
    with its comprehensible, coal-fired engine in its black
piston-shape, not even the new year's models of Chryslers
    and Buicks, but an airborne sound from the distance: Pearl
Harbor, jewel-lustrous, catastrophic syllables. Volunteers
    watched from Forest Service tower and rooftop, with manuals
to aid them, though the middle-aged eyes behind glasses confused one
    ircraft with another. But the boy on the roof of his father's
station recognized each type as by instinct – in the one-room
    house all windows, as he waited for apocalyptic sightings.
He imagined a desperate combat the whole country entered in,
    his somnolent South now wired by the phone line that
began at his own left hand to the military fathers, whose
    planes changed as quickly as the broadcasts: P-38's and
B-17's, the milk-jug P-47's, moving through the new marks,
    with armor and self-sealing tanks, machine guns and
cannon, stabilizer-fins extended. Young men training
    at Seymour Johnson nearby strained to learn control
of a fighter like a winged locomotive. One of these P-47's
    crashed in the edge of his county. He went with his father.
The boulderlike motor had broken from its mounts, an engine
    of two thousand horsepower rolling like the Juggernaut of
wartime, bowling down pine trees, letting in sunlight
    through the central, violated grove, toward the hollow,
frangible body. This Thunderbolt of a technical rhetoric

in a pastoral accumulated too vividly for scrutiny
illuminated a fuselage broken at the cockpit: a pilot's
        seat stark as an electric chair, where the throne
of this new succession stood jellied with blood.

James Applewhite

ON THIS DAY:

In 1941, Japan launched an air attack on the US Naval base at Pearl Harbor, Hawaii which brought the US into the Second World War.

Giovanni Lorenzo Bernini (1598–1680), Italian architect and sculptor, was born.

Joyce Cary (1888–1957), novelist, was born.

Hiding Beneath the Furze

(Autumn 1939)

Hiding beneath the furze as they passed him by,
    He drowned their talk with the noise of his own heart,
And faltering, came at last to the short hot road
    With the flat white cottage under the rowan trees:
And this can never happen, ever again.

Before his fever drowned him, he stumbled in,
    And the old woman rose, and said in the dialect, 'Enter'.
He entered, and drank, and hearing his fever roaring,
    Surrendered himself to its sweating luxuries:
And this can never happen, ever again.

There were bowls of milk, and (after such hunger) bread.
    Here was the night he had longed for on the highway.
Strange, that his horror could dance so gaily in sunlight,
    And rescue and peace be here in the smoky dark:
And this can never happen, ever again.

When he awoke, he found his pursuers had been,
    But the woman had lied, and easily deceived them.
She had never questioned his right – for who so childish
    Could ever do so wrong? 'He is my son,' she had said:
And this can never happen, ever again.

The days passed into weeks, and the newspapers came,
    And he saw that the world was safe, and his name unmentioned.
He could return to the towns and his waiting friends,
    The evil captain had fled defeated to Norway:
And this can never happen, ever again.

And this can never happen, ever again.
   He stands on the icy pier and waits to depart,
The town behind him is lightless, his friends are dead,
   The captain will set his spies in his very heart,
And the fever is gone that rocked inside his head.

Henry Reed

ON THIS DAY:

Britain, Australia and the United States of America declared war on Japan in 1941.

Henry Reed (1914–1986), poet, playwright and translator whose most popular verses drew on his wartime experiences, died.

How Soon Hath Time

How soon hath Time, the subtle thief of youth,
    Stoln on his wing my three and twentieth year!
    My hasting days fly on with full career,
    But my late spring no bud or blossom shew'th.
Perhaps my semblance might deceive the truth,
    That I to manhood am arrived so near,
    And inward ripeness doth much less appear,
    The some more timely-happy spirits endu'th.
Yet be it less or more, or soon or slow,
    It shall be still in strictest measure even
    To that same lot, however mean or high,
Toward which Time leads me, and the will of Heaven;
    As is, if I have grace to use it so,
    As ever in my great Taskmaster's eye.

John Milton

ON THIS DAY:

John Milton (1608–1674), poet and author of *Paradise Lost*, was born.

Clarence Birdseye (1886–1956), inventor of a deep-freezing process, was born.

Dame Judi Dench, actress and Oscar winner, was born in 1934.

December 10

What is Love?

Now what is love, I pray thee tell?
It is that fountain and that well
Where pleasure and repentance dwell.
It is perhaps that sauncing bell
That tolls all into heaven or hell:
And this is love, as I hear tell.

Yet what is love, I pray thee say?
It is a work on holy day.
It is December matched with May,
When lusty bloods in fresh array
Hear ten months after of the play:
And this is love, as I hear say.

Yet what is love, I pray thee sain?
It is a sunshine mixed with rain.
It is a toothache, or like pain:
It is a game where none doth gain;
The lass saith No, and would full fain:
And this is love, I hear sain.

Yet what is love, I pray thee show?
A thing that creeps, it cannot go;
A prize that passeth to and fro;
A thing for one, a thing for mo;
And he that proves must find it so;
And this is love, sweet friend, I trow.

Sir Walter Raleigh

ON THIS DAY:

Emily Dickinson (1830–1886), poet, was born.

Ernest H. Shepard (1879–1976), illustrator of *The Wind in the Willows* and *Winnie the Pooh*, was born.

Christmas Bells

I heard the bells on Christmas Day
Their old, familiar carols play,
    And wild and sweet
    The words repeat
Of peace on earth, goodwill to men!

And thought how, as the day had come,
The belfries of all Christendom
    Had rolled along
    The unbroken song
Of peace on earth, goodwill to men!

Till, ringing, singing on its way,
The world revolved from night to day,
    A voice, a chime,
    A chant sublime
Of peace on earth, goodwill to men!

Then from each black, accursed mouth
The cannon thundered in the South,
    And with the sound
    The carols drowned
Of peace on earth, goodwill to men!

It was as if an earthquake rent
The hearth-stones of a continent,
    And made forlorn
    The households born
Of peace on earth, goodwill to men!

And in despair I bowed my head;
'There is no peace on earth,' I said;
    'For hate is strong,
    And mocks the song
Of peace on earth, goodwill to men!'

Then pealed the bells more loud and deep:
'God is not dead, nor doth He sleep;
    The Wrong shall fail,
    The Right prevail,
With peace on earth, goodwill to men.'

Henry Wadsworth Longfellow

ON THIS DAY:

James II (1633–1701, reigned 1685–1688) abdicated the throne. He was succeeded by William III (1650–1702, reigned 1689–1702) and his wife, James II's daughter, Mary II (1662–1694, reigned 1689–1694).

In 1936, Edward VIII, later HRH the Duke of Windsor (1894–1972) abdicated in order to marry Mrs Wallis Simpson, and began a prolonged period in exile.

Two Sonnets *from* A Sequence of Sonnets on the Death of Robert Browning

The clearest eyes in all the world they read
    With sense more keen and spirit of sight more true
    Than burns and thrills in sunrise, when the dew
Flames, and absorbs the glory round it shed,
As they the light of ages quick and dead,
    Closed now, forsake us: yet the shaft that slew
    Can slay not one of all the works we knew,
Nor death discrown that many-laurelled head.

The works of words whose life seems lightning wrought,
And moulded of unconquerable thought,
    And quickened with imperishable flame,
Stand fast and shine and smile, assured that nought
    May fade of all their myriad-moulded fame,
    Nor England's memory clasp not Browning's name.

* * *

A graceless doom it seems that bids us grieve:
    Venice and winter, hand in deadly hand,
    Have slain the lover of her sunbright strand
And singer of a stormbright Christmas Eve.
A graceless guerdon we that loved receive
    For all our love, from that the dearest land
    Love worshipped ever. Blithe and soft and bland,
Too fair for storm to scathe or fire to cleave,
Shone on our dreams and memories evermore
The domes, the towers, the mountains and the shore
    That gird or guard thee, Venice: cold and black
Seems now the face we loved as he of yore.
    We have given thee love – no stint, no stay, no lack:
    What gift, what gift is this thou hast given us back?

Algernon Charles Swinburne

ON THIS DAY:
Robert Browning (1812–1889), poet, died.
In 1913 the *Mona Lisa* was found in Florence, Italy. It had been stolen from the Louvre in 1911. Vincenzo Perugia and three accomplices were arrested for the theft.

December 13

A Nocturnal upon St Lucy's Day, being the shortest day

'Tis the year's midnight, and it is the day's,
Lucy's, who scarce seven hours herself unmasks,
   The sun is spent, and now his flasks
    Send forth light squibs, no constant rays;
      The world's whole sap is sunk:
The general balm the hydroptic earth hath drunk,
Whither, as to the bed's-feet, life is shrunk,
Dead and interred; yet all these seem to laugh,
Compared with me, who am their epitaph.

Study me then, you who shall lovers be
At the next world, that is, at the next spring:
   For I am every dead thing,
    In whom love wrought new alchemy.
      For his art did express
A quintessence even from nothingness,
From dull privations, and lean emptiness
He ruined me, and I am re-begot
Of absence, darkness, death: things which are not.

All others, from all things, draw all that's good,
Life, soul, form, spirit, whence they being have;
   I, by love's limbeck, am the grave
    Of all, that's nothing. Oft a flood
      Have we two wept, and so
Drowned the whole world, us two; oft did we grow
To be two Chaoses, when we did show
Care to ought else; and often absences
Withdrew our souls, and made us carcasses.

But I am by her death (which word wrongs her)
Of the first nothing, the elixir grown;
   Were I a man, that I were one,

I needs must know; I should prefer,
    If I were any beast,
Some ends, some means; yea plants, yea stones detest,
And love; all, all some properties invest;
If I an ordinary nothing were,
As shadow, a light, and body must be here.

But I am None; not will my sun renew.
You lovers, for whose sake, the lesser sun
    At this time to the Goat is run
    To fetch new lust, and give it you,
        Enjoy your summer all;
Since she enjoys her long night's festival,
Let me prepare towards her, and let me call
This hour her vigil, and her eve, since this
Both the year's and the day's deep midnight is.

John Donne

ON THIS DAY:

Today is the feast day of St Lucy. In some countries her feast day has become a festival of light.

In 1904 the first electric tube train made its journey on the Metropolitan Railway from Baker Street to Uxbridge.

Winter

I, singularly moved
To love the lovely that are not beloved,
Of all the Seasons, most
Love Winter, and to trace
The sense of the Trophonian pallor on her face.
It is not death, but plenitude of peace;
And the dim cloud that does the world enfold
Hath less the characters of dark and cold
Than warmth and light asleep,
And correspondent breathing seems to keep
With the infant harvest, breathing soft below
Its eider coverlet of snow.
Nor is in field or garden anything
But, duly looked into, contains serene
The substance of things hoped for, in the Spring,
And evidence of Summer not yet seen.
On every chance-mild day
That visits the moist shaw,
The honeysuckle, 'sdaining to be crost
In urgence of sweet life by sleet or frost,
'Voids the time's law
With still increase
Of leaflet new, and little, wandering spray;
Often, in sheltering brakes,
As one from rest disturbed in the first hour,
Primrose or violet bewildered wakes,
And deems 'tis time to flower;
Though not a whisper of her voice he hear,
The buried bulb does know
The signals of the year,
And hails far Summer with his lifted spear.
The gorse-field dark, by sudden, gold caprice,
Turns, here and there, into a Jason's fleece;
Lilies, that soon in Autumn slipped their gowns of green,
And vanished into earth,

And came again, ere Autumn died, to birth,
Stand full-arrayed, amidst the wavering shower,
And perfect for the Summer, less the flower;
In nook of pale or crevice of crude bark,
Thou canst not miss,
If close thou spy, to mark
The ghostly chrysalis,
That, if thou touch it, stirs in its dream dark;
And the flushed Robin, in the evenings hoar,
Does of Love's Day, as if he saw it, sing;
But sweeter yet than dream or song of Summer or Spring
Are Winter's sometime smiles, that seem to well
From infancy ineffable;
Her wandering, languorous gaze,
So unfamiliar, so without amaze,
On the elemental, chill adversity,
The uncomprehended rudeness; and her sigh
And solemn, gathering tear,
And look of exile from some great repose, the sphere
Of ether, moved by ether only, or
By something still more tranquil.

Coventry Patmore

ON THIS DAY:

Michel de Nostredame, 'Nostradamus' (1503–1566), who made various prophecies in his lifetime about events in the centuries to follow, was born.

Prince Albert (1819–1861), consort of Queen Victoria, died.

George VI was born in 1895.

In 1918 women in Britain voted in a general election for the first time.

A Wife in London

She sits in the tawny vapour
   That the Thames-side lanes have uprolled,
   Behind whose webby fold on fold
Like a waning taper
   The street-lamp glimmers cold.

A messenger's knock cracks smartly,
   Flashed news is in her hand
   Of meaning it dazes to understand
Though shaped so shortly:
   He – has fallen – in the far South Land ...

'Tis the morrow; the fog hangs thicker,
   The postman nears and goes:
   A letter is brought whose lines disclose
By the firelight flicker
   His hand, whom the worm now knows:

Fresh – firm – penned in highest feather –
   Page-full of his hoped return,
   And of home-planned jaunts by brake and burn
In the summer weather,
   And of new love that they would learn.

Thomas Hardy

ON THIS DAY:

In 1899 the Boers defeated the British forces at the battle of Colenso.

Gustave Eiffel (1832–1923), designer of the Eiffel Tower in Paris, was born.

In 1916 the first battle of Verdun, which had begun in February, ended. Over 700,000 Allied and German soldiers lost their lives during this encounter.

Nothing is Lost

Deep in our sub-conscious, we are told
Lie all our memories, lie all the notes
Of all the music we have ever heard
And all the phrases those we loved have spoken,
Sorrows and losses time has since consoled,
Family jokes, out-moded anecdotes
Each sentimental souvenir and token
Everything seen, experienced, each word
Addressed to us in infancy, before
Before we could even know or understand
The implications of our wonderland.
There they all are, the legendary lies
The birthday treats, the sights, the sounds, the tears
Forgotten debris of forgotten years
Waiting to be recalled, waiting to rise
Before our world dissolves before our eyes
Waiting for some small, intimate reminder,
A word, a tune, a known familiar scent
An echo from the past when, innocent
We looked upon the present with delight
And doubted not the future would be kinder
And never knew the loneliness of night.

Sir Noël Coward

ON THIS DAY:

Sir Noël Coward (1899–1973), actor, playwright and lyricist, was born.

Sir John Berry (Jack) Hobbs (1882–1963), England cricketer and scorer of 197 first-class centuries, was born.

William Somerset Maugham (1874–1965), playwright and author, died.

Richard Dimbleby (1913–1965), broadcaster and journalist whose reporting exploits included a broadcast from a Lancaster bomber during a raid on Germany in the Second World War, died.

Belovèd, my Belovèd
from Sonnets from the Portuguese, XX

Belovèd, my Belovèd, when I think
That thou wast in the world a year ago,
What time I sate alone here in the snow
And saw no footprint, heard the silence sink
No moment at thy voice, but, link by link,
When counting all my chains, as if that so
They never could fall off at any blow
Struck by thy possible hand, – why, thus I drink
Of life's great cup of wonder! Wonderful,
Never to feel thee thrill the day or night
With personal act or speech, – nor ever cull
Some prescience of thee with the blossoms white
Thou sawest growing! Atheists are as dull,
Who cannot guess God's presence out of sight.

Elizabeth Barrett Browning

ON THIS DAY:
Sir Humphry Davy (1778–1829), chemist who invented the miner's safety lamp, was born.
Ford Madox Ford (1873–1939), poet and novelist, was born.

December 18

Tears of a Clown

I am a clown
But I have a heart too
And it makes me so sad
Because it beats so true
But no one wants to know
About how I may cry
They just want a squirty flower
And another custard pie.

Jonathan Caswell

ON THIS DAY:

The father of clowns, Joseph Grimaldi (1779–1837), comic actor, was born.

Antonio Stradivari (c.1644–1737), violin maker, died.

Francis Thompson (1859–1907), poet, was born.

Last Lines

No coward soul is mine,
No trembler in the world's storm-troubled sphere:
I see Heaven's glories shine,
And faith shines equal, arming me from fear.

O God within my breast,
Almighty, ever-present Deity!
Life – that in me has rest,
As I – undying Life – have power in thee!

Vain are the thousand creeds
That move men's hearts: unutterably vain;
Worthless as withered weeds,
Or idlest froth amid the boundless main,

To waken doubt in one
Holding so fast by thine infinity;
So surely anchored on
The steadfast rock of immortality.

With wide-embracing love
Thy spirit animates eternal years,
Pervades and broods above,
Changes, sustains, dissolves, creates, and rears.

Though earth and man were gone,
And suns and universes ceased to be,
And thou were left alone,
Every existence would exist in thee.

There is not room for Death,
Nor atom that his might could render void:
Thou – thou art Being and Breath,
And what thou art may never be destroyed.

Emily Brontë

ON THIS DAY:

Emily Brontë (1818–1848) died. Her sister, Charlotte, confirmed that '*Last Lines*' was the last poem Emily wrote.

In a drear-nighted December

In a drear-nighted December,
    Too happy, happy tree,
Thy branches ne'er remember
    Their green felicity:
The north cannot undo them,
With a sleety whistle through them;
Nor frozen thawings glue them
    From budding at the prime.

In a drear-nighted December,
    Too happy, happy brook,
Thy bubblings ne'er remember
    Apollo's summer look;
But with a sweet forgetting,
They stay their crystal fretting,
Never, never petting
    About the frozen time.

Ah! would 'twere so with many
    A gentle girl and boy!
But were there ever any
    Writhed not at passèd joy?
To know the change and feel it,
When there is none to heal it,
Nor numbèd sense to steel it,
    Was never said in rhyme.

John Keats

ON THIS DAY:

In 1928 Harry Ramsden's first Fish and Chip Restaurant opened in Guiseley, Leeds. The original building was nothing more than a tiny hut measuring 10 feet by 6 feet painted green and white. The company now has restaurants throughout Britain. The original building can still be seen at Guiseley.

John Steinbeck (1902–1968), writer and winner of the Nobel Prize for literature in 1962, died.

Snow in the Suburbs

Every branch big with it,
Bent every twig with it;
    Every fork like a white web-foot;
    Every street and pavement mute:
Some flakes have lost their way, and grope back upward, when
Meeting those meandering down they turn and descend again.
     The palings are glued together like a wall,
     And there is no waft of wind with the fleecy fall.

A sparrow enters the tree,
Whereon immediately,
    A snow-lump thrice his own slight size
    Descends on him and showers his head and eyes,
   And overturns him,
   And near inurns him,
And lights on a nether twig, when its brush
Starts off a volley of other lodging lumps with a rush.

The steps are a blanched slope,
Up which, with feeble hope,
A black cat comes, wide-eyed and thin;
    And we take him in.

Thomas Hardy

ON THIS DAY:

Benjamin Disraeli, Lord Beaconsfield (1804–1881), Prime Minister in 1868 and from 1874 to 1880, was born.

Joseph Stalin (1879–1953), revolutionary Russian leader, was born.

In 1902 the first transatlantic telegraph message was sent by Guglielmo Marconi to Edward VII.

December 22

Winter Nights

Now winter nights enlarge
　　The number of their hours,
And clouds their storms discharge
　　Upon the airy towers.
Let now the chimneys blaze,
　　And cups o'erflow with wine;
Let well-tuned words amaze
　　With harmony divine.
Now yellow waxen lights
　　Shall wait on honey Love,
While youthful revels, masks, and courtly sights
　　Sleep's leaden spells remove.

This time doth well dispense
　　With lovers' long discourse.
Much speech hath some defence
　　Though beauty no remorse.
All do not all things well:
　　Some measures comely tread,
Some knotted riddles tell,
　　Some poems smoothly read.
The Summer hath his joys,
　　And Winter his delights.
Though Love and all his pleasures are but toys,
　　They shorten tedious nights.

Thomas Campion

ON THIS DAY:

John Crome (1768–1821), landscape painter and founder of the Norwich School of Painting, was born.

J. Arthur Rank (1888–1972), film producer, was born.

Dame Peggy Ashcroft (1907–1991), actress, was born. One of her final acting roles was in Sir David Lean's film version of *A Passage to India*.

To a Locomotive in Winter

Thee for my recitative,
Thee in the driving storm even as now, the snow, the winter-day declining,
Thee in thy panoply, thy measur'd dual throbbing and thy beat convulsive,
Thy black cylindric body, golden brass and silvery steel,
Thy ponderous side-bars, parallel and connecting rods, gyrating, shuttling
    at thy sides,
Thy metrical, now swelling pant and roar, now tapering in the distance,
Thy great protruding head-light fix'd in front,
Thy long, pale, floating vapor-pennants, tinged with delicate purple,
The dense and murky clouds out-belching from thy smoke-stack,
Thy knitted frame, thy springs and valves, the tremulous twinkle of thy wheels,
Thy train of cars behind, obedient, merrily following,
Through gale or calm, now swift, now slack, yet steadily careering;
Type of the modern – emblem of motion and power – pulse of the continent,
For once come serve the Muse and merge in verse, even as here I see thee,
With storm and buffeting gusts of wind and falling snow,
By day thy warning ringing bell to sound its notes,
By night thy silent signal lamps to swing.

Fierce-throated beauty!
Roll through my chant with all thy lawless music, thy swinging lamps at night,
Thy madly-whistled laughter, echoing, rumbling like an earthquake, rousing all,
Law of thyself complete, thine own track firmly holding,
(No sweetness debonair of tearful harp or glib piano thine,)
Thy trills of shrieks by rocks and hills return'd,
Launch'd o'er the prairies wide, across the lakes,
To the free skies unpent and glad and strong.

Walt Whitman

ON THIS DAY:

Sir Richard Arkwright (1732–1792) was born. Arkwright invented a spinning frame used in the textile industry, which bore his name.

Anthony Fokker (1890–1939), aircraft engineer, died.

The Oxen

Christmas Eve, and twelve of the clock.
   'Now they are all on their knees,'
An elder said as we sat in a flock
   By the embers in hearthside ease.

We pictured the meek mild creatures where
   They dwelt in their strawy pen,
Nor did it occur to one of us there
   To doubt they were kneeling then.

So fair a fancy few would weave
   In these years! Yet, I feel,
If someone said on Christmas Eve,
   'Come; see the oxen kneel

'In the lonely barton by yonder coomb
   Our childhood used to know,'
I should go with him in the gloom,
   Hoping it might be so.

Thomas Hardy

ON THIS DAY:

John (1167–1216, reigned 1199–1216), youngest son of Henry II, was born.

St Ignatius of Loyola (1491–1556), founder of the Jesuit order, was born.

Matthew Arnold (1822–1888), poet, was born.

December 25

On The Morning of Christ's Nativity

This is the Month and this the happy morn
Wherein the Son of Heav'ns eternal King,
Of wedded Maid and Virgin Mother born,
Our great Redemption from above did bring;
For so the holy Sages once did sing,
  That he our deadly forfeit should release,
And with his Father work us a perpetual peace.

That glorious Form, that Light unsufferable,
And that far-beaming blaze of Majesty,
Wherewith he wont at Heav'ns high Council-Table
To sit the midst of Trinal Unity,
He laid aside; and here with us to be,
  Forsook the Courts of Everlasting Day,
And chose with us a darksom House of mortal Clay.

Say Heav'nly Muse, shall not thy sacred vein
Afford a Present to the Infant God?
Hast thou no verse, no hymn or solemn strain
To welcome him to this his new abode,
Now while the Heav'n by the Sun's team untrod
  Hath took no print of the approaching light,
And all the spangled host keep watch in squadrons bright?

See how from far upon the Eastern rode
The Star-led Wizards haste with odours sweet,
O run, prevent them with thy humble ode,
And lay it lowly at his blessed feet;
Have thou the honour first, thy Lord to greet,
  And join thy voice unto the Angel Quire,
From out his secret Altar toucht with hallowd fire.

John Milton

ON THIS DAY:

Sir Isaac Newton (1642–1727), scientist, was born.

Charles Pathé (1883–1955), film pioneer who introduced the newsreel, was born.

Humphrey Bogart (1899–1957), film actor, was born.

Good King Wenceslas

Good King Wenceslas looked out on the Feast of Stephen,
When the snow lay round about, deep and crisp and even.
Brightly shone the moon that night, though the frost was cruel,
When a poor man came in sight, gathering winter fuel.

'Hither, page, and stand by me, if you know it, telling,
Yonder peasant, who is he? Where and what his dwelling?'
'Sire, he lives a good league hence, underneath the mountain,
Right against the forest fence, by Saint Agnes' fountain.'

'Bring me food and bring me wine, bring me pine logs hither,
You and I will see him dine, when we bear them thither.'
Page and monarch, forth they went, forth they went together,
Through the cold wind's wild lament and the bitter weather.

'Sire, the night is darker now, and the wind blows stronger,
Fails my heart, I know not how; I can go no longer.'
'Mark my footsteps, my good page, tread now in them boldly,
You shall find the winter's rage freeze your blood less coldly.'

In his master's steps he trod, where the snow lay dinted;
Heat was in the very sod which the saint had printed.
Therefore, Christian men, be sure, wealth or rank possessing,
You who now will bless the poor shall yourselves find blessing.

J. M. Neale

ON THIS DAY:

Today is the feast day of St Stephen, now also known as Boxing Day.

Thomas Gray (1716–1771), poet, was born.

Henry Miller (1891–1980), author, was born.

In 1941 Winston Churchill (1874–1965) became the first British Prime Minister to address both Houses of Congress of the United States.

Autumn

I love to see, when leaves depart,
The clear anatomy arrive,
Winter, the paragon of art,
That kills all forms of life and feeling
Save what is pure and will survive.

Already now the clanging chains
Of geese are harnessed to the moon:
Stripped are the great sun-clouding planes:
And the dark pines, their own revealing,
Let in the needles of the noon.

Strained by the gale the olives whiten
Like hoary wrestlers bent with toil
And, with the vines, their branches lighten
To brim our vats where summer lingers
In the red froth and sun-gold oil.

Soon on our hearth's reviving pyre
Their rotted stems will crumble up:
And like a ruby, panting fire,
The grape will redden on your fingers
Through the lit crystal of the cup.

Roy Campbell

ON THIS DAY:

Johannes Kepler (1571–1630), astronomer whose name was given to three planetary laws, was born.

Thomas Guy (c.1645–1724), bookseller and printer who founded Guy's Hospital in London, died.

Charles Lamb (1775–1834), poet and essayist, died.

Louis Pasteur (1822–1895), scientist who discovered that micro-organisms can be destroyed by heat, a technique now known as 'pasteurisation', was born.

The first performance of *Peter Pan* by J. M. Barrie (1860–1937) was held in London in 1904.

Emmonsail's Heath in Winter

I love to see the old heath's withered brake
Mingle its crimpled leaves with furze and ling,
While the old heron from the lonely lake
Starts slow and flaps its melancholy wing,
An oddling crow in idle motion swing
On the half-rotten ash-tree's topmost twig,
Beside whose trunk the gypsy makes his bed.
Up flies the bouncing woodcock from the brig
Where a black quagmire quakes beneath the tread;
The fieldfares chatter in the whistling thorn
And for the haw round fields and closen rove,
And coy bumbarrels, twenty in a drove,
Flit down the hedgerows in the frozen plain
And hang on little twigs and start again.

John Clare

ON THIS DAY:

In 1879 a bridge spanning the river Tay in Scotland collapsed as a train was passing over it. More than seventy people lost their lives.

Woodrow Wilson (1856–1924), President of the United States 1913–1921, who played a leading part in the formation of the League of Nations and the negotiation of the Treaty of Versailles, was born.

Dame Maggie Smith, actress who has appeared in films such as *The Prime of Miss Jean Brodie* and *A Room with a View*, was born in 1934.

Remember

Remember me when I am gone away,
   Gone far away into the silent land;
   When you can no more hold me by the hand,
Nor I half turn to go yet turning stay.
Remember me when no more day by day
   You tell me of our future that you planned:
   Only remember me; you understand
It will be late to counsel then or pray.
Yet if you should forget me for a while
   And afterwards remember, do not grieve:
   For if the darkness and corruption leave
A vestige of the thoughts that once I had,
Better by far you should forget and smile
   Than that you should remember and be sad.

Christina Rossetti

ON THIS DAY:

Christina Rossetti (1830–1894), poet, and sister of Dante Gabriel Rossetti (1828–1882), died.

Thomas à Becket (c.1118–1170), priest and Archbishop of Canterbury from 1162, was murdered at Canterbury Cathedral on the instructions of Henry II.

William Ewart Gladstone (1809–1898), Prime Minister from 1868 to 1874, 1880 to 1885, briefly in 1886 and finally from 1892 until 1894, was born.

Pablo Casals (1876–1973), cellist, was born.

Harold Macmillan (1894–1986), Prime Minister from 1957 to 1963, died.

Passing away, saith the World, Passing away

Passing away, saith the World, passing away:
Chances, beauty and youth sapped day by day:
Thy life never continueth in one stay.
Is the eye waxen dim, is the dark hair changing to gray
That hath won neither laurel nor bay?
I shall clothe myself in Spring and bud in May:
Thou, root-stricken, shalt not rebuild thy decay
On my bosom for aye.
Then I answered: Yea.

Passing away, saith my Soul, passing away:
With its burden of fear and hope, of labour and play;
Hearken what the past doth witness and say:
Rust in thy gold, a moth is in thine array,
A canker is in thy bud, thy leaf must decay.
At midnight, at cockcrow, at morning, one certain day
Lo the bridegroom shall come and shall not delay:
Watch thou and pray.
Then I answered: Yea.

Passing away, saith my God, passing away:
Winter passeth after the long delay:
New grapes on the vine, new figs on the tender spray,
Turtle calleth turtle in Heaven's May.
Tho' I tarry, wait for Me, trust Me, watch and pray.
Arise, come away, night is past and lo it is day,
My love, My sister, My spouse, thou shalt hear Me say.
Then I answered: Yea.

Christina Rossetti

ON THIS DAY:

The battle of Wakefield (Wars of the Roses) took place on this day in 1460 and during the encounter with the Lancastrian forces Richard, Duke of York (1411–1460), father of Edward IV and Richard III, was killed.

Rudyard Kipling (1865–1936), writer, poet and winner of the Nobel Prize for literature in 1907, was born.

Sir Carol Reed (1906–1976), film director whose works included *The Third Man*, was born.

December 31

The Old Year

I

The Old Year's gone away
To nothingness and night
We cannot find him all the day
Nor hear him in the night
He left no footstep mark or place
In either shade or sun
Tho' last year he'd a neighbours face
In this he's known by none

II

All nothing every where
Mists we on mornings see
They have more substance when they're here
And more of form than he
He was a friend by every fire
In every cot and hall
A guest to every hearts desire
And now he's nought at all

III

Old papers thrown away
Or garments cast aside
E'en the talk of yesterday
Are things identified
But time once torn away
No voices can recall
The eve of new years day
Left the old one lost to all

John Clare

ON THIS DAY:

In 1879 the first public demonstration of the incandescent lamp was given by the inventor Thomas Edison (1847–1931).

Henri Matisse (1869–1954), artist, was born.

INDEX OF AUTHORS

INDEX OF FIRST LINES

INDEX OF TITLES

ACKNOWLEDGEMENTS

'Iron Age Flying' by James Applewhite from *Foreseeing the Journey* (Louisiana State University Press). Copyright © 1983 by James Applewhite. Reprinted by permission of Louisiana State University Press.

'News of Pearl Harbor' by James Applewhite from *A History of the River* (Louisiana State University Press). Copyright © 1993 by James Applewhite. Reprinted by permission of Louisiana State University Press.

'The Stone Beach' by Simon Armitage from *The Universal Home Doctor* (Faber & Faber Ltd). Copyright © Simon Armitage 2003. Reprinted by permission of Faber & Faber Ltd, London and David Godwin Associates, London.

'The Volunteer' by Herbert Asquith. Copyright © The Estate of the Hon Herbert Asquith. Reprinted by permission of Mr R. Asquith.

'Night Mail', 'Partition' and 'September 1, 1939' by W. H. Auden (Faber and Faber Ltd). 'Night Mail' copyright © 1938 by W. H. Auden. 'Partition' copyright © 1966 by W H Auden. 'September 1, 1939' copyright © 1940, renewed 1968 by W. H. Auden. Reprinted by permission of Faber & Faber Ltd, London and by permission of Random House, Inc., New York.

'Endpiece' by Brendan Behan from *The Hostage* by Brendan Behan (Methuen Publishing Ltd). Copyright © The Estate of Brendan Behan. Reprinted by permission of Methuen Publishing Ltd.

'By the Ninth Green, St Enodoc', 'Death of King George V', 'The Arrest of Oscar Wilde', 'The Heart of Thomas Hardy', 'Perp. Revival i' the North' by Sir John Betjeman from *Collected Poems*. Copyright © The Estate of John Betjeman. Reprinted by permission of John Murray Publishers.

'Edith Cavell', 'For the Fallen – September, 1914', 'The Burning of the Leaves' by Laurence Binyon. Reprinted by permission of The Society of Authors, Literary Representative of the Estate of Laurence Binyon.

'Roman Fountain' by Louise Bogan from *The Blue Estuaries* by Louise Bogan. Copyright © 1968 by Louise Bogan. Copyright renewed 1996 by Ruth Limmer. Reprinted by permission of Farrar, Straus and Giroux, LLC, New York.

'August 6, 1945' by Millen Brand published in the *American Poetry Review* (vol. 4, no. 4, 1975). Copyright © The Estate of Millen Brand.

'Late Lamented Fame of the Giant City of New York' [translated by Frank Jones] and 'Of Poor B. B.' [translated by Michael Hamburger] by Bertolt Brecht from *Poems 1913–1956* [translated by John Willett and Ralph Manheim] (Methuen Publishing Ltd). Reprinted by permission of Methuen Publishing Ltd, Routledge Inc. and Suhrkamp Verlag.

'The Water Seller's Song' by Bertolt Brecht from *Poems and Songs from the Plays* (Methuen Publishing Ltd). Reprinted by permission of Methuen Publishing Ltd, Routledge Inc. and Suhrkamp Verlag.

'London under Bombardment' by Greta Briggs published in *Other Men's Flowers* (Pimlico). Copyright © Greta Briggs.

Excerpt from 'History of the Twentieth Century' by Joseph Brodsky from *Collected Poems in English* by Joseph Brodsky. Copyright © 2000 by the Estate of Joseph Brodsky. Reprinted by permission of Carcanet Press Ltd and Farrar, Straus and Giroux, LLC, New York.

'Autumn' by Roy Campbell, published by Ad Donker Publishers, Johannesburg. Reprinted by permission of Jonathan Ball Publishers, South Africa.

'Tears of a Clown' by Jonathan Caswell. Copyright © 2006 by J. R. Caswell. Reprinted by permission of Mr J. R. Caswell.

'Armistice Day' and 'At The British War Cemetery, Bayeux', by Charles Causley from *Collected Poems* (Macmillan). Reprinted by permission of David Higham Associates, Ltd.

'The Donkey' and 'The Rolling English Road' by G. K. Chesterton. Reprinted by permission of A. P. Watt Ltd on behalf of The Royal Literary Fund.

'South Pole' by Richard Church. Copyright © The Estate of Richard Church. Reprinted by permission of Pollinger Ltd and the Proprietor.

'Blueberrying in August' by Amy Clampitt from *Collected Poems of Amy Clampitt* by Amy Clampitt. Copyright © 1997 by the estate of Amy Clampitt. Reprinted by permission of Alfred A. Knopf, a division of Random House Inc., New York and by permission of Faber & Faber Ltd, London.

'1901', 'Lie in the Dark and Listen', 'When I have Fears' and 'Nothing is Lost' by Sir Noël Coward from *Collected Verse* (Methuen Publishing Ltd). Copyright © The Estate of Sir Noël Coward. Reprinted by permission of Methuen Publishing Ltd.

'Mad Dogs and Englishmen' and 'The Stately Homes of England' by Sir Noël Coward from *The Complete Lyrics* (Methuen Publishing Ltd).

Copyright © The Estate of Sir Noël Coward. Reprinted by permission of Methuen Publishing Ltd.

'At Melville's Tomb' by Hart Crane from *The Complete Poems of Hart Crane* by Hart Crane edited by Marc Simon (Liveright Publishing Corp, New York). Copyright © 1933, 1958, 1966 by Liveright Publishing Corporation. Copyright © 1986 by Marc Simon. Reprinted by permission of the Liveright Publishing Corporation.

'Talkies' by Robert Crawford from *Talkies* (Chatto and Windus). Reprinted by permission of The Random House Group Ltd.

'Maple and Sumach' by C. Day-Lewis from *The Complete Poems by C. Day Lewis* published by Sinclair-Stevenson (1992). Copyright © 1992 The Estate of C. Day Lewis. Reprinted by permission of The Random House Group Ltd.

'The Scarecrow' by Walter de la Mare from *The Complete Poems of Walter de la Mare 1969* (USA 1970). Reprinted by permission of the Literary Trustees of Walter de la Mare and the Society of Authors as their representative.

'Armistice' by Paul Dehn from *The Fern on the Rock* by Paul Dehn (Hamish Hamilton). Copyright © The Estate of Paul Dehn.

'Midnight: May 7th, 1945' by Patric Dickinson from *Stone in the Midst* by Patric Dickinson. Reprinted by permission of Mrs V. K. Lindley.

'On a Return from Egypt' by Keith Douglas from *Complete Poems* edited by D Graham (Faber & Faber Ltd). Copyright © by the Estate of Keith Douglas. Reprinted by permission of Faber & Faber Ltd, London & by permission of Faber & Faber Inc., an affiliate of Farrar, Straus and Giroux, LLC, New York, USA.

'Moonlit Apples' by John Drinkwater. Reprinted by permission of Samuel French Ltd, London on behalf of the Estate of John Drinkwater.

'The Fury of Aerial Bombardment' by Richard Eberhart from *Collected Poems 1930–1976* by Richard Eberhart. Copyright © 1976 by Richard Eberhart. Reprinted by permission of Oxford University Press, Inc, New York, USA and by permission of Mr D. Eberhart and Ms G. Cherington.

'Homage to the British Museum' and 'Note on Local Flora' by Sir William Empson from *Collected Poems* by William Empson (The Hogarth Press). Reprinted by permission of The Random House Group Ltd.

'Fleet Fighter' by Olivia Fitzroy. Copyright © The Salamander Oasis Trust. Reprinted by permission of the Salamander Oasis Trust, London.

'The Road not Taken' by Robert Frost from *The Poetry of Robert Frost* edited by Edward Connery Lathem, published by Jonathan Cape. Copyright 1916, © 1969 by Henry Holt and Company, copyright 1944 by Robert Frost. Reprinted by permission of The Random House Group Ltd and by permission of Henry Holt and Company, LLC, USA.

'Breakfast' by Wilfrid Gibson from *Collected Poems*. Reprinted by permission of Macmillan, London, UK.

'The Next Poem' by Dana Gioia from *The Gods of Winter*. Copyright © 1991 by Dana Gioia. Reprinted by permission of The Graywolf Press, Saint Paul, Minnesota, USA.

'A World Where News Travelled Slowly' by Lavinia Greenlaw from *A World Where News Travelled Slowly* by Lavinia Greenlaw (Faber & Faber Ltd). Copyright © Lavinia Greenlaw. Reprinted by permission of Faber & Faber Ltd, London.

'The Mangel-Bury' by Ivor Gurney from *Collected Poems* (Carcanet Press Ltd). Reprinted by permission of Carcanet Press Ltd.

'November' by F. W. Harvey. Copyright © The Estate of F. W. Harvey. Reprinted by permission of Mr P. Harvey.

'The Railway Children' by Seamus Heaney from *Station Island* (Faber & Faber Ltd). Copyright © 1984 by Seamus Heaney. Reprinted by permission of Faber & Faber Ltd, London & by permission of Farrar, Straus and Giroux, LLC, New York.

'Moon-Man' by Dorothy Hewett from *Collected Poems* (Fremantle Arts Centre Press, Australia, 1990). Copyright © The Estate of Dorothy Hewett. Reprinted by permission of the Fremantle Arts Centre Press, Australia.

'The Eve of St Mark' by Geoffrey Hill from *Collected Poems* by Geoffrey Hill (Penguin Books 1985). Copyright © Geoffrey Hill 1985. First published in *Tenebrae* by Geoffrey Hill. Copyright © Geoffrey Hill 1978. Reprinted by permission of the Penguin Group (UK). 'The Eve of St Mark' from *New & Collected Poems 1952–1992* by Geoffrey Hill. Copyright © 1994 by Geoffrey Hill. Reprinted by permission of Houghton Mifflin Company. All rights reserved.

'Requiem for the Plantagenet Kings' by Geoffrey Hill from *Collected Poems* by Geoffrey Hill (Penguin Books 1985). Copyright © Geoffrey Hill 1985. First published in *For the Unfallen*. Copyright © Geoffrey Hill 1959. Reprinted by permission of the Penguin Group (UK). 'Requiem for the Plantagenet Kings' from *New & Collected Poems 1952–1992* by Geoffrey Hill. Copyright © 1994 by Geoffrey Hill. Reprinted by permission of Houghton Mifflin Company. All rights reserved.

'Photograph of Haymaker, 1890' by Molly Holden. Copyright © Alan Holden. Reprinted by permission of Mr A. Holden.

'Walking in Autumn' by Frances Horovitz from *Collected Poems* (Bloodaxe Books 1985). Reprinted by permission of Bloodaxe Books Ltd.

534

ACKNOWLEDGEMENTS

'Loveliest of Trees' by A. E. Housman. Copyright © The Estate of A. E. Housman. Reprinted by permission of The Society of Authors as the Literary Representative of A. E. Housman.

'Song at the Beginning of Autumn' by Elizabeth Jennings from *Collected Poems* (Carcanet Press Ltd). Reprinted by permission of David Higham Associates Ltd.

'Cathedral' by Richard Jones from *The Blessing: New and Selected Poems*. Copyright © 2000 by Richard Jones. Reprinted with the permission of Copper Canyon Press, PO Box 271, Port Townsend, WA 98368-0271, USA.

'Beech Tree' and 'October' by Patrick Kavanagh from *Collected Poems* edited by Antoinette Quinn (Allen Lane, 2004). Reprinted by kind permission of the Trustees of the Estate of the late Katherine B. Kavanagh, through the Jonathan Williams Literary Agency, Dublin.

'The Way Through the Woods' by Rudyard Kipling. Reprinted by permission of A. P. Watt Ltd, on behalf of The National Trust for Places of Historic Interest or Natural Beauty.

'The Scientists are Wrong' by Abba Kovner (translated by Shirley Kaufman) from *My Little Sister and Selected Poems 1965-1985* (Oberlin College Press, 1986). Reprinted by permission of Oberlin College Press, Ohio, USA.

'Going, Going' by Philip Larkin, from *High Windows* by Philip Larkin (Faber & Faber Ltd) and *Collected Poems* by Philip Larkin. Copyright © 1988, 2003 by the Estate of Philip Larkin. Reprinted by permission of Faber & Faber Ltd, London and Farrar, Straus and Giroux, LLC, New York.

'February Evening in New York' by Denise Levertov from *Collected Earlier Poems 1940–1960*. Copyright © 1957, 1958, 1959, 1960, 1961, 1979 by Denise Levertov. Reprinted by permission of New Directions Publishing Corp. and by permission of Pollinger Ltd and the Proprietor.

'Buna' by Primo Levi (translated by Ruth Feldman and Brian Swann) from *Collected Poems*. English translation copyright © 1988 by Ruth Feldmann and Brian Swann. Reprinted by permission of Faber & Faber Ltd, London and by permission of Farrar, Straus and Giroux, LLC, New York.

'Grace at Gloucester' by Oscar Lloyd from *The Poetry of Cricket* (Macmillan 1964). Copyright © The Estate of Oscar Lloyd.

'The Miner's Helmet' by George Macbeth from *Collected Poems 1958–1982* by George Macbeth (Hutchinson). Copyright © George Macbeth 1989. Reprinted by permission of Sheil Land Associates Ltd.

'Ars Poetica' by Archibald MacLeish from *Collected Poems 1917–1982* by Archibald MacLeish. Copyright © 1985 by the Estate of Archibald

MacLeish. Reprinted by permission of Houghton Mifflin Company. All rights reserved.

'In Carrowdore Churchyard' by Derek Mahon from *Collected Poems* (1999). Reprinted by kind permission of the author and The Gallery Press, Loughcrew, Oldcastle, County Meath, Ireland.

'Autumn Ploughing', 'Number 534', 'Sir Winston Churchil' and 'The West Wind' by John Masefield. Reprinted by permission of the Society of Authors as the Literary Representative of the Estate of John Masefield.

'Old Photograph' by Hugh McMillan from *Oxford Poets 2002: An Anthology* edited by David Constantine, Hermione Lee and Bernard O'Donoghue (Carcanet Press Ltd). Reprinted by permission of Mr H McMillan.

'The British Museum Reading Room' and 'Star-gazer' by Louis MacNeice from *Collected Poems* (Faber & Faber Ltd). Reprinted by permission of David Higham Associates Ltd.

'Seed' by Paula Meehan from *The Man Who Was Marked By Winter* (1991). Reprinted by kind permission of the author and The Gallery Press, Loughcrew, Oldcastle, County Meath, Ireland.

'Spring' by Edna St Vincent Millay from *Collected Poems* (HarperCollins). Copyright 1921, 1948 by Edna St Vincent Millay. All rights reserved. Reprinted by permission of Elizabeth Barnett, Literary Executor.

'Poetry' by Marianne Moore from *Collected Poems* by Marianne Moore. Copyright © 1935 by Marianne Moore; copyright renewed © 1963 by Marianne Moore and T. S. Eliot. Reprinted by permission of Scribner, an imprint of Simon & Schuster Adult Publishing Group and by permission of Faber & Faber Ltd, London.

'Aberdeen Train' by Edwin Morgan from *Collected Poems* by Edwin Morgan (Carcanet Press Ltd). Reprinted by permission of Carcanet Press Ltd.

'Morse' by Les Murray from *Four Australian Poets*. Copyright © 1991 by New Directions Publishing Corp. Reprinted by permission of Carcanet Press Ltd and by permission of New Directions Publishing Corp. and by permission of Margaret Connolly, Australia.

'Cinema Paradiso' by Ann Nadge from *Corrugations* (Ginninderra Press, Australia). Copyright © Ann Nadge. Reprinted by permission of Ms A. Nadge.

'The War Films' by Sir Henry Newbolt. Reprinted by permission of Mr P. Newbolt.

'Halley's Comet' by Norman Nicholson from *Collected Poems* edited by Neil Curry (Faber & Faber Ltd). Reprinted by permission of David Higham Associates Ltd.

'After the Shipwreck' by Alice Ostriker from *The Little Space: Poems Selected and New, 1968–1998*

ACKNOWLEDGEMENTS

by Alice Ostriker. Copyright © 1998 by Alice Ostriker. Reprinted by permission of the University of Pittsburgh Press.

'Hiding Beneath the Furze' by Henry Reed from *Collected Poems: Henry Reed* (1991) by Henry Reed, edited by Jon Stallworthy. Reprinted by permission of Oxford University Press.

'Stanley Matthews' by Alan Ross. Reprinted by permission of Mrs J. Ross.

'Jarrow' by Carol Rumens from *Poems 1968–2004* by Carol Rumens (Bloodaxe Books 2004). Reprinted by permission of Bloodaxe Books Ltd.

'Blunden's Beech' by Siegfried Sassoon from *Collected Poems of Siegfried Sassoon*. Copyright © 1918, 1920 by E. P. Dutton. Copyright © 1936, 1946, 1947, 1948 by Siegfried Sassoon. Reprinted by permission of the Barbara Levy Agency and by permission of Viking Penguin, a division of Penguin Group (USA) Inc.

'Autumn' by Vernon Scannell. Copyright © Vernon Scannell. Reprinted by permission of Mr V. Scannell.

'February 13, 1975' by James Schuyler from *The New York Poets An Anthology* (Carcanet Press Ltd) and *Collected Poems* by James Schuyler. Copyright © 1993 by the Estate of James Schuyler. Reprinted by permission of Carcanet Press Ltd and Farrar, Straus and Giroux, LLC, New York.

'Groundsmen' by David Scott from *Selected Poems* by David Scott (Bloodaxe Books 1998). Reprinted by permission of Bloodaxe Books Ltd.

'To Sir Len Hutton' by Colin Shakespeare from *A Breathless Hush* (Methuen Publishing Ltd). Copyright © Colin Shakespeare. Reprinted by permission of Mr C. Shakespeare.

'The Other Little Boats – July 1588' by Edward Shanks. Copyright © The Estate of Edward Shanks.

'Why are the Clergy…?' by Stevie Smith from *Collected Poems of Stevie Smith*. Copyright © The Estate of James MacGibbon. Copyright © 1972 by Stevie Smith. Reprinted by permission of Hamish MacGibbon, James & James (Publishers) Ltd, London and by permission of New Directions Publishing Corp.

'In Front of Chagall's 'America Windows'' by Christopher Southgate from *Easing The Gravity*

Field: Poems of Science and Love by Christopher Southgate (Shoestring Press, 2006). Copyright © 2004 by Christopher Southgate. Reprinted by permission of Mr C. Southgate.

'Muhammed Ali at the Ringside, 1985' and 'Your Logic Frightens Me, Mandela' from *Selected Poems* by Wole Soyinka and *Mandela's Earth* (Methuen Publishing Ltd and by permission of Random House, Inc.). Copyright © 1988 by Wole Soyinka. Reprinted by permission of Methuen Publishing Ltd and Random House, Inc., New York and by permission of the author c/o Rogers, Coleridge & White Ltd, 20 Powis Mews, London.

'Lost Poems' by Wole Soyinka from *Samarkand and Other Markets I Have Known* by Wole Soyinka (Methuen Publishing Ltd). Copyright © 2002 Wole Soyinka. Reprinted by permission of Methuen Publishing Ltd and by permission of the author c/o Rogers, Coleridge & White Ltd, 20 Powis Mews, London.

'At the Bomb Testing Site' by William Stafford from *The Way It Is: New and Selected Poems*. Reprinted by permission of Graywolf Press, Saint Paul, Minnesota, USA.

'Poem in October' by Dylan Thomas from *Collected Poems* (Dent). Copyright © 1945 by the Trustees for the copyrights of Dylan Thomas. First published in *Poetry*. Reprinted by permission of David Higham Associates Ltd, London and by permission of New Directions Publishing Corp.

'First Snow in Alsace' by Richard Wilbur from *The Beautiful Changes and Other Poems*. Copyright © 1947 and renewed 1975 by Richard Wilbur. Reprinted by permission of Harcourt, Inc and by permission of Faber & Faber Ltd, London.

'Piazza di Spagna, Early Morning' by Richard Wilbur from *Things of this World*. Copyright © 1956 and renewed 1984 by Richard Wilbur. Reprinted by permission of Harcourt, Inc and by permission of Faber & Faber Ltd, London.

'An Irish Airman Forsees His Death', 'Easter 1916' and 'The Wild Swans at Coole' by W. B. Yeats. Reprinted by permission of A. P. Watt Ltd on behalf of Michael B. Yeats.

'February' by Francis Brett Young. Reprinted by permission of David Higham Associates Ltd.

Publisher's note

We acknowledge with thanks the permissions granted to reproduce in this publication poems that are protected by copyright. Every effort has been made to trace all current copyright holders but in some cases that has not been possible. We apologise for any unintended omissions and would be pleased to receive information that would enable us to rectify any inaccuracies.

Methuen
11–12 Buckingham Gate
London SW1E 6LB